MW01127890

THE WAGES OF HISTORY

A VOLUME IN THE SERIES
Public History in Historical Perspective

EDITED BY
Marla R. Miller

THE WAGES OF HISTORY

Emotional Labor on Public History's Front Lines

AMY M. TYSON

UNIVERSITY OF MASSACHUSETTS PRESS
Amherst and Boston

Copyright © 2013 by University of Massachusetts Press
All rights reserved
Printed in the United States of America

ISBN 978-1-62534-024-5 (paper); 023-8 (hardcover)

Designed by Sally Nichols
Set in Monotype Apollo and Monotype Engravers
Printed and bound by Thomson-Shore, Inc.

Library of Congress Cataloging-in-Publication Data

Tyson, Amy.
    The wages of history : emotional labor on public history's front lines / Amy M. Tyson.
        pages cm. — (Public history in historical perspective)
    Includes bibliographical references and index.
    ISBN 978-1-62534-023-8 (hardcover : alk. paper) — ISBN 978-1-62534-024-5 (pbk. :
    alk. paper) 1. Historical reenactments—Psychological aspects—Minnesota—Fort
    Snelling. 2. Historical reenactments—Psychological aspects—Case studies. 3. Historic
    sites—Interpretive programs—Psychological aspects—Minnesota—Fort Snelling. 4.
    Historic sites—Interpretive programs—Psychological aspects—Case studies. 5. Public
    history—Minnesota—Fort Snelling. 6. Acting—Psychological aspects—Case studies.
    7. Fort Snelling (Minn) — History. I. Title.
    F614.F7T97 2013
    977.6'57—dc23
                                      2013002452

British Library Cataloguing-in-Publication Data
A catalogue record for this book is available from the British Library.

Publication of this book and other titles in the series Public History in Historical Perspective
is supported by the Office of the Dean, College of Humanities and Fine Arts, University of
Massachusetts Amherst.

In memory of Dr. Andy Helmich Sr., former Fort volunteer and paid interpreter, who told me, "You've got to write it, you've got to put it out there, you've got to draw on the people."

CONTENTS

ILLUSTRATIONS

ACKNOWLEDGMENTS

I owe a debt of gratitude to two women who have been instrumental in seeing this book come to print. Cathy Stanton has been this project's champion, a model of intellectual generosity, and my sure-footed guide as I journeyed through the process of reshaping the ideas contained here. Not insignificantly, Cathy introduced me to Marla Miller, the series editor for Public History in Historical Perspective at the University of Massachusetts Press. Marla expressed an early interest in the project, and has since shepherded it through many, many drafts. I am grateful to both women for their excellent mentorship, and their provoking ideas, as well as for pushing me to clarify the story told in these pages, and for helping me have the confidence to think big.

Also at the University of Massachusetts Press, I am grateful to editors Clark Dougan and Carol Betsch, and to my copyeditor, Mary Bagg, for their help, support, and guidance at various stages of publishing this book. I am also grateful to James Green and the additional anonymous peer reviewer who both provided many useful suggestions and critiques at an early stage of the manuscript, giving me a lot to chew on. Thanks are also owed to the group of graduate students in public history at the University of Massachusetts who attended my talk at the university in April 2012. The conversation we had inspired my thinking about future implications of the study, the fruits of which are scattered throughout the manuscript, and especially in the epilogue. Christopher Benning, Jeff Robinson, Jessie MacLeod, Michella Marino, Laura Miller, Emily Oswald, Kate Preissler, and Stephania Villar: Thank you for thinking with me.

Some of the material found here has appeared in print before— although my conclusions may now be somewhat different and my analyses have since shifted focus. From *Museum and Society,* I want to thank Gordon Fyfe and the anonymous reviewers who lent insights on my past scholarship that have informed this present work. Likewise, from the volume *Enacting History* (University of Alabama Press, 2011) thanks are owed to Scott Magelssen, Rhona Justice-Malloy, and the peer reviewers who worked with that project.

The intellectual and emotional support that I have received from colleagues these last few years at DePaul University has been a gift. In particular, I am grateful to Lisa Z. Sigel who mentored me through the publication process and read an early draft of the Introduction; Jim Wolfinger who helped me map out the larger social implications of the work; Kerry Ross who read an almost final draft of a much-revised chapter in a pinch; and Margaret Storey who helped me clarify historical details regarding the Dred Scott Decision of 1857. Roshanna Sylvester and graduate students in her Capstone Seminar read and reviewed the uncompleted manuscript, which led to a productive conversation that informed my edits during my last month of writing. Thank you Roshanna, Ian Burns, David Magee, DJ Marty, Lauren McCaugherty, Sanskruti Patel, William Radke, Lauren Schlueter, Kathleen Tallmadge, Erin Tubbs, and Kevin Whitman. Thanks are also owed to Thomas Foster and Onie Green-Givens in the Department of History for allowing student worker Lucero Garabay to help me complete some transcription work in the final hour.

For supporting this work in its earliest stages I owe a debt of gratitude to American studies and history professors at the University of Minnesota who equipped me to approach this project in a truly interdisciplinary way, especially Thomas Augst, Lary May, Kevin Murphy, David Noble, Jean O'Brien, Jennifer Pierce, and Dave Roediger. Jennifer and Kevin in particular provided intellectual influence and guidance that enabled me to bring public history and emotional labor scholarship together in this book.

I am also grateful to the fellow members of Jennifer Pierce's writing group, for the "Piercing Insights" that helped form this project (Hokulani Aikau, Pam Butler, Sara Dorow, Karla Erickson, Felicity Grabiel-Schaeffer, Peter Hennen, Nalo Jackson, Ryan Murphy, Deb Smith, Miglena Todorova, and Chia Vang), as well as to my other graduate student comrades who offered a more than passing enthusiasm for this project when it was in development (Matt Becker, David Gray, Scott Laderman, Sharon Leon, Julia Musha, Dave Noon, and Mary Rizzo).

Deserving special mention for their help when the project looked much different are Steve Ashcroft, Jon Keljik, and Aaron Windel, who each read substantial portions of the project long before it was ready to be a book. I still remain grateful for their ideas and suggestions.

Financial support has been helpful at different stages of the project. I want to thank the University of Minnesota College of Liberal Arts and the Department of American Studies for two grants that provided early research funding. More recently, DePaul University funded a summer research fellowship that supported key research trips and follow-up interviews. This fellowship also gave me funds to hire Elizabeth Boden, who worked as my undergraduate research assistant and tirelessly transcribed many of the interviews (thank you, Lizzy!). In 2009, a University Competitive Paid Research Leave funded time off from teaching and service so I could rewrite substantive portions of the manuscript, and in 2012, a Competitive Research Grant from the University Research Council covered the services of a professional indexer.

From Historic Fort Snelling, I would like to thank my co-workers throughout the years, especially those interpreters who allowed me to interview them and whose thoughts and words have profoundly shaped this book. I would name you each individually, if I hadn't promised to make all narrators anonymous. I am also grateful to the staff of the Minnesota Historical Society's archives and library, as well as to Jeff Boorom, Eric Ferguson, Thomas Lalim, Jean Hewlett-Moline, Kevin Maijala, Erik Olsrud, Steve Osman, and John Waldo for providing me with copies of Fort-related paper-based materials not in those archives. Pat Cierna, Eric Ferguson, and David Wiggins went out of their way to respond to my online and email queries about worksite history before my time.

Friends who had no good reason to read the manuscript offered to do so. I am grateful to Andy Urban and Emily Callaci for reading and commenting on several sections of the manuscript and helping me refine ideas along the way. Leah Lopez read and commented on my first attempt at getting the manuscript together to send out to readers. Paula Dempsey took over from there, and read the revised manuscript cover to cover—offering line edits and smart suggestions for new ways of framing analyses. Finally, Ellen Baker acted as literary midwife for the book during my final stages of writing. She read multiple drafts of some chapters (even when jet-lagged in Paris), and in addition to massaging my prose in places, she told it to me straight. I am grateful that she shared her considerable gifts with me.

I also want to acknowledge those who morally supported this book even though they did not read it (until now). I am grateful to each of those wonderful Cedarleafs for their love and support, and their many trips to visit me while I labored in costume at the Fort. I am also grateful to my husband's family (Sue Smith, Jim Smith, Valerie Kenlay, Dick Kenlay, and Ted Nunn) for keeping me on my toes by frequently asking, "How's the book going?" My sister Kim Claire, and her children, Anna and Ty, provided much-welcomed distraction from writing when I was back home in California, which was a great help. I am also grateful to my parents, Candy and Craig Tyson, who taught me about the importance of seeing labor from an early age. My father worked in the trades as a union electrician, and made considerable sacrifices for his family in exchange for a wage. My mother worked as a frontline secretary at a middle school where she performed (often difficult) emotional labor on a daily basis. My mother showed me the value of supporting workers at all levels of an organization's hierarchy; twice she took me to picket lines at the district office—once to show her support of teachers, and once to protest projected lay-offs of janitorial and cafeteria staff, the most vulnerable workers at her school. My parents, each in their own ways have inspired me to feel like I was doing something of value in the process of writing a book whose aim is to bring attention to a group of workers whose labor is often invisible, undersupported, and undervalued.

Finally, my husband, Brent Nunn, has shaped this work profoundly. Throughout the process of my writing this book, he has worn multiple hats as a late-night editor, reference librarian, wordsmith, provider of welcome distractions, motivational speaker, provocateur, and short-order cook. He has mulled over key ideas with me more times than both of us wish was necessary. I am grateful that he gave so much of himself— and to me—in this process. And I am humbled that he did so because he cares deeply about the book's implications for the importance of nurturing frontline culture workers so that our world might be a richer, more humane, and more deeply engaged place for us all to live.

THE WAGES OF HISTORY

INTRODUCTION
Customer Service Superstars

APRIL 2, 2001

After initial greetings in the lobby of the Fort Snelling History Center, my co-workers and I take our seats in the auditorium. Nearly fifty people—mostly seasonal workers hired either as gift shop clerks or costumed guides—are gathered for the annual spring training at this Minnesota historic site. Behind me, I hear male co-workers joking about the costume-measurement forms we guides are filling out: "Hey, what are you putting for your bust size?" In a caricatured, effeminate voice someone responds, "Let's see . . ." While this might have offended me during my first season, now I'm familiar with the juvenile humor of some of male guides on staff. Although I am mildly annoyed with the co-workers in the row behind me, I am glad to see so many familiar faces among the workers gathered as I turn to scan the room.

After sitting through presentations addressing changes in the Minnesota Historical Society's Historic Sites Divisions, we come to the high point of tonight's training session; we are going to learn how to become superstars at Historic Fort Snelling, that is to say, Customer Service Superstars. Our manager takes the podium. Behind him, emblazoned on a white screen, is this message: "The customer is paying for personal service as the product, rather than 'carry-away merchandise.'" That personal service, the manager stresses, sets the Fort apart from and above similar attractions. He tells us: "Our visitors leave with a smile on their face. We hope that our corporate culture here makes customer service your priority at all times."

The manager presses "play" on a remote to start a corporate training *video called "Customer Service Superstars," which features a package-delivery worker named Bradley. In a parody of the fictional hero Indiana Jones's recovery of archaeologically significant objects, Bradley lassos objects and descends staircases on a bicycle in order to ensure timely package delivery. The takeaway message is that Bradley risks life and limb in order to exceed customer expectations because he is an intrinsically motivated worker whose reward is the emotional satisfaction of a job well done.*

Following the twelve-and-a-half minute video, our manager asks us if we know of any workers at Historic Fort Snelling who may already be superstars. Several of us raise our hands and share observations. To a large extent workers describe situations in which they have seen co-workers emotionally connecting with visitors, or making a sacrifice to meet visitors' needs. Among the highlights: Arthur is praised for foregoing his lunch break in favor of speaking with children about his replica musket; Craig is recognized for directing conversations to subjects that interest the visitors; Oliver is said never to be seen with a frown on his face; and Kathleen is recognized for her unstoppable energy at birthday parties. Smiling and gratified, Kathleen says: "You just have to love your job, that's all."

Kathleen may love this job, but she also needs it. During a break, Kathleen mentions to me that her daughter has just come out of a three-week coma. The hospital bills are draining her, so Kathleen needs to work a lot of hours at the Fort this season to help make ends meet. To be able to attend the Fort's training session tonight, she had to skip an event at the school where she teaches. She is afraid that there might be repercussions for missing the school event, but she did not want to jeopardize her chances for a job with the Fort this summer; although she's worked here several seasons already, management made it clear that these preseason training sessions were mandatory. While Kathleen's knowledge and experience add value to her work at the Fort, she nonetheless feels devalued and senses that she could easily be replaced. Certainly, as we've been told a number of times, more people apply for these jobs than there are positions available.

To conclude the evening we play Minnesota History Bingo, a game that management has designed to serve both as an icebreaker and as a low-stakes training exercise related to ground-floor knowledge about Minnesota history. For correctly filling out our bingo cards, we are tossed candy bars. As far as training goes, I'd rather be down at the Fort in costume, learning interpretive skills on the job from my co-workers and relaying history

through conversations with visitors. That chance will come soon enough.
In the meantime, when I catch a candy bar that is tossed in my direction,
I can't help but feel a bit like a performing dolphin at a Sea World show.

In April 2001, I was both enrolled as a graduate student in American
Studies at the University of Minnesota and employed (for a second season)
as an interpreter at Historic Fort Snelling. I recorded my impressions of
the April 2 training session as part of my early research on the Fort,
unaware of how the session foreshadowed complex themes that, I have
now come to understand, shape this site and others like it—including
gender tension, co-worker surveillance, emotional investment, feeling
devalued, and making games out of history. What did strike me at
the time was how the corporate values espoused at this historic site
varied little from those at other worksites where I had been employed
previously. Whether as a singing waitress at a Michigan dinner theater
or as a school district employee for a youth summer program called
Friendship Connection, I repeatedly had been trained to produce unique
but meaningful experiences for clientele, and had been encouraged to
become an emotionally invested customer service superstar. Despite the
many similarities between these seemingly disparate jobs, there was a
key difference: working as a living history interpreter for the Minnesota
Historical Society felt *important*. Even though I was dressed in a costume,
educating the public about Minnesota history in a restored 1820s fortress
carried a much weightier sense of cultural significance, than did singing
"Time for Salad" at the dinner theater, dressed as Brunhilde. Through
observations over the course of the seven years I worked at Historic
Fort Snelling, and vis-à-vis thirty-two interviews with workers and
managers at the site, it became clear that other interpreters felt much
the same way, and like Kathleen they generally "loved their jobs."[1]

But while the living history interpreters I came to know at the Fort
found themselves gratified by their jobs, many also found themselves
upset, dissatisfied, or troubled by their work lives in equal measure.
Though many interpreters aimed to provide personalized service to
each visitor who walked through the Fort's gates, many felt regarded as
replaceable cogs in the machine of the cultural economy. When visitors
refused to engage with them, when managers hinted that they could be
easily replaced, or when co-workers found fault in their interpretive

decisions, the cuts ran deep. But despite often feeling undervalued or unappreciated—either by the public, by management, or by their co-workers—most interpreters continued to invest emotionally in their jobs, sometimes at a cost to their lives out of costume. Like Kathleen, they invested in their jobs not only because they needed the income in the insecure and low-wage economic sectors they inhabited, but because they loved history, because they took pleasure in the creative expression afforded by "living history" itself, and because they strongly believed in the importance of the cultural role they performed for the public. Significantly, because they understood their cultural work of connecting with visitors about the past as a privilege, they also tended to refrain from confronting the material circumstances of their working lives.

This book examines museum interpreters as service workers and cultural producers. At first glance the jobs of the costumed workers who are the focus of this study might seem as far removed from relevant contexts as the starched day caps upon their heads, but examining their labor yields wider insights into how labor is reproduced in the cultural and service sectors of the new economy. Exploring how people negotiate significant workplace issues alongside desires to contribute to something meaningful through their work is at the heart of this study. Workers I knew at the Fort found pleasure in connecting with visitors through the medium of history and were also deeply gratified by opportunities to perform old-world skills like blacksmithing or hearth cooking. Such opportunities to personally connect and creatively express themselves were key to the compensation many workers sought from their jobs.

Individuals of all stripes seek outlets for creative expression, of course, whether those outlets satisfy a solely emotional need or provide a monetary reward: business professionals attend community arts and music classes at the end of their workdays, for instance, and Internet-savvy artisans across the globe sell their wares in online marketplaces like Etsy. Such creative expressions may take place in either on- or off-the-clock contexts. But cultural workers at mission-driven, nonprofit institutions often expend energy, both on and off the clock, on work-related projects. These extra labors (i.e., the public historian who leads a neighborhood walking tour, the kindergarten teacher who preps the crafts for students, the librarian who arranges a poetry reading, the humanist blogger who posts thoughtful insights that help us make sense of our world), intensify the value of the jobs for the workers who get paid to do them. But these labors of love also add value to our world by making it a more meaningful and fulfilling place for us all to live. Those drawn to work in the nonprofit sectors of the cultural economy are hungry for opportunities to connect with people, to find outlets for creative expression, and to make a positive difference in the world, so that when they find a job in today's economy that pays them—however little—to do this kind of meaningful work, they hold on tight, and feel like one of the lucky ones.

Despite feeling lucky, these workers are faced with issues of insecurity and devaluation. Though they often have a strong work identity and a keen desire to be part of something bigger than themselves by serving as content holders and knowledge producers, these same workers are confronted by work–role boundaries and perceptions. For example, they are often regarded as little more than routine service workers, more often called on to offer reassurance or to relay tidbits of information, rather than being asked to contribute real knowledge. Here I am thinking of the academic who is increasingly expected to be on call to respond to panicked student emails (which are often generated because the student has not consulted the syllabus), or the information technology employee who is relied upon to calm down agitated co-workers whose tech problems too often stem from user error.[2] Similarly, a highly educated reference librarian at an East Coast college campus once quipped to me that he had a very important job: showing people how to find the pencil sharpener. Like the workers in my study, this man really did love his job and treasured the moments when he was singled out to add value to student learning and faculty research. But his comment betrays how he often felt that those whom he was called to serve rarely understood his job as a knowledge producer; they did not recognize that skills and training he possessed held value not only for him but for them as well.

A core problem exists for cultural workers because labor involving interpersonal interaction, emotional work, and caretaking behavior is often perceived as feminized (even when it is performed by men), the value of which is not only widely unappreciated on a social level but often goes unarticulated even within one's own organization.[3] In addition to having an impact on pay, this devaluation affects the influence these workers have on their workplace, as well as their professional identity and their ability to gain access to organizational support inside or outside their work environments. Moreover, in the wake of shrinking resources for cultural institutions, there are not enough positions available to meet demand, which exacerbates the devaluation of these workers.[4]

In other sectors of the economy, such as manufacturing, when workers are not provided sufficient training in meaningful skill development (or when they do not receive adequate organizational support), direct, realizable costs are easily tracked. For example, if a skilled worker in manufacturing is replaced with a less trained worker, production slowdowns or assembly-line mistakes can be easily attributed to the lack of experience in the workforce. In this context, retaining and supporting a more skilled and supported workforce can be justified given the high costs of fixing mistakes in production. It is harder to trace the cumulative effect of a devalued workforce on the front lines of the culture industry. Are there social costs that might not be easily recognized? What are the costs for replacing a highly trained knowledge producer with someone who is equipped with less-relevant knowledge? What if citizens do not come in contact with thought-provoking or nuanced history from museum interpreters? What if a patron is misinformed about the resources available at the local library because a skilled reference librarian has been replaced with an unskilled student worker? Does it matter if this knowledge about access to information is simply lost? And on a larger scale, what does it mean for society when knowledge about the past is regarded as a product that can be delivered by interchangeable and low-paid workers? How does this follow the trend toward deskilling and standardizing educational and learning experiences of all kinds?

Field/Work: *Working and Researching at the Fort*

I first took a job at the Fort, Minnesota's premiere living history attraction, in 1999. I had no idea that I would ultimately return for a total of seven seasons, even as I became intrigued by the following questions: Why were the workers at the Fort so dedicated to their jobs? What kind of meaning did this job of interpreting history infuse in the lives of the workers? And how might examining public history as work yield insight into historic interpretation—that is, the process of translating the past to others?

To deeply understand the rewards, costs, and consequences of working on public history's front line, I decided in 2001 that once again I needed to participate as a historic interpreter at the Fort. This decision to reapply did not come easily; I'd found my first season as a Fort interpreter only somewhat enjoyable, but intensely (emotionally and physically) exhausting. That first season, because I primarily considered the job a way to earn summer income, I chose not to participate much in the larger culture of the worksite, such as attending after-hours parties, or—as a female employee—becoming proficient in needlework, knitting, or hearth cooking. As a "fresh fish" (what Fort "veterans," adopting military parlance, called newcomers to the job), parts of the workplace culture perplexed and sometimes troubled me; in particular the job seemed to encourage a much deeper investment of one's self than I was then willing to give for the hourly wage of $9.42.

But as my research interests about living history's place in the service economy grew stronger, I was driven to return as a costumed interpreter by the quest for field notes and contacts with Fort workers. While absorbing the values and techniques of the museum workforce in my summer duties, I learned the values and techniques of cultural anthropology in my graduate studies. My research brought the latter to bear on the former. I decided that in order to better understand the site's unique work culture, I would employ the extended case method, which meant that I needed to engage in participant observation at the Fort over an extended period of time.[5] As part of the extended case method, researchers begin their participant observation fieldwork with the intent to improve existing social theory. And so I entered into my participant observation with a concern about how workers experienced and produced emotions at their worksite, and a focus on the ways in which they emotionally invested in their jobs. I recorded field notes with special attention to these factors.

This on-the-ground perspective focusing on the emotional labor of a history museum's frontline workforce is a departure from the groundbreaking ethnographies of history museums. Richard Handler and Eric Gable's ethnography of Colonial Williamsburg, and Cathy Stanton's ethnography on Lowell National Historic Park, offer critical and broader analyses on the inner workings of their respective field sites from an outsider perspective (although Stanton sometimes felt as though she were part of the staff).[6] Likewise, Laura Peers's important ethnography of North American living history museums does draw on insights from frontline workers, but her overarching purpose was to gauge how First Nations peoples and Native Americans were portrayed at her field sites.[7] And while Stephen Eddy Snow's *Performing the Pilgrims* offers relevant observations from his experience as an interpreter at Plimoth Plantation, his book primarily examines Plimoth as an example of environmental theater that "constantly improves in its historical accuracy," without fully analyzing the labor of his pilgrim subjects within broader economic contexts.[8] While gleaning insights from these important museum ethnographies for my work on *The Wages of History,* I also draw on the anthropology of service work more broadly—from food service to the travel industry—to better understand living history interpreters as a workforce, albeit one with unique demands given the special nature of the visitor-interpreter relationship, and the charge of performing the past. Ultimately, as a case study, I designed this book to intimately examine the work experiences of public history's front line alongside analyses of the wider forces shaping those experiences.

When my case study officially began in 2001, I openly disclosed to management and co-workers that I was using the Fort as a field site for my participant-observation research on the work of living history. Happily, my fellow interpreters tended to be very supportive of my heightened curiosity about the Fort's worksite culture, which was particularly evident in their willingness to be interviewed. With the promise that all informants would be assigned a pseudonym, my interview requests were never rebuffed,[9] and, ultimately, I was able to conduct thirty-two interviews with interpreters and supervisors at the site.[10]

Some found my research into the Fort's work culture inspiring, and several individuals went out of their way to provide me with copies of documents that were not formally on file at the Minnesota Historical Society Archives, where I conducted the bulk of my archival research.[11] These individuals—drawn from both the interpretive staff and management team—provided me with copies of memos, written personal observations, personal notes, as well as electronic files for the full run of newsletters produced by the Minnesota Historical Society Interpreter's Caucus (an interpreter-rights organization from the 1990s).[12] The Fort's management team (both during and after my tenure) was supportive and assisted me with conducting archival research at the Fort itself. A bevy of old memos, work schedules, training notes, and interpretive plans were among the wide variety of ephemera that I examined in the boxes of records made available to me.[13] Along with my own participant observations and the interviews, these additional documentary sources shed light onto the history of the Fort's work culture.

The seven years I spent working at the Fort provided me with a wealth of experience on the front lines of living history (offered here as part of the case study). This long-term commitment also afforded me the unique opportunity to build workplace relationships with managers and workers, and I may not have gained access to many archival sources or been granted interviews had I not built these relationships over time.[14] Drawing from this range of sources, *The Wages of History: Emotional Labor on Public History's Front Lines* offers a level of insight into the front lines of public history heretofore unseen.[15]

The Emergence of Living History and the Work Display

As historian Denise Meringolo has argued, we can trace the roots of what we have come to call the field of "public history" back to federal preservation efforts of the nineteenth century.[16] But the field as we now understand it was profoundly affected by concerns of the post–civil rights era, wherein many historians sought to produce more-inclusive histories "from the bottom up" that mined the experiences of, for instance, workers, minorities, and women. The proliferation of public history in the 1970s should also be seen as a response to the shrinking academic job market, wherein professional historians were forced to look beyond the ivory tower and toward places like museums, historical societies, and preservation agencies if they wanted to be employed in their field.[17]

While the modern public history movement directly descended from social historical concerns, it would not have been possible without the preceding postwar preservation and tourism booms, which created new worksites that would call on the skills of a new professional class of historians. One was the living history museum. In the early decades of the twentieth century, only a handful of living history museums, such as Henry Ford's Greenfield Village in Dearborn, Michigan (1923), and the Rockefeller-funded Colonial Williamsburg in Virginia (1927), were founded. But in the years during and after World War II, there was a veritable boom in this museum genre, including the founding (in Massachusetts) of Old Sturbridge Village (1946) and the Plimoth Plantation (1947), as well as Living History Farms in Iowa (1970) and El Rancho de las Golondrinas in New Mexico (1972).[18] Likewise, the expanding National Park Service (NPS) took a particular liking to living history as a method of interpretation at its sites. By the early 1970s, living history programming had been formally established at several NPS military forts—including Fort Laramie (Wyoming), Fort Davis (Texas), Fort Pulaski (Georgia), Fort Union (New Mexico), and Fort Vancouver (Washington). Writing in 1982, folklorist Jay Anderson estimated that in North America there were, all told, "perhaps 650 institutions that regularly present[ed] living-history programs and could be considered serious 'living museums.'"[19]

In the United States, these new museums were directly linked with the expansion of the service and knowledge economies. For tourists, these living museums offered opportunities for discretionary spending on leisure "time travel" through which they could immerse themselves in the everyday lives (especially the work lives) of people of the past. For public historians these museums offered a chance to work in their chosen field, researching, designing, and planning the programming. Given public history's roots in social history, its professionals tended to steer the interpretation of living museums toward a focus on the lives of everyday people—the soldier, the laundress, the blacksmith—rather than (solely) on history's elites. That practice helps account for the kind of history interpreted at these sites beginning in the late 1960s.[20] Living history museums also offered opportunities for historians working within the academy to become laborers themselves in off-site knowledge production, for instance by publishing journal articles that criticized the emerging museum genre for oversimplifying the past, or for failing the public in terms of historical authenticity.[21]

Significantly, the professional public historians described above were not generally charged with delivering face-to-face content at living history museums. Rather, living historical programming was, and continues to be, performed by a relatively new class of paraprofessionals (costumed tour guides or living history interpreters), whose labor centers on producing what social theorist Dean MacCannell has called a "work display," that is, the display of someone else's labor for the delight of the tourist. To MacCannell, such work displays signal that industrial capitalism was entering a new phase in which labor was being transformed "into cultural productions attended by tourists and sightseers who are moved by the universality of work relations . . . as it is revealed to them at their leisure through the displayed work of others."[22] Living museums doubly produce work displays—first, through the expected costumed demonstrations of industrial or preindustrial labor (blacksmithing, musket drills, churning butter), and second, through performances of service encounters (conversations between costumed interpreters and museum guests that are often—though not always—related to the site's history). When working public history's front lines, interpreters earn an hourly wage, and receive on-the-job training regarding how to perform their double function work displays: the physical labor from bygone eras, and the emotional labor and knowledge work that colors interpersonal interactions with museum guests.

Public History and the Service Economy: *The Emotional Proletariat*

Originally called Fort Saint Anthony, Fort Snelling was created as one of a chain of military forts established at the edge of the frontier, following the end of the War of 1812.[23] As such, its first front line comprised soldiers and officers of the 5th Regiment of the United States Infantry. Built at the confluence of the Minnesota and Mississippi rivers in the early years of the 1820s, Fort Snelling was intended to house the army that was sent to the hinterlands of the Northwest Territory (which was originally incorporated in 1787 to include lands that cover the modern-day states of Ohio, Indiana, Michigan, Wisconsin, northeastern Minnesota) to support the United States' economic interests in the territory's lucrative fur trade—the driving force of the economy at the time. It would take 150 years—and two major economic shifts—before the Fort's front line would include service workers hired to perform Fort life during the era known as the Early Republic.

After being heavily used during World War II, the Fort was decommissioned in 1946 and declared a National Historic Landmark in 1960—one of the hundreds of sites to benefit from the postwar focus on patriotism and historic preservation. By the 1970s, the historic site found new life and purpose as a tourist destination managed by the Minnesota Historical Society. In conjunction with the expansion of the service economy during the last decades of the twentieth century, from 1970 onward living history interpreters have been hired to work as the Fort's *new* front line, as they interacted with visitors as costumed as figures from the Fort's frontier past—including soldiers, laundresses, officers, domestics, keel boat captains, immigrant refugees, and occasionally American Indians.[24]

The Fort saw peak tourism during the nation's bicentennial year of 1976, when Americans had a keen desire for patriotic pageantry and the Fort welcomed 158,894 visitors through its gates. Attendance has not reached such heights since then. According to the Minnesota Historical Society, in 1977 visitation "dropped to 113,384. While there was a slight improvement in 1984, when the Fort attracted 135,207 visitors, attendance declined to 105,625 in 1988; 99,950 in 1992; 85,728 in 1999; and 72,756 in 2004."[25] This visitor decline is consistent with other living history museums in the United States. Williamsburg, for example was drawing around a million visitors each year throughout the 1970s, but by 2005 they were counting an average of 734,000 visitors a year.[26] How museums and historical sites responded to this decline marks their entrance into the slipstream of changes in the broader economy.

The former vice president of Colonial Williamsburg, Cary Carson (who is also a public historian), has noted that although the reasons we see such a marked decline in history museum attendance may be anybody's guess, history museum administrators should be nonetheless prompted to consider a "Plan B" to ensure that their programming speaks more intensely to modern visitor's learning preferences and their persistent desires to connect to the past.[27] Along these lines, documented decline of visitor attendance at Old Sturbridge Village encouraged museum administrators to develop a new business model founded on user-directed services "from signage to hands-on activities to a judicious introduction of technology" to attract a new customer base (and not incidentally, to help compensate for staffing reductions).[28] By 2009 it seems this new business model approach was working, when Old

Sturbridge Village president and CEO James E. Donahue announced that the "living history museum's January and February 2009 attendance jumped 32 percent over the same period last year, giving OSV its best start in seven years."[29]

Similarly, in 2009 Conner Prairie Interactive History Park (formerly Conner Prairie Living History Museum) boasted that it was "thriving despite the economic downturn. Attendance, revenue and membership sales [were] up significantly [and that as] of Nov. 1, 2009, general admission attendance at Conner Prairie was 11 percent higher than last year at the same time."[30] As does Sturbridge, Conner Prairie credits its success to adopting a new business model that pushed the "History Park" to widen its customer base and to stress the importance of training front-line staff in the tenets of excellent customer service, focusing especially on preparing the workers to make meaningful emotional connections with museum guests who navigated the Park's free-choice learning environment.[31] As Conner Prairie's experience manager Dave Allison (the job title itself telling evidence of Conner's service economy rebranding) and chief operating officer Ken Bubp have noted of the living history site's recent changes, "the concept that visitor's needs should come first became inculcated into Conner Prairie's culture."[32]

Adjusting to meet visitor's needs and expectations is a key way that living history museums are working to stay relevant. Tellingly, the 2012 Call For Papers for the Annual Meeting of the Association for Living History, Farms and Agricultural Museums (ALHFAM) was "Maintaining Relevance in a Digital Age." Though learning the ropes of Facebook, tweeting, and YouTube might seem out of step with the antiquarianism often associated with living history, conference attendees to the 2012 ALHFAM conference were promised "an opportunity to learn how the historical community maintains its sense of relevance in an ever changing world filled with tweets, tubes and online friends you've never met in person."[33] And yet, while the nearly 400 institutional members of ALHFAM looked to remain relevant through the use of digital technologies, for prospective clientele no amount of digital media could ever fully replace the experience of visiting a living history site and interacting with the interpreters working there.

Ultimately, interpreters are the linchpins of any site's ability to ensure the *personalized* delivery of history. As interactive service workers, that is, those who relate directly with customers either through voice time (as with telemarketers) or through face time (as with restaurant servers, retail clerks, or living history interpreters),[34] the living history interpreters who are the focus of this study are also part of what sociologists Cameron Lynne MacDonald and Carmen Sirianni have termed the "emotional proletariat."[35] Asked to perform what sociologist Arlie Hochschild first described as "emotional labor" (when workers are asked to use their own emotions to create feeling states in clientele), the emotional proletariat are frontline service workers who "are given very explicit instructions concerning what to say and how to act," while both customers and managers "watch to ensure that these instructions are carried out."[36] For example, Sacramento City College's student employee training guide instructs employees to "answer the phone by the third ring, and smile. Smiling actually makes you sound friendlier!" The employee manual for the company that jointly owns Sbarro and Subway implores workers: "Always greet the customer with a pleasant smile. Be friendly and happy that they cam [sic] in to do business with you. The customer MUST be greeted within 3 seconds of the time they enter our doors."[37]

Such corporate-style guidelines and manuals represent a Taylorized stage of the knowledge and service economy, wherein knowledge and services of all kinds (including emotions) are being subjected to a new kind of scientific management and oversight. The *Staff Administrative Handbook* at Historic Fort Snelling, for example, instructs its trainees with the following directive: "Feelings and attitudes and facial expressions are highly communicable to the visitor. Active staff members who obviously are enjoying their job create an ideal environment for learning. Slouching, frowning or bored tour guides create the opposite. You obviously won't be expected to smile while making soap or chopping wood, but do smile when a visitor asks if that is a real fire you are cooking over."[38] Although one would have to make a few changes depending on the worksite, similar instructions can be found in any employee manual that relies on the labor of the emotional proletariat, including the wider training literature published for museum practitioners and interpreters.

In *Thriving in the Knowledge Age: New Business Models for Museums and Other Cultural Institutions,* for example, museum practitioners and education scholars John H. Falk and Beverly Sheppard suggest ways in which frontline staff should be encouraged to manipulate their personalities, and to identify with their worksites. Falk and Sheppard recognize that "unfortunately, at the bottom of the employee pecking-order [at museums] are the floor staff, whether volunteer or paid. These individuals, who generally receive the least pay and the least training in the organization, are actually the ones we count upon to support the public experience."[39] Though the authors find the low wages of front-line staff unfortunate, the new business model approach of their book focuses on the importance of improving employee training in customer service. According to the authors, museums should strive to train front-line workers (including "the guards, the ticket takers, the coat room clerks" to feel "true ownership for the institution") by empowering them "to make decisions, and to go the extra mile to ensure that the best interests of the organization are served."[40] Empowering workers as such allows for the flourishing of creativity from the museum staff members who deal with the public, which can be rewarding both to visitors and frontline workers alike. The successful service delivery hinges, how-ever, on the museum staff being empathic with and responsive to visi-tor needs. "Again," Falk and Sheppard emphasize to their readership of museum managers and directors, "at the heart of service is emotion."[41]

In a related vein, museum specialists William T. Alderson and Shirley Payne Low's *Interpretation of Historic Sites* provides a list of thirteen "Do's and Don't's of Interpretation," which addresses how interpreters can correctly manage their personality and emotions in their interac-tions with the visitor. These "Do's and Don't's" lessen the burden of managers by providing interpreters with ways to self-manage their per-sonalities, while the guidelines simultaneously highlight ways for the interpreters to manage the public. Number 3 suggests that if an inter-preter makes a mistake they should "say so and laugh it off [because] visitors identify with the human qualities of an interpreter who is not infallible," while number 7 suggests that interpreters "speak in a natu-ral, informal way, never in singsong. Try to give the impression that you just happened to think of a particular point that visitors might enjoy hearing about." Number 10, the most empowering of the "Do's and Don't's" emboldens the interpreter: "Remember that you are the historic site, so far as visitors are concerned—the front line. You can make or break visitor's interest in the site."[42] This instructive "Do" casts interpreters not merely as arbiters of history, but as the site itself; it urges them to connect emotionally with visitors and to define their own sense of *self* with their place of work.

Similarly, the introductory lines of the *Staff Administrative Handbook* at Historic Fort Snelling, assigns interpreters the task of fulfilling the expectations of the State:

> You have been selected as a member of Minnesota Historical Society's Historic Fort Snelling with the confidence that you will give the best possible service to the visitor touring the fort. The State of Minnesota and the Minnesota Historical Society funds the site each biennium for two reasons: the education and recreation of its visitors. It will be your job to give the visitor an understanding of history of the fort and the region and an empathy for the inhabitants of the area. At the same time you will make each visit as enjoyable as possible.[43]

Here it pays to notice the ways in which Fort interpreters are encouraged to construct their identities as workers. They are not only charged with the responsibilities of educating and entertaining the public, but they are obliged by the state of Minnesota to carry out those duties. This is certainly raising the tasks of interactive service work—at roughly $10/hour—to great heights, and points to one of the contradictions for the poorly paid but generally well-educated and committed workers who ply their trade on public history's front line.

Working to Connect: *Why Frontline Interpreters Matter*

Visiting a living history museum is just one of many ways one might choose to spend an afternoon; visitors to Historic Fort Snelling might otherwise elect to drive five miles down the road to the Mall of America—a mecca of global consumerism that boasts more than 400 chain stores. But time spent at local history sites signals modern desires to experience life in ways that are seemingly unmediated by mass culture. Indeed, Historic Fort Snelling and local history sites like it are part of what historian Tammy S. Gordon has identified as a "backlash against the perception that globalization has homogenized culture and a backlash against the perception that culture is produced by big companies everywhere."[44]

Drawing on information gleaned from contemporary audience surveys, Cary Carson has observed that "modern museum-goers" yearn "to imagine themselves back in the past, and their expectation that their pretended persona will share history's trials and tribulations with the historical figures they meet there."[45] Helping us make sense of these longings to connect with the past, Dean MacCannell has posited that tourist rituals embody efforts "to overcome the discontinuity of modernity"[46]—that is, to overcome the ways in which our modern world makes us feel disconnected from authentic connections with each other and our past. And while MacCannell denies the possibility of actually overcoming that discontinuity through tourism (because tourism is always staged, and so, always already inauthentic), he persuasively shows that behind touristic excursions (whether to see Monticello, Machu Picchu, or the *Mona Lisa*) lie deep desires to connect more intimately with—and to build a "fragile solidarity" in—the present.[47]

Those of us who have participated in touristic rituals of guided tours know how deeply disappointing it can be to feel disconnected from one's tour guide, and to sense that the guide is just going through the motions without caring much about our needs or interests. By contrast, tour guides and interpreters also have the capacity to deeply enrich a visitor's experience of a site—particularly when they can fulfill the visitor's wish, in the words of the National Park Service's interpretive sage Freeman Tilden, "not so much to be talked at as talked *with*."[48]

But inspiring visitors toward a greater understanding of a site is not the only function of the interpreter-visitor interaction. Anthropologist Cathy Stanton, in her ethnographic study of Lowell National Historic Park, concluded that the park's history professionals, and "especially, but not exclusively, the frontline rangers" were participating in "rituals of reconnection" through their cultural work at the park.[49] In these rituals of reconnection, employees valued their own personal connections with the site's history, and emotionally bonded with visitors who were moved by the historical narratives imparted at the site. Stanton maintains that interpreter-visitor interaction at the industrial history site helped both parties "to locate themselves and their work more firmly in the present day."[50]

In a related vein, Tammy S. Gordon's work on local history exhibits shows that visitor encounters with nonwhite (or ethnic) curators at historical venues such as Shoshone-Bannock Tribal Museum in Idaho, or

Olde Mill House Gallery and Printing Museum in Florida, have proved
personally transformative for many visitors. To take one example,
an elderly repeat visitor (presumably white) to the Olde Mill House
Museum reported that the African American curator there "helped her
overcome a lifetime of prejudiced thinking."[51] Although this example
places the burden of responsibility on nonwhite museum workers to
serve as ambassadors of their culture for white clientele, anthropologist Laura Peers's ethnography of First Nation and American Indian
interpreters at Canadian and US living history museums suggests that
many native interpreters seek out this kind of work not only because
they value seeing their own history represented, but also because they
seek opportunities to teach non-native people about indigenous culture,
which, as a ritual of reconnection, they find personally fulfilling.[52]

In my field notes I recorded one particularly poignant experience
recounting my own desire to emotionally connect with a visitor. In the
following excerpt, I am describing my encounter with a family who was
visiting the Fort with their elderly mother named Joan. I was portraying a domestic from 1827 that day, and Joan, I learned, had worked as a
domestic early on in her life:

> The four of us ended up on the back porch of the house, and even-
> tually I broke character because they wanted to know who I really
> was. Joan asked if she could write me, if we could keep in touch. I
> promised her we could if she wrote me. I had no qualms about giving
> her my address. I skipped my lunch break to continue talking with
> them. I didn't eat until I was off the clock at 1:30. History was defi-
> nitely secondary here. It was that personal connection that mattered
> to me, even though I did manage to tell the stories of the Fort at first,
> but the visitors seemed to want me to drop the facade and just talk
> to them: to connect, I suppose.[53]

In this scenario, the sacrifice of the lunch break is but one symbol that
I was invested in connecting with visitors through the raw material of
history. Alas, Joan never wrote me, and as such, the connection was
fleeting. But the encounter itself bespeaks a deep desire on both the visitors' and my behalf "to connect." This is certainly an effort—through a
ritualistic, touristic encounter—to repair the wounds of disconnection
that are symptomatic of our modern world.

But the moment where this mending fails for the worker is at the point where the seemingly authentic encounter is taken and repackaged as a sign of his or her place in the service economy: at the moment where emotional labor defines the worker not as part of a deeply connected society—but as a customer service superstar.

At the 2001 training session at the Fort, when Arthur was praised for foregoing his lunch break in favor of speaking with children about his replica musket, when Oliver was singled out for never being seen with a frown on his face, or when Kathleen was recognized for her unstoppable energy at birthday parties, these workers were labeled *customer service superstars*. Through additional self-sacrifice performed in a workplace that already demanded emotional labor, these individuals rose to the top of the frontline corporate culture.

But being touted *customer service superstar* does not necessarily encourage workers to see how they might be part of a worker collective bound by common interests. True, by performing or sharing the stories of our mutual past, cultural workers—such as living history interpreters—and tourists come together in ritualized encounters that help both parties make meaning of their lives. And yet because these encounters take place within the marketplace, they also spur new tensions and conflicts about working conditions and benefits.

Caught in the Machine

The frontline workers who are the focus of this book tended to frame their cultural work of connecting with visitors through the mechanism of history as a privilege; in so doing they also tended to avoid confronting the material conditions of their working lives, including pay, job security, benefits. At other times those who saw their work as a privilege but nevertheless chose to confront the material conditions of their work, still tended to concede the conditions of their employment, however grudgingly. Like many who work in the nonprofit cultural sector of the new economy, workers sacrifice themselves for the love of the job, for the love of meaningful work that contributes to society, for the love of history. Significantly, the promise of external monetary rewards or benefits is not what inspires people to pursue or perform this work—although many, like Kathleen at Fort Snelling (and me as well), need what economic remuneration these jobs provide.

In his empirical study of datasets from for-profit and nonprofit firms, economist Matthias Benz concluded that nonprofit workers are drawn to their jobs because of "substantial non-pecuniary work benefits"—emotional in nature—which intrinsically motivate workers to thought-fully interact with and produce meaningful experiences for the public.[54] Ryan, a costumed interpreter at the Fort, alluded to this kind of intrin-sic motivation in his interview with me: "There have been times when myself and several others have stayed later than what was necessary just to make sure things were done [right], when we were doing things off the clock, just to make sure that the site is the best that we can offer."[55] Workers like Ryan find their interactive cultural work fulfilling because it allows for creativity, for intellectual challenges, and for opportunities to positively affect the lives of others. Unlike more routinized service workers such as the fast-food workers that sociologist Robin Leidner has studied, cultural workers in the service economy tend to be able to personalize their interactions with the public so that each interaction is memorable and tailored to meet users' needs.[56] Notably, Ryan named those parts of the job that *were* routinized—such as doing a series of seven-minute presentations for school groups throughout the day (the bulk of spring and fall work)—as his least favorite part of working as a living history interpreter at the Fort, namely because he experienced no real interaction with the public during those presentations, but rather the drudgery of saying and "doing things over and over and over again." In contrast, Ryan relished "doing normal interpretation to the public" because he was "always interacting, and [never knew] what the next question [was] going to be."[57] This nonscripted interaction is fulfilling to both interpreter and visitor. Such personal individuation is why tour-ists continue to visit living history sites, why students value personal interactions with their professors, and why patrons seek individual assistance from reference librarians.[58] In our current culture, shaped as it is by corporatization, hypermobility, and technological mediation of our social lives, that personalized service is important and even sacred work. And so, when the workers I encountered sensed that they were not valued, or when their creativity was not allowed to flourish—they felt that what was sacred and special about their work had evaporated and history was turned into a product to be bought and sold. Though sometimes troubled by the material and emotional hazards of the job, these same workers tended to be much more emotionally invested in their jobs than one might expect from someone employed in what the Bureau of Labor Statistics considers a low-wage service job.[59]

Although one sign of emotional investment could be seen in the ways female interpreters engaged in caretaking behavior, for instance by laboring at the Fort's historic hearth in order to cook a particularly tasty meal that would earn them individuating compliments from co-workers during a break,[60] other signs could be seen in the ways the job affected interpreters' identities off the clock—something performance studies theorist Stephen Eddy Snow also identified as happening to interpreters at Plimoth Plantation.[61] One interpreter who had worked at the Fort for more than two decades described parts of his tenure:

> When we had a full six months of near full time employment [at
> the Fort], we would get unemployment in the winter, and that was
> a lifestyle for a while. Some of us took it seriously and we did a lot
> of serious research in the winter; we'd go on trips to New Orleans
> or Tippecanoe; we'd actually have monthly meetings at [someone's]
> house to do a sewing bee or a cooking demonstration, or a historical
> roundtable or something like that. So we took the lifestyle seriously,
> and more recently with the cuts in hours [at the Fort], a lot of us just
> work on other jobs [until the spring season begins again].[62]

Many Fort interpreters returned to the historic site for years and valued the job for more than the financial remuneration it offered. The interpreter quoted above described spending countless unpaid hours in the off season doing research and acquiring supplemental knowledge that benefited his organization; this betrays a deep intrinsic motivation. Although Fort interpreters were seasonal workers, those who deeply invested in the job spent the off-season in meaningful reflection about their work.

Like many worksites in the knowledge and cultural sectors—even in the face of insecurity, and often experiencing a sense of being devalued—the Fort offered some workers opportunities to experience meaningful connections with co-workers and the public, to have creative autonomy to apply their unique knowledge sets to their working lives, and to have the space to think, reflect, and make meaning. In addition to receiving a wage for doing something they loved to do, the realization of this fulfillment drives both the expansion of many jobs that are in the crosshairs of the service and nonprofit cultural sectors, even while it results in the overproduction of cultural workers who, rather than seeing the ways in which they are part of a shared enterprise, are often preoccupied with protecting their own little piece of turf within the cultural and knowledge economies. The challenge for public historians is to see how their labor is connected to the work of others across a range of worksites, and even within a climate of shared and limited resources to nurture one another across the hierarchy of job titles. This effort may well start with taking the time here to understand, appreciate, and analyze the experiences of a group of interpreters who once labored on the front lines of public history, at a work site they simply called "the Fort."

With an eye toward examining public history's front line and the consequences of their emotional investment in their work, the book is divided into two parts: "Part I: Public History's Emotional Proletariat (1960–1996)" draws largely on archival evidence; and "Part II: Historic Fort Snelling's Front Line (1996–2006)" draws extensively from interviews and my own participant observation working on public history's front line.

Part I begins with Chapter 1, "Performing a Public Service: From Historic Site to Work Site (1960–1985)," which focuses on the history of the Fort beginning when it emerged as a new tourist destination in the 1960s. At this time, training documents for a new type of service worker (living history interpreters) were being drafted alongside materials that would dictate how the site's larger history would be disseminated to the public. This chapter examines these materials in tandem in order to show the relationship between the production of history and customer service directives at the Fort. Chapter 2, " 'Our Seat at the Table': Interpreter Agency and Consent (1985–1996)," gives us a window into crucial workplace issues concerning Historic Fort Snelling's frontline interpreters. This chapter offers a case study of how some living history interpreters in this era organized to improve their conditions as workers in the service society, and it analyzes why larger collective organizing efforts among Minnesota Historical Society interpreters may have failed.

Part II of the book draws largely on the thirty-two extensive interviews with interpreters and supervisors, and on my own participant observation as a worker there. Chapter 3, "The Wages of Living History: Rewards and Costs of Emotional Investment," critically examines how workers at the Fort juggled the demands of servicing and educating the public while also pretending to be characters from the past. Interpreters I encountered were extraordinarily loyal to their places of work and took seriously the work they performed, often at the expense of their personal lives out of costume. I probe this contradiction by asking why living history interpreters invested themselves as such and by examining the emotional costs of that investment. This chapter offers insight on how the labor process is reproduced and worker subjectivities are shaped in the new economy. Interpreters may have been loyal to the site, but that loyalty was fraught with complication and ambivalence.

Chapter 4, "Pursuing Authenticity: Creative Autonomy and Workplace Games," takes a ground-level approach to understanding how authenticity was used as a kind of worksite "game" at the Fort. Striving to acquire authentic knowledge and skills bolstered interpreters' work identities and benefited the overall organization, but in this organizational culture of top-down supervision that focused on disciplining workers rather than nurturing them, "authenticity" was also used as a policing mechanism. In this manner, we see the horizontal fragmentation of public history's frontline workers whose energies were often focused on infighting about authenticity, even as they yearned for an organizational culture that would harness their creative potential.

The fifth and final chapter, "Interpreting Painful Histories: Emotional Comfort and Connecting," examines how, during my time as a guide, the site promoted a pain-free programming that naturalized unequal power relationships. Chapter 5 also analyzes how interpreters used additive knowledge, their own ideological positions, various levels of emotional investment in their jobs, and shifting conceptions of self—all of which they brought to bear in interactions with the public about emotionally painful histories.

Drawing on archival research, my participant observation, and interviews with Fort interpreters and supervisors, this book argues that those who chose to invest themselves in the worksite did so because they found it emotionally fulfilling to connect with others through the medium of living history, and also because the structure of the worksite encouraged these workers to create strong self-identities (rather than collective identities) that were embedded in the larger workplace culture. In order to truly understand the historical form and content at living history museums, we need to understand the larger contexts that shape the working lives of those delivering that content: public history's front line. Ultimately, the emotional fulfillment that interpreters seek from their jobs profoundly affects the way the past is translated to the public. In the end, this study may be about frontline workers at one living history museum, but the implications of this study extend beyond the walls of the Fort. The study yields insight to the work of public history writ large, while it is also emblematic of a whole class of labor relationships in the modern world where a growing class of quite highly qualified (and emotionally invested) workers are expected to be more and more entrepreneurial by deeply investing—emotionally and financially—in their own job and professional skills through unpaid internships, volunteer positions, and low-wage frontline jobs. Increasingly, those seeking meaningful work in the culture industries find an economy that is providing fewer opportunities for it, in so far as jobs that provide meaning are increasingly standardized and oversupplied. To find meaning in our working lives, our economy wages a high price to get it.

In the front lines of public history—as elsewhere—in order to invest in the profession, public historians need to communicate the value that this kind of frontline worker investment brings, not only to the organizations but also to the larger field and the field's impact on the public good. Teaching the public about the nuances of history is important to cultivate an informed and engaged citizenry. Frontline workers need knowledge as well as skills to translate the past effectively to the public by meeting them where they are. The social costs of a vulnerable and devalued frontline workforce are hard to trace, however. A case study approach offers an opportunity for us to answer difficult questions about complex issues by examining frontline culture workers at the micro level. In so doing, we gain far-reaching insights about the changing meaning of labor, and with respect to this case study, especially about the wages of history work in our time.

PART I

Public History's
Emotional Proletariat
(1960–1996)

CHAPTER I
PERFORMING A PUBLIC SERVICE
From Historic Site to Work Site (1960–1985)

O n a spring Sunday in 1965, Mr. Richard J. Weiss—a life-
long resident of Minnesota—visited Fort Snelling to fly
kites with his children. While there, he and his family toured the old
Fort's buildings and visited the newly opened Fort Snelling State Park,
which lay at the confluence of the Minnesota and Mississippi rivers. Dismayed by what he saw, Weiss wrote a concerned letter to the Minnesota
Department of Conservation noting that he had "never seen a historical
place in such *poor* shape."[1]

Weiss described his visit to the state park as a disappointing "long
walk through uninteresting bottom lands" that ended "at a despicable dump," and he found his tour of the old Fort—a National Historic
Landmark since 1960—similarly wanting. In 1965, of the Fort's four
original buildings only one was being actively renovated, while two of
the buildings—Weiss was dismayed to discover—were "inhabited by
doctors and VA [Veterans Administration] personnel free loading [*sic*] in
these historical places for a pitance [*sic*]" paid in rent. Ultimately, Weiss
wanted to see more evidence of planning at the historic site and park;
specifically, he wanted the dump buried, the VA evicted, and the buildings and furnishings of the original Fort restored and reconstructed.
Little could Weiss have predicted that by 1970 the Fort would have
several restored buildings and a fledgling workforce of living history
interpreters who were hired to interact with tourists and perform work
displays appropriate to the 1820s.

Focusing on the period from 1960 to 1985, this chapter examines archival materials related to Historic Fort Snelling's early interpretive programming, qualitative data, and training materials developed for the site's growing cadre of living history interpreters, all of which draw attention to the relationship between the production of public history and the performance of customer service. The chapter provides a window into several areas of tension that significantly affected the experience of living history for both workers and consumers.

One of those areas of tension lay in the gendered work displays at the living history museum. While the labor of male and female interpreters attempted to represent the historical divide between male and female labor at the post in the 1820s, not only were some of those purportedly historical performances misleading, they also led to differing expectations for male and female interpreters with regard to the emotional work displays required of them. And in the male workforce, internal tensions arose as the military chain of command enacted was used for social control of the Fort's contemporary workforce (so that, for instance, male interpreters playing the roles of soldiers with the rank of private on the bottom of that chain were expected to follow orders from co-workers assigned to play their superiors).

While some workers may have taken pleasure in this slippage between past and present, examining the archival evidence alongside qualitative data reveals an interpretive workforce divided between those who took pleasure in the job primarily because it provided opportunities for "playing soldier," and those who valued it for the opportunities it afforded to provide a "public service." Gradually, the Fort's interpretive workforce shifted to include more individuals from this latter group as changes in interpretive policy and higher wages attracted a new demographic of applicants who saw opportunities for meaningful employment on public history's front line.

Fort Snelling: *Minnesota's Williamsburg*

Throughout its history, the Fort was mostly a quiet post; indeed, its primary purpose in 1858 was to pen sheep.[2] Though this army post never entered into the larger historical consciousness of most of the American public, the Fort did play a role in a few key historical events (fig. 1). For

Figure 1. "The Second Minnesota State Fair at Fort Snelling: Cassius M. Clay Is Delivering the Address," 1860. Photograph by Moses C. Tuttle. Courtesy Minnesota Historical Society.

example, the enslaved couple Dred and Harriet Scott repeatedly sued for their freedom from 1846 to 1857 on the basis that they had several times lived on free soil—in Illinois and at Fort Snelling, where the couple met (and where they had lived for much of the 1830s). Thus the geographic location of the Fort in "free territory" (per the Northwest Ordinance of 1787, and the Missouri Compromise of 1820) helped lay the groundwork for the United States Supreme Court's Dred Scott Decision of 1857, which declared that "a negro of African descent, whose ancestors were of pure African blood, and who were brought into this country and sold as slaves," were not entitled to national citizenship even if living in a free state or territory (and therefore had no legal right to sue in federal courts), and that the federal government had no constitutional basis to prohibit slavery in the territories.[3] The Fort also played a significant role in national events during the winter of 1862–63 when the U.S. Army imprisoned approximately 1,700 Dakota Indians (mostly women, children, and elders) just below the Fort's walls. In the concentration camp at Fort Snelling some three hundred Dakota died as a result of inadequate shelter and poor conditions.[4]

Figure 2. "Streetcar passing by the Round Tower, Fort Snelling," circa 1915, postcard, Acmegraph Company, Chicago. Courtesy Minnesota Historical Society.

Figure 3. "Visitors Viewing Exhibit at the Round Tower Museum," circa 1958. Courtesy Minnesota Historical Society.

Figure 4. "Aerial View of Fort Snelling," November 25, 1959. Photograph by St. Paul Dispatch & Pioneer Press. Courtesy Minnesota Historical Society.

From 1866 to 1911, the Fort headquartered the Department of Dakota, which oversaw all military activities in the state of Minnesota and the territories of Dakota and Montana. After World War I, the fort was used as quarters, and one of its four original buildings—the Round Tower, dating to the 1820s—was briefly converted into both a beauty shop and residence (fig. 2). During the 1920s Fort Snelling earned notoriety as the so-called Country Club of the Army because of the extensive polo grounds on its upper post,[5] and by the end of the 1930s the old Round Tower, converted from a residence to the "Round Tower Museum," featured Works Progress Administration murals (fig. 3).[6] During World War II, the Fort was bustling again with activity when it served as a Military Intelligence Service Language School and a recruiting, reception, and induction station.[7] At the close of the war, however, in 1946, the U.S. military officially decommissioned the Fort as a military post, and the Veterans Administration assumed management.[8]

Meanwhile, the Fort's existing structures had long been compromised by a road and bridge that ran through the center of the grounds (fig. 4). In 1956, the four buildings that remained from the early complex were further threatened by proposals to build a cloverleaf turnpike around the Fort's iconic Round Tower. Weary of urban renewal projects rapidly and dramatically altering the downtown landscapes of the Twin Cities, Minnesotans voiced their displeasure at the prospect of seeing their state's foremost historical structure blemished by modern freeway construction.

Public outcry led the state to abandon the freeway plans and also to begin discussions on how, in the words of one Smithsonian archaeologist in 1956, "to free the parade ground of the objectionable heavy traffic by way of the Seventh Street bridge, which now bisects the historic nuclear area."[9] Governor Orville L. Freeman, after meeting with representatives from interested state agencies, asked the highway department to redraft construction plans to reroute traffic through a tunnel underneath the historic area of interest, in order to "leave the old fort site free of roads."[10]

Traffic rerouting was completed by 1958, at which time the Minnesota Statehood Centennial Commission provided the funds needed for the Minnesota Historical Society to excavate 10 percent of the old post. Excavations unearthed many of the Fort's original foundations, and positioned the post to become Minnesota's first designated National Historic Landmark in 1960. But even in the wake of landmark designation and the federal government's "willingness to transfer the Round Tower and substantial acreage at the Fort to the State for park purposes," Minnesota still had no established course of action for the preservation, restoration, or interpretation of the historic area.[11]

In 1963, however, with hopes that Minnesota could enjoy a larger piece of the tourist-economy pie, the Minnesota legislature established the Minnesota Outdoor Recreation Resources Commission (MORRC), whose Fort Snelling Committee lobbied hard to halt proposed new construction on the Fort's old polo field; state representative William J. O'Brien, who chaired the committee, reflected on how this preservation victory put into sharp relief the many unanswered questions that were "vital to legislative consideration" in order for additional Fort grounds to be put on the path toward eventual preservation or restoration. In partnership with the Minnesota Historical Society (MHS), MORRC established a subcommittee, the Fort Snelling Restoration Committee (FSRC), whose mission was to research and produce a report regarding the projected costs of the Fort's physical restoration and maintenance, the major uses of the Fort after restoration, and ideas for interpretive programming.[12]

From the outset, the fifteen professional architects, historians, archaeologists, business leaders, and legislators of the all-male FSRC leaned away from merely preserving the four existing Fort structures as they had changed over time and toward a full-scale restoration and reconstruction.[13] As part of their research, the FSRC studied "the more than 50 fort restorations across the country" and paid particular attention to those which "attained the quality that Fort Snelling seeks to achieve," including Fort Laramie (Wyoming), Fort Michilimackinac (Michigan), Fort Mackinac (Michigan), Fort Osage (Missouri), and Fort Ticonderoga (New York)—restorations that all were host to living history encampments and military pageantry in the 1960s.[14] Fort Michilimackinac, for example, hosted its first reenactment pageant in 1962.[15] But while the FSRC targeted military historic sites to help them estimate projected staff size and costs, development costs, maintenance costs, attendance, and admissions income, they also took inspiration from other sites.

Fort Snelling historian John Grossman—who developed much of the early interpretive programming materials—noted that, "Program ideas and precedents were borrowed from places such as Williamsburg, Virginia, Old Sturbridge Village, Massachusetts, and Fort York and Fort Henry, Ontario, where personnel have had experience in interpretations. The people at Fort York were particularly helpful with military training, equipment, and demonstrations."[16] Likewise, in remarks to the Minnesota Planning Association in 1965, FSRC chairman William J. O'Brien began his presentation by showing a film about the restoration and reconstruction of Colonial Williamsburg—the Rockefeller-funded project that aimed to recreate (a white-washed vision of) Virginia's colonial capital through restoration and reconstruction. "That's how it's done, being done at Williamsburg," noted O'Brien to the group of Minnesota planners: "Fort Snelling is Minnesota's Williamsburg."[17] In 1965, the FSRC's report and recommendations persuaded the legislature to appropriate $200,000 from the natural resources fund to allow the MHS to begin a full-scale reconstruction and restoration of the stone walls and of the sixteen buildings that had originally made up the 1820s frontier Fort. In all, the plan was projected to take ten years and to cost $10 million.

On a national scale, this restoration project was not unique. Through-out the 1960s and 1970s, as historian Mike Wallace quipped, everyone was "doin' it."[18] With the postwar economic boom, the nation saw an exponential growth in the numbers of Americans who were setting out in their automobiles on family vacations, with cash in their pockets. Investors and developers met demand by funding and creating more tourist destinations. Locations touched by history were prime targets.

With a coalition of middle-class advocates and funding partners ready to back development, city squares, districts, and main streets lined up to receive historic facelifts designed to attract the modern tour-ist. Likewise, crumbling industrial centers looked to profit from their own historic pasts by rebranding themselves as postindustrial tourist destinations. In 1978, for example, Lowell National Historic Park—which included "a series of buildings and open spaces within the down-town area and along the canal system that had once powered the tex-tile mills"—became what anthropologist Cathy Stanton has called "the flagship project of Lowell's culture-led redevelopment."[19] This kind of historic rebranding was aided by the passage of three major federal acts in 1966: the National Historic Preservation Act of 1966, the Department of Transportation Act, and the Demonstration Cities Act, which collec-tively buoyed preservation efforts by creating more safeguards before properties could be demolished (especially via highway construction or urban renewal) and by providing funding to survey areas with potential historic significance.

The initial funds for the Fort Snelling restoration were allocated in 1965, and by October 1966 Minnesotans were invited to celebrate the opening of "Minnesota's newest and oldest school house"—the first reconstructed building on the old post grounds.[20] Russell W. Frid-ley, director of the Minnesota Historical Society, spoke at the Satur-day morning dedication ceremony whose audience included Governor Karl Rolvaag, as well as educators who were attending the 14th Annual Teachers' Institute in Minnesota History.[21] In typed notes prepared for the ceremony, Fridley opined that it was "very fitting that the school house [was] the first of the major buildings to rise" because it sym-bolized a major aim of the restoration project: a "desire to share and acquire knowledge." Betraying perhaps the slightest chip on his shoul-der regarding Cold War educational trends to aggressively support the hard sciences, Fridley made a plug for the value of pursuing historical knowledge, which, in his words, were "as important as the knowledge yet to be uncovered by the scientists and our adventurers, our pioneers to the moon."[22]

Building the Scaffolding for a Living History Workforce

As the abbreviated account above regarding the pulse of historic preservation during the 1960s and 1970s suggests, the altruistic pursuit of knowledge was not the sole reason the Fort found financial support in the Minnesota legislature. The MORRC report poised Fort Snelling to become Minnesota's first open-air museum—a heritage site that would help stimulate the state's economy through projected tourist dollars. As such, the dual goal of the Fort as a platform for educating and entertaining tourists would be fused with the site even before its reconstruction.[23]

As elsewhere in the nation, the Fort Snelling Restoration Committee determined that once the restoration of the historic properties was complete, "pageantry or 'live' exhibits" would be "highly desirable to promote attendance and strengthen the educational impact upon visitors."[24] Thus, interpretation at the Fort was slated not only to include "life-sized dioramas inside reconstructed buildings" but also "military pageantry" afforded by costumed interpreters who would demonstrate drill and cannon firings. Likewise, "in order to add atmosphere and give the participating staff a sense of history," it was recommended that the interpreters "be uniformed in period dress."[25] This vision was akin to that which was gradually being realized at National Park Service (NPS) military forts during the 1960s and 1970s. For example, when Fort Laramie's living history program began in 1966, a living history atmosphere was created vis-à-vis a NPS ranger who conducted periodic firings of historic weapons. The following summer, two seasonal employees were hired to wear historic costumes and present talks in Fort Laramie's guardhouse about frontier and military life at the post in 1876. In 1971, military pageantry was solidified as the focus of the site when "a soldier field camp was added [and] manned by soldiers throughout the summer [who] portrayed rigors of campaign life through discussion of clothing, equipment, food, weapons, and field service."[26]

At Historic Fort Snelling (HFS) the interpretive program that immediately followed the 1966 reconstructed schoolhouse opening was not on too grand a scale—nor did it incorporate living history interpretation. During the 1967 summer season, a handful of tour guides—many recruited from local high schools—were hired to interpret the history of the Fort for the visiting public. Loren Johnson, director of the restoration, reported that the resulting program "left a great deal to be desired."[27] In Johnson's estimation, the staff members were not only poorly selected, they were also inadequately trained in both historical content and customer service: "the tour guides seemed to hide in the schoolhouse, waiting for the public to contact them, rather than making an active attempt to contact the public."[28] Much to Johnson's chagrin, the chief tour guide seemed to model this behavior: "This young man's personal motivation and initiative were negligible in the extreme, although there was nothing wrong with his ego and self-esteem. These latter qualities were of no benefit to either the tour program or to the Society's image, as [the guide] had difficulty in condescending to speak with the 'illiterate public.'"[29] Johnson recommended that the historical society improve the interpretive programming by instituting a more ambitious training program for a group of more shrewdly selected guides. These guides were to wear uniforms and would need to be "closely supervised" to ensure that they conform to an established set of "rules and regulations outlining their duties and governing their conduct."[30] These rules and regulations would be drafted alongside materials that would dictate how the site's larger history would be disseminated to the public. As HFS would start to take its new place in the postindustrial knowledge and service economy, it would simultaneously cultivate what I term a *public history proletariat* who would be hired to carry out the educational mission of the historic site while also delivering individualized customer service to its clientele.

As the 1970 sesquicentennial of the laying of the Fort's cornerstone approached, pressure mounted for the Minnesota Historical Society to more satisfactorily develop its interpretive programming. A Fort Snelling Sesquicentennial Committee chartered by the state recommended that the summer of 1970 be one where visitors could come to see costumed guides who would portray "life at the fort as it was 150 years ago."[31] In their 1969 report, the Fort Snelling Sesquicentennial Committee, which comprised sixteen community leaders, worked "to justify the request for public funds to finance partially the commemoration" and also "to indicate to the Governor and to the Legislature the direction of the committee's thinking"—especially with regard to the proposed budget and the ideas for commemorative activities.[32] Suggested activities included—but were not limited to—developing a "top-notch documentary film on the history of Old Fort Snelling," mounting interpretive exhibits and markers, and procuring "appropriate costumes for guides as well as other furnishings and equipment."[33]

While the ongoing restoration projects and the continued occupancy of the Veterans Administration may have made it difficult for some visitors to suspend disbelief, the scaffolding for the Fort's future living history program emerged during the sesquicentennial year when an eight-man "Guard" was ultimately hired to reenact drills and guard duties. Along with the Guard, four women were also hired at the hourly wage of just over a dollar an hour (the same as the men), to demonstrate domestic chores such as cooking, sewing, and laundering. The women also demonstrated candle dipping in the schoolhouse and served as cashiers at the post's reconstructed sutler's (civilian merchant's) store, which was structurally completed in 1970.

Female interpreters were also part of the living history programming at Fort Laramie. The author of this NPS site's administrative history notes that in 1971, "Mrs. Nadya Henry portrayed the role of an officer's wife," and in 1972, "an officer's maid began interpreting facets of the role of women employed at the post."[34] Similarly, at Fort Pulaski in Savannah, Georgia (run by the NPS), "in 1972, living history at the park consisted of a uniformed soldier giving musket demonstrations and performing roving interpretations and a small group of women in period clothing serving hardtack, pea soup, and coffee."[35]

By contrast, at Fort Ticonderoga (a living history museum in New York, managed by "a private, non-profit foundation") visitors had long encountered third-person interpreters "dressed as French soldiers of the 1750s as well as fife and drum corps members clad in American uniforms of the 1770s," but they would not encounter a female interpreter at Fort Ticonderoga until 1993, when Fran Davey decided to portray a nineteenth-century woman at the (eighteenth-century) military post.[36] Thus, by the time that Davey and co-author Thomas A. Chambers published their 1994 *Gender and History* article, " 'A Woman? At the Fort!'

A Shock Tactic for Integrating Women's History in Historical Interpretation," which discussed Ticonderoga's foray into interpreting women's roles, other military posts elsewhere in the nation—including Fort Snelling—had already been "shocking" visitors with female living history interpreters (though not necessarily fully realized women's history programming) for more than two decades.

In addition to the men and women that HFS hired as its first crew of living history interpreters, the Fort also recruited costumed volunteers to flesh out the look of the garrison, and to save the Minnesota Historical Society the cost of hiring additional workers.[37] Betraying a similar concern about the costs of hiring interpreters, beginning in 1973 Fort Vancouver (Washington) defrayed staffing costs of its living history program through an innovative work-study program with Portland Community College. Through this work-study program, the NPS hired students as seasonal interpreters while "the college agreed to pay 25% of the students' salaries."[38]

Emotional Requirements and Early Interpretive Programming

At HFS, the foray into costumed interpretation and historical demonstration for the sesquicentennial prompted the first comprehensive interpretive-program planning document for the Fort: "An Interpretive Program for Fort Snelling Restoration."[39] This 1970 interpretive program (henceforth, IP) set forth the goals, policies, and the general plot for the interpretation; outlined the personnel needs; defined how the structures should be used following their restoration or reconstruction; and proposed a biennial budget for 1971–72.

Parts of the IP were never executed. To cite a few examples, the program suggests that various barracks might "be occupied by full-time interpretive staff if they wish to live on the post"—a suggestion that might not have seemed so farfetched in 1970 given that VA staff members *were* living in the Officer's Quarters.[40] Likewise, the overall concept for interpretation never took hold. From our future vantage point, it would seem that the author of the IP had a case of sesquicentennial fever, as the IP suggested that the interpretive programming be overhauled on a yearly basis so that every year would be a sesquicentennial at the post. Thus visitors would experience an interpretation of the year 1820 in 1970, but in 1971 they would experience the year 1821, and so on. These changes were proposed to continue for a fifty-year cycle, ending in the year 2020. While these and other details did not come to pass, the overarching goals of the IP did take hold.

Pointing to the author's desire to have a professional workforce of interpreters guided by sound interpretive principles, the author frames his goals by drawing on the NPS's guru of heritage interpretation, Freeman Tilden, whose treatise *Interpreting Our Heritage* became an instant classic when it was published in 1957. In short, Tilden's philosophy of interpretation asks that it not be "sterile" for the visitor and that interpretation be conceived of as a teachable art form whose "chief aim . . . is not instruction, but provocation."[41] The IP, and subsequent articulations of interpretive philosophy for the Fort, adopts this outlook, noting that interpretation at the Fort Snelling Restoration would move beyond the mere reporting of facts; metaphorically speaking, the IP's author writes, guides would be called "to SHOW the sunset, not to define it." The plan's author then quotes Tilden directly: " 'The use of history is internal,' says Freeman Tilden in *Interpreting Our Heritage,* 'not what you can do with history, but what history does to you.' The goals of this interpretation are, first to *show* an accurate portrayal of life in Minnesota in the early nineteenth-century and second, to *stimulate* the visitor to ask himself, 'what would I have done, what would have been my fate, under these circumstances?' "[42]

To these empathy-building ends, the proposed Fort Snelling staff would be trained in two main areas: how to convincingly portray someone from the past and how to deliver excellent customer service as appropriate to the outdoor museum environment (figs. 5 and 6). Thus, staff members were to "assume period names, biographies, appearance, speech and manners, much in the way actors do, in order to interpret the spirit of the period to the audience," while they were also expected to enthusiastically engage the public by "talking *with* rather than *at* the visitors."[43] The IP's "policies of interpretation" also contain the familiar service economy dictum: "Every visitor to the Restoration is a guest, not a mere customer."[44]

An early 1970s training document for Fort Snelling guides reinforces the Tilden-esque emotional requirements for tour guides, as it instructs them "not to teach but to stimulate" by telling stories, making guests "feel comfortable," and by recognizing when guests were "losing their

Figure 5."Fort Snelling Staff Training Session," 1974. Courtesy Minnesota Historical Society.

Figure 6. "Soldiers and Laundresses in Schoolhouse, Fort Snelling," April 6, 1976. Photograph by John Grossman. Courtesy Minnesota Historical Society.

interest" so that guides could "change the subject, [and] move on to something that [the visitor] may be more interested in."[45] Likewise in 1970, guides at the Ramsey House (another historic site managed by the Minnesota Historical Society) were evaluated not only on their ability to present accurate knowledge about the history of the historic home and the Ramsey family, but also on their abilities to make "guests feel welcome," to show "enthusiasm about the house on the tour," and to adjust "the tour to the age and interests of the individuals taking the tour."[46]

Performing Gender

The IP also differentiated the emotional requirements of the job according to gender. While the male Fort Snelling Guard was expected "to greet and assist all the visitors" seven days a week, the plan predominately focused on what actions would need to be taken for the Fort's interpretive program to faithfully represent a company in the army. No doubt it was a formidable task to assemble a corps of twenty-six male interpreters who could convincingly "demonstrate the more elaborate, crowd-pleasing ceremonies, such as evening parade (tattoo)." Muskets, cannons, and period-appropriate uniforms would need to be procured, and staff would have to be trained to perform according to early nineteenth-century drill specifications. But the focus on believable military pageantry would unintentionally reinforce a tension between guides who cared less about "playing soldier" and more about interacting personally with the public.

While four pages of the IP address the Guard, two pages from the IP are devoted to the portrayal of "post dependents" (referring to army wives who generally worked as laundresses or domestics). Here—as with the Guard—the author notes what costumes and equipment would be needed for the "post dependents" program: dresses; 400 pounds of wax for candle-dipping; and 100 pounds of soap for laundry. Notably, these two pages conclude by offering a justification for portraying female post dependents in what had historically been a predominantly male environment. According to the IP's author, portraying women's roles was important, not only because modern female visitors were presumed to enjoy watching domestic arts demonstrations more than watching military drill, but also because women on the post "contribute tone and gentility to what would otherwise be a brusque and careless man's world. . . . Their smiles, visits, and apparel make everyone feel welcome."[47]

The language in the document is ambiguous as it conflates the imagined historic role of females on the post with the expected emotional output of the modern-day female interpreter. It is unlikely that early nineteenth-century laundresses were at all concerned with affecting an air of gentility as they pounded away with their dolly pins at the soldiers' fatigue frocks, but in the document the author imagines that the presence of females at the historic post would have softened the man's world of the Fort. A modern female interpreter was similarly expected to soften the Fort's atmosphere by producing pleasant feelings in Fort's paying visitors through "smiles, visits, and apparel."

In 1986, Patricia West—a curator at Lindenwald, President Martin Van Buren's New York estate—discussed the museum's move to include "young Irish servants" into their interpretive program, noting that they were doing so in order to raise "the issues of ethnicity, gender, class and work, which we consider to be significant interpretive material illustrating the incorporation of 'the new social history' into a house museum."[48] By contrast, the Fort's IP suggests that the decision to represent women's roles ("post dependents") was chiefly driven by a customer service mandate, rather than by the concerns of social history. The IP justified the inclusion of post dependents because they were presumed to please female visitors, and because it was presumed that the mere presence of smiling females dressed in period costume would be a successful way to make everyone feel welcome.

This is not to say that the male employees were not expected also to make visitors feel welcome, but at this early stage in the Fort's history, the burden of doing so through personal interactions may have lain more heavily with the female staff who more frequently interacted one-on-one with visitors. The male staff seldom interpreted alone. Not only were they required to frequently perform musket and artillery drills, but—in the spirit of verisimilitude—it was also discouraged for male interpreters portraying soldiers to walk alone anywhere; they were supposed to walk in unison with at least one other interpreter wherever they went. By contrast, whether they were laundering, candle dipping, or selling goods in the sutler's store, female guides were not often scheduled to work with other interpreters. They therefore had more

Figure 7. "Fort Snelling Sutler Store," 1982. Photograph by Stan Waldhauser.
Courtesy Minnesota Historical Society.

opportunities to interact directly and personally with guests than did
many of the male interpretive staff.[49]

Notably, while male staff members occasionally portrayed the post sutler, female interpreters were usually the ones to staff and clerk the sutler's
store (fig. 7).[50] While this would have been historically inaccurate for the
early nineteenth century (both sutlers and clerks were historically male),
it placed the twentieth-century public and interpreter in a familiar gendered relationship. Since the 1890s, women had been increasingly sought
after to work as saleswomen and retail counter clerks because—as historian Susan Porter Benson has argued—they were considered a "relatively
cheap and supposedly docile labor" force.[51] Even during my tenure at the
Fort from 1999 to 2006, women were most often staffed to tend the cash
register at the admissions office, although by that time male interpreters
did regularly portray the sutler and his cadre of middling-class clerks.

Sessions in the 1970s trained female interpreters to perform both clerical and domestic work as part of their interpretive duties. For example,
at the 1979 training sessions, the laundresses were scheduled on Fri-
day, April 20, at 11:00 a.m., to learn "Admissions and tour registration
procedures, recording attendance and receipts, [and] making deposits,"

while the next day, after learning about laundry, ironing, and quilting, at 10:30 a.m. they were to learn the "Operation of the Sutler Store, plus cleaning shelves and merchandise/Publications and sales procedures." At the same time that their female counterparts were learning about admissions, male interpreters were scheduled to report for drill call. And when female interpreters were learning about the sutler store sales procedures, the men rotated by squads through several military stations, including musket cleaning. It is possible that the male interpreters learned the clerical procedures more informally, but the training session schedules only show female interpreters being trained as such.[52]

Thus while women were represented as having been *present* at the post, interpretation of the actual roles that women played at the post were less developed, and even misleading. A 1989 symposium published in the *Oral History Review* about the "Representation of Women's Roles at the Oliver Kelley Farm" (a living history site managed by the Minnesota Historical Society), suggests that this somewhat generic approach to women's history seems to have been occurring at the Kelley Farm as well (at least, in the 1980s).[53] Despite ample evidence to support a complex interpretation of the roles that the Kelley women played at the farm— from domestic duties, to frequently managing and running the farm—at least one visitor to the farm in 1986 (professor of linguistics Amy Sheldon) went away with superficial impressions of nineteenth-century farm women: "When I visited the farm, I was listening for the story of the women. What I found was a generic view, an already familiar stereotype of women's lives. . . . Nothing in my visit to the farm with the children had led me to expect that any of these women had been invested with management responsibility or power in running the farm."[54]

Early interpretation of women's roles at the Fort also reproduced familiar stereotypes. Another area in which we can see superficiality is the site's early cooking program. One interpreter, Candyce, who had prior work experience at a prominent living history museum with a developed cooking and foodways program, noted that the women's cooking program at the Fort was woefully inadequate when she began working there in 1990: "The cooking program was basically making up cookie dough and baking some cookies, and that was all [female interpreters] did all day long." According to Candyce, this limited interpretation of women's roles not only misrepresented domestic skills, it also had a negative effect on the female staff's morale. Compared to male interpreters who could learn to demonstrate skilled crafts by working in the blacksmith or carpenter's shops, the women "didn't feel like we were contributing much to the staff or the interpretation and so [developing a cooking program] gave us a real kind of craft and added to the Fort and the duties that we do." It wasn't until the early 1990s that Candyce and her female interpretive colleagues helped invent "the cooking program at the Fort based off of past experiences [with hearth cooking]."[55]

Throughout the 1970s, historical verisimilitude was more carefully cultivated in the Fort's military program than it was in the portrayal of historically accurate women's work. This could be seen not only in the programming, but in the early costumes as well. The costumes for interpreters portraying soldiers generally conveyed an accurate impression of Army regulars in the 5th Regiment in the 1820s, but accurate costumes for female interpreters were not fully developed until the 1980s, when the MHS hired an assistant site manager at the Fort who specialized in period costumes. He was instrumental in procuring petticoats, stays, neckerchiefs, and more appropriate headgear for the female interpretive staff. The prioritizing of military history and men's roles at this military post is not surprising. Certainly, cultivating an authentic 1820s living history military program reflected the public's expectations for pageantry. But the focus on military history had effects that were initially unintended, with regard to how the guides would to be controlled and managed at the worksite.

Past Meets Present: *The Chain of Command*

During the 1970s, the Fort's program manager—fresh out of college when he was hired in 1971—was the only full-time supervisor at the site, which gave him the formidable task of being responsible for the more than fifty paid staff members and volunteers, and also for general operations at the site. Notably, during these years when the programming focused on the display of military pageantry, the Fort offered minimum hourly wages to would-be employees, supporting Alderson and Low's observation that "wages paid to interpreters in historic sites have been notoriously low."[56] Partly because of the low wages, the Fort initially attracted a workforce comprised chiefly of high school students.

As a means of expediency to supervise and discipline the Fort's staff and volunteers, the program manager "encouraged intense development of a mid-1820s military recreation" that served a dual function; it not only provided structure to the interpretive programming, it also "facilitated supervision of an ever growing number of guides by minimal full time staff."[57] It accomplished the latter by creating a workplace culture in which a military chain of command was enforced among interpreters. In essence, the management was referred to (and treated) as officers (e.g., lieutenants), while some senior interpretive male staff members were referred to (and treated as) as non-commissioned officers (e.g., sergeants or corporals).

During the 1970s, this chain of command would first be reinforced to new male interpreters through the overnight training sessions that lasted three consecutive days in the early 1970s, tapering off to two consecutive days by the decade's end. Based largely on the regimented schedule of early soldiers at the post (including all-night guard duty), the training sessions were intended to provide an immersion experience for interpreters, so they could internalize their roles and learn the practical details of interpreting at the site. One interpreter who portrayed a musician during the 1975 season recalled the following about the start of day 2:

> I didn't get much sleep, maybe an hour and a half. At 4:40 smoke rose through the floor from the kitchen below. This made sleeping hard. Later at 5:45 [the lieutenant] came through to my bunk. (There were three 2-bed bunks. Mine was on the left, looking at the wall. I was on top.) He woke me up. I groped my way through the smoke and dark and put on my bootees and chacos. (I wore my clothes during the night.) Peter, Dan, and I sounded reveille. We all awakened and were filmed by Channel 9 (ABC). Next came roll call. "Murdock, Born, Brovold, Dienst," the first sergeant called. When someone's name is called, he must answer, "Here, Sergeant!"[58]

Although the immersion experience could be useful for perfecting the modern-day work display of portraying a nineteenth-century soldier, for the Fort's overburdened manager, encouraging the staff to internalize the military chain of command proved useful to keep his modern-day costumed workforce literally and figuratively "in line."[59]

At least one worker at the Fort in the early 1970s questioned the usefulness of the immersion training weekends. In a three-page typed memo (signed "Percy") that was delivered to management, Percy critiqued the training weekend on the basis that it did a very poor job of preparing the staff to interpret history to tourists, and because—as this interpreter saw it—it also actually worked toward cultivating a workforce that was more like an actual army than staff at a twentieth-century tourist site:

> By starting the year with the attitude that tourists are secondary to our own little soldier group, it will be that much more difficult to later get the men to accept their roles as "aggressive interpreters." In a job that requires a very happy outgoing type personality, this weekend will tend to make the men sullen and bitter. . . . If 48 hours with virtually no sleep in such close proximity to the other men (to the point of sharing bunks), with poor food, under extremely trying working conditions, for a wage of .43 cents per hour—if all of that does not end up in at least a few fights by Sunday afternoon I will be very much surprised. A fourth aspect of the weekend which I think points out the harm which will be caused is the fact that much of the work we are required to do doing the summer is very UNmilitary.[60]

Thus, early on in the Fort's history as a living history worksite, Percy identified one of the keys tensions at the site—there were those who emotionally invested in the Fort because they viewed it primarily as an opportunity for "playing soldier," and those who emotionally invested in the Fort because they viewed it as a "state supported historic site" geared toward "public service."[61]

This divide in the interpretive staff between those who prioritized the role-playing, and those, like Percy, who prioritized the "public-service" might best be understood as evidence that the staff comprised individuals who more closely resembled a "reenactor" contingent and those who resembled the "interpreter" contingent—both of which Jay Anderson named as integral to the wider "world of living history."[62] Generally, the term "reenactors" refers to those whose living historical performances are recreational and inwardly focused, whereas the term "interpreters" denotes those whose more professionalized living history services are primarily intended to engage the public.[63] That both reenactor-types and interpreter-types were represented on the

Fort staff in the 1970s is not surprising. On a national scale, efforts to professionalize the field of interpretation are seen not only in the NPS's 1957 publication of Tilden's *Interpreting Our Heritage*, but also in the formation of professional associations, such as the Association of Interpretive Naturalists and the Western Interpreters Association—which were founded in the 1950s and 1960s (a 1988 merger between the two organizations resulted in the founding of the National Association for Interpretation). Contemporaneous to these early measures to advance the field of interpretation as a profession, the hobby of reenactment became increasingly popular. Civil War reenactment, in particular, was popular across the nation in the early 1960s as the nation celebrated the centennial of the Civil War, and battle reenactments served as key components to large-scale celebrations, like the restaging of First Manassas in July 1961, wherein 3,000 reenactors performed a "sham battle" for a crowd of 35,000.[64] Following the end of the Civil War Centennial in 1965, we see the founding of scores of reenactment divisions. For example, the "First Minnesota Volunteer Infantry" was formally established as a nonprofit organization in 1973. Notably, the Fort regularly "drew from the ranks" of this reenactment unit, when it recruited both staff and volunteers.[65]

Percy's 1973 memo to management suggests that very early on there was a tension between the inwardly focused reenacting contingent (those who were, in Percy's view, primarily interested in "playing solider") and the professionalizing interpretive contingent (those who primarily considered their work as a job for which they were paid to engage with the public). This tension would persist throughout the decade, but does not appear to be addressed at the Fort throughout the 1970s—in part because MHS resources were more sharply directed to the Fort restoration efforts, not to professionalizing the Fort's workforce of interpreters.

Aside from Percy's memo, the archives are fairly silent as to how tensions between reenactor-types and interpreter-types may have surfaced at the worksite during the 1970s. However, Charles, an informant who worked at the Fort during this era, recalled there was at least one formal effort on behalf of some of the interpretive staff to lobby for workplace protections, such as overtime pay, and compensation for training:

> There was a time in the midseventies (I am thinking about 1977) when it was common for people to work as much as possible if they wanted to earn a lot of money at our low wages. [Around that time] . . . a group of the newer troopies began to form into a guardhouse lawyers' clique and decided to call MHS on their violation of labor laws. They were led I believe by [three interpreters who would later become a prosecutor, a judge, and a University of Minnesota regent] and were successful in winning a fairly sizable amount of money for all the overtime pay [that was] due at time and a half [for] people [who] had accumulated [hours] by both these long marathon stretches and simpler violations of work week rules. This was significant in that it really changed the relationships between the MHS and the fort staff into a much more formal one, and it helped to end the culture of us simply working as much as we wanted.[66]

This incident likely also alerted the Minnesota Historical Society to the fact that there was not much formal oversight of the interpretive workforce on the grounds of the restored fortress. In 1980, when the Fort's Restoration was nearly complete, the MHS more deliberately shifted its focus to the site's interpretive programming. With that shift came top-down directives to create more supervisory positions at the Fort, and also to hire a workforce that would primarily be composed of service-oriented interpreters.

Shifting Demographics: *Hiring Practices and Turnover*

In 1980—the same year that the Fort's Commanding Officer's Quarters were first opened—the MHS created a new position at the Fort, called a site technician, whose duties included "overall daily supervision of all Historic Fort Snelling guides in the Program Manager's absence."[67] This new site technician came with several years of experience working as a third-person interpreter at Murphy's Landing, a living history museum in Shakopee, Minnesota, that was founded in 1969.[68] He would prove to have a profound impact on the interpretive programming of the Fort, as he worked to expand the Fort's civilian roles, and helped usher away the site's use of strict first-person interpretation (wherein interpreters were prohibited from ever breaking character)—two interpretive shifts that would help attract individuals to apply for hire in the interpretive workforce from a wider range than those primarily interested in "playing soldier."

Another way that a demographic shift in the interpretive workforce began to be realized was through the MHS's already established hiring practices. At HFS, until the late 1990s, all interpreters were automatically laid off at the end of each season—a practice that gave management the opportunity each April (theoretically at least) to start from scratch. An interoffice memo dating from March 5, 1982, suggests that the hiring practices had previously resulted in "the majority of those [interpreters] hired being totally new to the program."[69] Program notes intended to introduce HFS interpreters to the 1982 season built an expectation of turnover into the description of how the worksite operated: "Staff turnover also used to keep program active. Guides many times burn out after 2 to 4 years on site. We aim for a 30–40% turnover rate each season to spark alive and bring new talent into the program."[70] In her pioneering study of the condition called burnout, psychologist Christina Maslach described how workers experienced it as an emotional exhaustion, and identified it as especially common amongst workers who had to constantly interact with others.[71] At HFS, workers who experienced burnout either withdrew their consent and chose not to apply for rehire, or they were not invited to return. Rather than investing in training opportunities, or in trying to prevent burnout (as is often done for professional staffs—through work retreats, staff appreciation days, etc.), the Minnesota Historical Society purposefully built turnover into the personnel structure of the Fort, which reinforced interpreters' precarious position on public history's front line.

While job security was precarious for interpreters at HFS, the built-in possibilities for turnover gave Fort leadership the opportunity to change staff demographics in terms of age and experience, particularly once the MHS began to offer higher wages.[72] In 1976 the starting hourly wage for guides was at the level dictated by the federal minimum wage ($2.30); by 1981 the MHS offered starting hourly wage to $4.48/hour, over a dollar above the federal minimum wage of $3.35. As wages increased throughout the 1980s, "older and better-educated" interpreters joined the Fort staff, including "school teachers, actors, and graduate students."[73] Gavin, who was hired in 1981, was part of this transition when the Fort hired (in his words) "several people like me who had been out of school for years and were doing other things."[74]

Insurgent Workforce: Keeping the World Safe from Company H

But the workplace culture of the Fort did not immediately transform even with the addition of a new supervisor and the several new post-college-aged interpreters, in part because a number of former paid-staff interpreters, who were *not* rehired as staff, were still "hanging around as volunteers."[75] Representing those who might more closely resemble the reenactor contingent described above, this group of men called themselves Company H,[76] and, much to Gavin's confusion, these former employees showed up at "training sessions and all the special events and all the holidays" and continued working at the Fort as volunteers "under assumed names, some real, some fictional, some historical."[77] As the interpretive framework was strictly first-person during Gavin's first year at the site in 1981, he found it difficult to tell who was an actual employee and who was not, especially since many of those who had prior experience working at the Fort either did not readily break character, or their identities were so fused with the site that there was little difference between the soldiers they portrayed and their off-duty selves—a boundary-blurring that Stephen Eddy Snow also noted as being common among Plimoth's interpreters.[78] So deeply invested were they in the inwardly focused games of historical fantasy that the site's strict first-person "dogma"[79] offered, the former employees who formed Company H refused to stop working at the Fort. They were willing to enter the nonpaid workforce of volunteerism in exchange for the opportunity to continue investing in the games of playing soldier—games that allowed them to emotionally connect with history, as well as to their Company H comrades.[80]

In short, during his first couple of years at the Fort, Gavin saw the Fort treated as a worksite by some and as a playground by others. As an example of this playground atmosphere, Gavin recalled the "unauthorized cannon drill of 1982" wherein a few of the "lads" (both employees and members of the aforementioned Company H) thought it would be amusing to procure a full charge of 1¾ pounds of black powder, load the charge into one of the Fort's 6-pound cannons, and fire the cannon from a distance of only about 15 feet away, into his face and one of the "sergeants."[81] Granted, there was no cannonball, but significant injury from such a large powder charge (not to mention hearing damage) could have resulted nonetheless. Apparently, these lads were trying to get even with their "sergeant" for having beat them the night before at a game of "Wooden Ships and Iron Men, or Conquest, or one of those big imperial-age games in which you plot your armies and navies against each other."[82] While I analyze the larger significance of this enduring masculine and military culture at the Fort in Chapter 3, I use this example to point out the playground/worksite culture of the Fort in its early years as a living history museum. Indeed, when I asked Charles—who had worked at the Fort for most of the 1970s—about the most prevailing concern he had as an employee at the Fort, he replied (only half-jokingly) that his biggest concern was worrying about who he wanted to date.[83]

From Playground to Worksite

As the 1980s wore on, however, the shifting cadre of interpreters increasingly regarded the living history museum more as a professional worksite than as the playground some had previously treated it. The year 1982 marked a significant moment in this reconceptualization. State budget cuts forced management to reduce the number of interpret-ers, which made it difficult for the Fort to believably carry out its mili-tary pageantry programming.[84] This inspired new thinking about how to effectively interpret the Fort with a smaller staff. Gradually, under the guidance of the Fort's site technician, character roles expanded to address early settlement in the region and the fur trade—roles that did not demand a large staff to carry out visually believable interpretations. Likewise, with the (re)opening of the Commanding Officers Quarters in 1983, female interpreters had opportunities not only to portray laun-dresses, but also to portray "ladies" like Abigail Snelling (the "First Lady" of the Fort who lived there with her husband, Colonel Snelling, from 1820 to 1827), and also to portray domestics in that same space.[85] Thus, as the sheer numbers of interpreters diminished, so did the Fort's once nearly exclusive focus on its military programming. And so, as we see the "broadening of educational themes," we also see the inevitable de-enlistment of the Company H volunteers and the weeding out of additional hardcore first-person military enthusiasts.[86]

By the end of the 1980s, guides were no longer expected to interpret to the public in a strict first-person persona, but instead were encouraged to "break out of character whenever a visitor's question or a given situation requires, then to step back into period again."[87] Gavin attributes this major programming shift to older, educated workers like him who, in the early 1980s, chose to "defiantly and pigheadedly" break out of character to better suit the needs of the public.

I do not doubt that individual public-service-oriented interpreters were key to the emergence of this new interpretive style, but, by the late 1980s, breaking character was not considered defiant, and interpreters were schooled in what would come to be known as "modified first-person" interpretation, wherein interpreters were instructed to break character whenever necessary in order to serve the needs of the customer. This technique found favor with Fort leadership precisely because it quelled the tendency for some interpreters to see the Fort as a first-person playground where their aim was to cast a "carefully constructed historic spell" through elaborate portrayals of 1820s soldiers and laundresses.[88] While strict first-person interpretation can certainly be an effective interpretive technique for communicating to visitors about the past, enforcing the interpretive technique of *modified* first-person more directly focused the goal of interpretation on meeting visitors' needs. To an extent, the bloom was off the rose for strict first-person living history programs elsewhere in the country as well. For example, even while strict first-person sites such as Plimoth Plantation remained popular, by the mid-1980s living history demonstrations at, for example, Cabrillo National Monument in California "went quietly out of fashion—deemed by a later administration to be 'somewhat contrived and . . . often more "cute" than appropriate.'"[89]

At the beginning of the 1980s, with the Fort fully restored and reconstructed, the Minnesota Historical Society focused more intensely on the Fort's interpretive programming. Throughout this decade, the MHS increased the Fort's supervisory leadership from one to three (a site manager, an assistant site manager, and a site technician), raised its base hourly wage for interpreters, shifted its workforce demographic to include far fewer high school students, and extended its interpretive focus beyond the military pageantry that had been its bread and

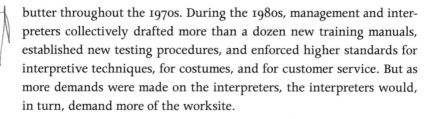

butter throughout the 1970s. During the 1980s, management and interpreters collectively drafted more than a dozen new training manuals,
established new testing procedures, and enforced higher standards for
interpretive techniques, for costumes, and for customer service. But as
more demands were made on the interpreters, the interpreters would,
in turn, demand more of the worksite.

CHAPTER 2
"OUR SEAT AT THE TABLE"
Interpreter Agency and Consent (1985–1996)

In 1980, Gavin saw an ad in one of the local Twin Cities newspapers advertising a job for a blacksmith at Historic Fort Snelling. College educated and in his early thirties, Gavin admittedly did not have experience blacksmithing, but he had read books on the subject with great interest. He applied for the position, got the job, and began his first season at the Fort in 1981. Thrust into a living history work culture that—given the antics of Company H—he described as "literally, a madhouse," Gavin nonetheless relished this new job, which not only allowed him the opportunity to learn blacksmithing skills, but also gave him a chance to engage in meaningful public service, a charge which he took seriously: "We are serving those people who walk in by themselves, or with their families or their groups, and want to see a historic site that is preserved for them by public money."[1]

Although he loved his job at the Fort, for many years working as a historic interpreter at Historic Fort Snelling did not guarantee full-time seasonal employment, nor did it offer job security. Every year for two decades, Gavin formally applied to the Minnesota Historical Society to be considered for work at the Fort from spring through fall. He did so, he noted in an interview in September 2002, always with a bit of fear that he might not be asked back: "[Until 2001, we] always had to get rehired, and had to apply to work at Fort Snelling every spring. At the discretion of the management we would either be, or not be hired. And it tended to work out that as a surprise every year, they would dump somebody just to keep the rest of us in line, and sometimes they'd dump several people." In his interview Gavin referred to the times when Fort management did not rehire several former employees at once as "periodic purgings." Gavin himself may have benefited from one such periodic purging, as he and the "five or six others who were hired with [him]" were given a chance when several of the Fort's regular "troopies" were not hired back for the 1981 season.[2]

In Gavin's recollection, the "next big periodic purging" occurred after several Fort workers (some of whom had worked at the Fort for about a decade) were not rehired after having expressed concerns about state budget cuts that were trickling down to affect work hours available for interpreters at Minnesota historic sites around the state.[3] In fact, they had expressed these concerns on Minnesota Public Radio, during a live call-in portion of an interview with a top Minnesota Historical Society administrator, and confronted the administrator on the radio (and, apparently, during the lunch break) about why historic sites were seeing cuts even as the MHS was embarking on plans for a new multi-million dollar building. As one interpreter who worked at the Fort at the time noted, "several troopies and troopettes called in to ask . . . why their hours had been reduced 25% while the society was spending so much money on a new building. [The administrator] was not amused."[4]

The new building that was drawing the ire of some interpreters in the wake of cuts to historic sites, was a yet-to-be-constructed "large new facility called the History Center," which would be located in the heart of St. Paul, a half-mile from Minnesota's majestic capitol building.[5] Intended to further the MHS mission of preserving and promulgating Minnesota history (a regional story told within the context of the developing nation-state),[6] the building was slated to have space dedicated "to the storage, maintenance, exhibition, and study of collections ranging from canoes and thimbles to books, diaries, maps, and government records" as well as for "attractive and convenient public amenities, such as a restaurant and museum stores."[7] By 1986, the MHS's vision for its History Center was poised to become real, after the legislature "approved a bonding bill appropriating $50 million to construct the center, $5 million of this amount contingent upon the Society matching the sum from nonstate sources" in the private sector.[8] That same year the Upper Sioux Agency historic site (a MHS historic site near Granite

Falls) and the Meighen Store (a MHS historic site in Forestville State Park) were both closed—causing anxiety among those employed in the MHS historic sites division about whether their jobs or sites would face the chopping block next.[9] It was in 1987 that the four veteran interpreters voiced their concerns live on the radio.

According to Gavin, of the four veteran interpreters who called in to the radio show that day, three were not rehired the following season when they reapplied to work at the Fort. No hard evidence proves that the calls were the reason they were not rehired, but interpreters found it difficult to believe that there was no correlation. To Gavin, the net result of what he considered a "purging" was mixed. On the one hand, "the periodic purgings caused anger among the staff and dismay and low morale." On the other hand, the purgings also galvanized some interpreters to come together to exercise their agency as workers, eventually leading to "the movement to get a union at Fort Snelling, and among all the historic site guides in the Minnesota Historical Society."[10]

Gavin had it only partly correct. MHS historic site guides may have largely led the union drive, but they made up only one-fifth of the designated bargaining unit, which ultimately included anyone and everyone who held a nonsupervisory position at the MHS. Organized with the help of American Federation of State, County and Municipal Employees (AFSCME), by 1992 the organizing campaign had completely fizzled, defeated by a bargaining unit that could not find common ground. It would seem that job descriptions and job titles were too varied for these MHS workers to feel solidarity with each other, notwithstanding that the bargaining unit was spread throughout the entire state.

Even so, following the fizzled union drive, the historic site guides who were at the drive's helm continued to agitate the next several years for improved working conditions on behalf of those who labored on public history's front line in Minnesota. Drawing on employee-produced newsletters, MHS archives, and personal accounts, this chapter examines a MHS grassroots collective of historic site interpreters who called themselves the Caucus.[11] Formed in 1993, the Caucus initially included all historic site interpreters—a group of approximately a hundred employees—from the seventeen historic sites across Minnesota. In 1994, when it began collecting an annual $5 dues fee to defray costs of mailing the monthly newsletter, the Caucus still maintained about

30 percent membership, with membership drawing from each of the seventeen sites. This was true throughout its tenure as an employee-run organization, which lasted until July 1, 1996. While the Caucus lasted only a few short years, examining why it formed (and why it declined) provides a window into understanding not only how some interpreters exercised their agency as workers, but also why and how other interpreters conceded to the terms of their seasonal employment.

Illusory Raises, and Reclassification

Throughout the 1980s and 1990s, federal and state government purse strings tightened with regard to the distribution of funds to nonprofit "cultural" institutions. As a result, public schools, universities, arts programs, and museums were forced to compete with one another as they vied for their piece of the government's shrinking pie.[12] To make ends meet, nonprofits also had to fight for support from individual and corporate sponsors in addition to finding additional ways to increase their earning potential.[13]

To reduce operating budgets, nonprofits almost always made cuts that affected staff. A 2004 survey conducted by the Minnesota Council of Nonprofits, for example, found that of the 350 nonprofits surveyed, 73 percent "found it necessary to make some kind of staffing change—28% of all survey participants reported reducing hours, 37% reported leaving vacant positions open—and 43% reported actually laying off staff."[14] Nonprofit workers keenly felt the effects of these cuts, and not just in their paychecks. Many also felt disenfranchised and betrayed. Nonprofit researchers Jan Masaoka, Jeanne Peters, and Stephen Richardson's study of nonprofit workers found that many nonprofit employees did not feel they had a real voice in their organization. As one of their informants phrased it: "I think nonprofits are already changed. They don't work like they say they do. Like 'we're small, we're different.' They say they're not corporate but then they tell us things by memo. That's not why I came to work here."[15]

Alongside workers in the service economy more broadly,[16] some nonprofit employees responded to the conditions of their labor through collective bargaining efforts as major unions expanded organizing strategies to include segments of the workforce that were growing the fastest on the domestic front—namely, service workers, professional and technical workers, and workers from the nonprofit sector.[17] Across the country, many employees in these sectors affiliated themselves with major unions and launched union organizing campaigns as a way to gain a voice at worksites that had previously been unlikely spaces for the staging of union campaigns—as was the case with cultural institutions such as universities, museums, and historical societies.[18]

In Minnesota, for example, the American Federation of State, County and Municipal Employees (AFSCME) successfully organized a 3,200-person bargaining unit of University of Minnesota clerical workers whose high profile campaign asserted: "The University Works Because We Do!"[19] This campaign ended on February 20, 1991, when workers voted for union representation, and favored representation by AFSCME over the International Brotherhood of Teamsters. As a result, AFSCME Local 3800 became one of the largest bargaining units in Minnesota history.[20] But while the AFSCME Local 3800 campaign made history, aforementioned efforts to unionize nonsupervisory MHS employees, in a nutshell, did not.

In 1993, a year after the MHS union campaign dissolved, the MHS raised the base wage of historic site guides to $9.18 an hour—several dollars above the minimum wage (and more than a dollar higher than their interpretive counterparts at Colonial Williamsburg were earning).[21] Notably, Gavin, who worked with others on the union campaign, did not consider the pay increase a gain won because of the unionization effort: "Some of the things that happened, like pay increases, happened anyway because the people of the state of Minnesota said, 'Well you're getting state funding, you meet certain criteria, Mr. MHS, so you're going to have to pay your people more.' I think improvements in the workplace were more due to outside influences and the state requirements than to any of our efforts."[22]

With regard to the 1993 pay raise, Gavin appears to be correct. At first glance the pay raise seems to contradict the trend for nonprofits to scale back on human resources in the wake of budget cuts. In fact, the trend to make cuts affecting staff played out. The hourly raise for historic site guides was illusory, because MHS simultaneously planned to cut $345,000 in funding to the historic sites division for the 1993–95 biennium, which would reduce available work hours for interpreters who hoped to work forty hours a week.[23] Although the budget cuts to historic sites may have been proportionate to cuts elsewhere within the MHS, the funding cuts were experienced as pay cuts for workers at the historic sites—a bitter pill for some interpreters to swallow as they saw "$5.6 million . . . spent on public programs at the new History Center" that was completed in 1992, while only "$4.3 million a year [was allocated] to operate 17 historic sites around the state."[24]

Alongside the illusory pay raise and the slated funding cuts, additional changes were initiated in 1993 when MHS reclassified its seasonal employees as "Project Employees"—that is, the historical society formalized seasonal employees as temporary workers who were hired annually and formally terminated at the conclusion of their "project" in the fall. More than a rhetorical gesture, this reclassification absolved the MHS from any ongoing relationships with seasonal workers. In addition to deflating the morale of employees like Gavin who had then worked at the Fort for a dozen years, being reclassified as Project Employees had the practical effect of stripping seasonal workers of any sick and vacation time that they had earned working at their historic site in previous seasons.

Prior to fiscal year 1993, if seasonal workers were rehired, their vacation time refreshed at the beginning of each season, and unused vacation time was paid off at the end of each season. Thus, employees who did not use their vacation time received an extra week of wages at the end of the season in November. Sick time, in contrast, accrued from year to year so that it would carry over if workers were rehired the following season. While some seasonal employees had health insurance through other jobs, many did not. For many seasonal workers, the sick and vacation time that they had earned as MHS employees, was the "closest thing [they] had to a health plan."[25] In the wake of this policy change in particular, during the summer of 1993 interpreters from historic sites across the state of Minnesota formed the Minnesota Historical Society Interpreters Caucus, as a grassroots solution to address and redress workplace issues and grievances.

Building the Caucus's Platform

The Caucus formed in 1993 largely in response to the immediate issue at hand: "to the reclassification and the resulting perception that we were not seen by the MHS as valuable professionals."[26] Adopting the language of professionalization for the interpretive workforce at the Fort would have been unthinkable two decades before, but its use in the early 1990s is less surprising, given the gradual demographic shift toward an older and more educated workforce throughout the 1980s. The Caucus's rhetoric of professionalization is also in step with larger trends. On a national level, the National Association for Interpretation (NAI) formed in 1988 to merge two organizations that had largely focused on naturalist interpretation: the Association for Interpretive Naturalists and the Western Interpreters Association, which were founded in 1954 and 1965, respectively. With a mission "to advance heritage interpretation as a profession," the NAI holds professional development workshops, conferences, and certification training for membership, which "includes volunteers, docents, interpreters, naturalists, historians, rangers, park guards, guides, tour operators, program directors, consultants, academicians, planners, suppliers, and institutions."[27] Occasionally the Caucus held business meetings to discuss issues and problems related to the workplace and conducted seminars to improve professional development and interpretive skills.[28] Outside of working to raise the legitimacy of historic interpretation as a profession, however, the NAI was not founded to function as a forum to redress workplace grievances, as the Caucus was trying to do.

In terms of membership, the Caucus initially defined itself as including all historic site interpreters from each of the seventeen MHS historic sites (about a hundred employees). Founded in 1993, before the Internet was a fixture in American households, the Caucus used monthly printed newsletters and meetings (held at the various sites around the state) as its major forms of communication and organizing.[29] By 1994, elected Caucus leadership began to collect $5 in annual dues—which amounted to signing up for a formal newsletter subscription (i.e., the dues covered the costs of printing and mailing newsletters to MHS interpreters across the state). After dues were instituted, roughly 30 percent of all MHS interpreters became dues-paying members, but since the Caucus continued to draw members from each of the seventeen sites, it is possible that the newsletters circulated informally among those who did not formally join.

Once formed, Caucus members began developing a platform. Throughout its tenure as an employee-run organization, "low morale" was a key issue. Caucus members valued their jobs and prized themselves for the effort and dedication they had put into their work—but they did not feel that those efforts were recognized or valued by their employer. In his February 1994 editorial, "Priorities for the Coming Year," then thirty-one-year-old newsletter editor Eric Ferguson placed improving morale as a top priority for interpreters, as he was concerned that deflated morale among staff would not only negatively impact job performance once the season began, but also adversely affect involvement in the Caucus:

> So what should we do this year? I believe the first thing we have to concern ourselves with is improving morale. The low morale we all suffered the past year seems not to have abated thus far in the off-season, and is bound to cause problems. First off it is bound to affect our performance on the job. We may do only an adequate job but not do that extra bit for our visitors, or start to slack off on cleaning and maintenance, such subtle ways as that. Also, I have noticed that participation in the Caucus rises and falls with the morale. People who are discouraged or even downright numb after bad news just want to leave the workplace and go home. This bodes ill for anything we might want to accomplish. We must find the means within our reach to improve morale.[30]

It is clear from the Caucus's newsletters that MHS interpreters struggled with morale across its historic sites division.

In the April 1994 Caucus newsletter, for example, interpreter Marco Good, from MHS's Forest History Center (an interpretive center featuring a living history logging camp in Grand Rapids, Minnesota), wrote a letter to the newsletter's readership reporting that in the Forest History Center's first meeting of the season, morale was a key concern among interpretive staff, and he notably links flagging morale as a response to top-down decisions. In the meeting that Good describes, site managers and veteran interpreters—"some seasoned as many as 15 times as 1900 lumberjacks, camp cooks, 1934 foresters, and river pigs"—gathered in order "to discuss the past and future work of entertaining and educating our visitors about the history of the Northwoods of our state." Cuts to employee hours as well as issues of ongoing job security were the main agenda items for the meeting wherein interpreters learned that "overall staff numbers w[ere to] be significantly reduced except at times of peak visitation, and although [their] season continue[d] after Labor Day until October 15, a skeleton crew of interpreters w[ere] then [to] be on hand."[31] In light of cuts, Forest History Center management also discussed the prospect of relying more heavily on the free labor of volunteers and youth workers. No doubt, especially for those interpreters who had worked as many as fifteen seasons at the site, learning that cuts in their hours would be addressed through soliciting free volunteer labor did not sit well. No wonder, then, that the meeting concluded with a discussion of the staff's low morale. Writes Good:

> The probable past causes of flagging morale were run up the pole one more time, as well as the issues of lack of advancement and recognition for interpreters who return year after year. Anxiety and confusion about our exact status at MHS with regard to rehire or lack thereof, and suspension of vacation and sick pay benefits continue to be perceived as sore spots among our staff, and any discussion of morale problems inevitably must include those issues.
>
> We appreciate the hard work and organizational effort so far advanced by the Caucus, and hope to keep the lines of communication open.[32]

Three months after Good sent his report in from the Forest History Center (FHC), in Grand Rapids, Minnesota, the MHS Interpreters Caucus held its monthly meeting there on July 25, 1994.

A true Minnesota gathering, "the meeting was preceded by a pot luck supper, the conversation of which was segued into the meeting."[33] Perhaps fueled by hearty Minnesotan hot-dish, the meeting was a productive one: the Caucus gained five new members, discussed the interpreters' survey that was slated for an August distribution date, and enjoyed the solidarity that came with meeting with interpreters from across the state. For example, at the meeting, "The FHC staff mentioned feeling that they were considered to be troublemakers by the rest of the MHS staff. They were pleased to learn that other staffs have had the same feeling and none of us are alone in this."[34]

At the meeting on July 25, 1994, the Caucus also unanimously passed a resolution intended to outline the concerns that the Caucus would most want to focus on in the months ahead: "The changes in

MHS policies most desired by the Interpreters Caucus are the establishment of permanent employee status for seasonal staff, the restoration of
sick and vacation time, and the improvement of management/employee
communications by the inclusion of interpreters on MHS committees
and consultation on matters affecting interpreters."[35] This resolution
worked its way into the lead question on Marco Good's survey, which
was distributed to all MHS interpreters with the August newsletter; the
results were shared in the November 1994 newsletter.

What a Guide Wants: *The Survey Results*

As of November 5, forty-four interpreters from MHS historic sites
(roughly half of all interpreters) responded to the six-question Caucus
survey although, unfortunately, "not all respondents answered all questions."[36] While the survey's quantitative section has some shortcomings,
the survey has qualitative merit. Of the forty-four who returned the
Caucus's survey, eleven respondents wrote in additional comments, and
most of those who commented were supportive of the Caucus's efforts.

Respect, Sick Leave, and Automatic Rehire

One respondent used the comments section of the survey to express
his frustration with the MHS administration, and what he[37] perceived
as their lack of respect for the work that interpreters did, particularly
with regard to interpreters who had returned year after year to work at
the MHS historic sites:

> We are getting a message loud and clear from the director of Historic
> Sites that we who return to this job as regular seasonal employees
> are not valued for our depth of experience, study, and skill. We have
> worked hard and sometimes sacrificed other opportunities, and over
> the years many of us have studied hard to present the best possible
> historical interpretation to our visitors. For most of us who do return,
> it has taken years to build in off-season work that complements the
> season. The strength of this experience, and our depth of subject
> knowledge [are] feature[s] at our site for which our visitors give us
> constant enthusiastic feedback, and we would not get that if we had
> less experienced staff, who would be less trouble to the administra-
> tion only because they care less about the job they were doing.[38]

This passionate respondent clearly identified strongly with his inter-pretive job. While he notes receiving emotional remuneration from site visitors, he expresses a similar yearning to feel valued by MHS admin-istration, whose members he felt did not adequately acknowledge or appreciate interpreters' skills or how their devotion to the job, year after year, benefited the MHS at large.

Though this respondent did not specifically note actions that he wanted MHS administration to take in order to redress his particular concerns, other respondents were more explicit about how they wanted the material conditions of their employment to change—specifically with regard to sick leave and job security:

> For sure, restoration of sick leave we have already earned! Believe we
>   have a right to what we earned.
> We deserve our sick leave, which we have already earned. How can
>   it be taken away after earning it?
> We would really like to keep our sick leave; if not the future time,
>   the time we have already earned would be great.[39]

Restoration of sick leave benefits was clearly an important issue for many employees (all quotes in this section are excerpted from the individual survey results and responses published in the November issue of the Caucus newsletter), but one respondent noted that he felt that the issue of instituting an automatic rehire system should take precedence over working to reinstitute vacation and sick leave: "Of the sites I've visited I know that the majority of the people work there because they really enjoy working at that site. They study hard and enjoy their work. I miss the vacation and sick leave though I can live without." Though this respondent felt that he would continue to consent to work as an inter-preter even without the vacation and sick leave, he nonetheless found it "very upsetting to know that this year and from now on" employees would have to continue to fill out applications if they wanted to return to work at their site the following year: "It also adds to more paperwork for MHS. For employees at MHS a simple memo of do you wish to rehire should be sufficient. If you decide not to then that is in your file."

Non-Committal Relationships and Debates over Automatic Rehire
Not everyone agreed that the Caucus should pursue automatic rehire

for the interpretive workforce. One interpreter felt that the Caucus's resolution to seek permanent status for seasonal employees only "somewhat" spoke to his interests. In short, he "wonder[ed] about permanent employee status" because while he "agree[d] it is nonsense to go through rehire if management asks" someone to return, he feared that permanent status might require management to rehire someone even though "in their judgement [sic] an employee has not performed up to the expectations or is otherwise undesirable."[40] This respondent also felt that job security should not necessarily be a perk of seasonal employment; with his final remark he suggested that efforts to increase benefits of any kind might ruin an otherwise "good" employment situation:

> Personally I do not see a job that is advertised as seasonal as being a career choice—but others may. I would not think a seasonal employment would call for vacation, medical or other benefits. I would call the salary generous for the work performed, the local situation, and the necessary background. To depend on seasonal employment is a choice that is made by weighing all factors involved, and the freedom to choose that route and that lifestyle involves obvious sacrifices. I respect those who choose it but if there is no benefit to permanent employment why commit to that. Nearly all of us [here] are "second incomes"—valuable to maintain lifestyles. We work hard and are loyal to [the] society and it should respect our needs and our contribution to the work of the society. We give to them in many ways, in our own ways, and I do not look at it as a "regular" job. Let us not spoil a good thing for many to serve the wishes of a few.[41]

 While the respondent felt that the MHS should give interpreters respect because they worked hard for and were loyal to the society, he did not necessarily see this job as a "career choice," which may be read as code for a "real job." We can see an undercurrent of derision for those employees who considered this second-income job as worthy of engaging in collective resistance so as to improve conditions. In this way of seeing circumstances, if interpreters were not happy with conditions at this seasonal job, it was their own fault for choosing to work there; individuals did, after all, have the responsibility of "weighing all factors involved"[42] and then the freedom to exercise their full agency with regard to whether they want to depend on temporary, seasonal employment.

In fact, workers in the new economy may not simply be able to choose—as though from a catalogue—a full-time job with a good salary and full benefits. The rhetoric of the above survey respondent conforms to the tenets of neoliberalism, wherein citizens are governed by adhering to ideologies of individualism and freedom. Political theorist Wendy Brown describes the neoliberal citizen as "the rationally calculating individual [who] bears full responsibility for the consequences of his or her action no matter how severe the constraints on this action."[43] Thus, if you have failed to "navigate impediments to prosperity" the neoliberal assumption is that that failure is yours alone.[44] Because real power is depoliticized, the citizen is rendered more and more passive and complacent. The survey respondent above, who did not see his interpretive role as a "regular job," is one such citizen—a rational individual who presumes to have chosen the extent to which he will "depend on seasonal employment."[45] In his view, those who have elected to depend on seasonal employment have made the deliberate choice to mismanage their lives. This employee may especially not have wanted "permanent status" as a seasonal interpreter, because to have a "permanent" job as an interpreter may have disrupted his own sense of pride that *this* job was not his career choice; he was just passing through.[46]

This notion was echoed by another respondent who claimed to "represent the group of interpreters who [we]re students and [who] appreciate[d] this job for its seasonal benefits." This respondent felt that working as an interpreter was "a fantastic job," notwithstanding "serious Executive Management problems," but did not want to see seasonal employment go to permanent status: "I prefer this job as a seasonal non-committal relationship that provides me with a fine salary and excellent educational opportunities."[47] Here, when the respondent describes his job as a "non-committal relationship" pursued alongside other "real jobs," he casts the cultural work he performed as if it were a mistress to the private sector.[48]

Both of these survey respondents noted that they were satisfied with their jobs as seasonal interpreters for the MHS, and were happy to consent being classified as temporary Project Employees. In addition to whatever emotional remuneration they got from their cultural work, both praised the salary as meeting their needs, and neither saw the value in having a "permanent" classification for seasonal work. I maintain that, for these two interpreters (and for others who may have shared their views), resisting automatic rehire was tied up with their conceptions of self. In seeking the "non-committal relationship" inherent to their jobs as interpreters, they distanced themselves from the identity of being seasonal interpreters on a permanent basis, because identifying as such would signal a mismanagement of their lives.

Lending insight into this claim is sociologist Jackie Rogers's study of identity formation among those working in the temporary workforce. Although many of Rogers's interviewees had worked extended periods of time as temps (i.e., individuals, usually with office and clerical skills, who are hired out to companies/firms/offices through so-called Temp Agencies), "no one actually identified himself or herself as a temporary worker," in part, Rogers argues, because "by its very definition, *temporary* is a condition that cannot be part of a solidified or stable identity."[49] One way that individuals in Rogers's study resisted identifying as a temporary worker was by using what she calls "cover stories":

> Part of each "cover story" told by temporaries is the notion that they are not "just a temp." Rather, they are an artist, a teacher, a student, an actor, an upwardly mobile yet unrecognized talent—a professional who has been laid off. Temporary workers who invoke these cover stories are not lying; rather, they are rejecting the label of temp and its associated stigma. The larger implication of these identity struggles is the individualization of temporaries. Temporaries do not feel or act as part of the group "temporaries" but feel attached to the groups they identify in their cover story. Changing the conditions of temporary employment is much less a priority for many temporaries than is getting out of temporary employment.[50]

Thus, as a means to craft an identity that they themselves could respect, temporary workers embraced their "cover stories," thereby rejecting identifying with other temporaries. As a result of their own individualization, temporaries were unlikely to feel solidarity with their fellow workers. Even while temporaries at large experienced similar work-related grievances, such as low wages, no benefits, and unwarranted/sudden dismissal from their temporary jobs, Rogers, who conducted participant observation as a temporary worker, found that resistance among temporary workers was highly individualistic. In this manner, temps often chose to work longer or harder than the terms of their work agreements specified, as a way to prove their worth as a good worker despite their transience: "If collective resistance or solidarity derives out of identification with one's job and not from opposition, we can understand why temporary workers use individualistic resistance. Like other temporaries, I did not wish to identify with my job, so I did not enter into collective resistance to protect it."[51]

While there are significant differences between the work performed by most temps and that of historic interpreters, Rogers's research into resistance and identity formation among temporary workers offers insight into the two respondents to the Caucus's survey who did not want MHS interpreters to have permanent employee status. Like temporaries who did not want to identify with their jobs, the two respondents resisted fully identifying as interpreters. One of the respondents even invoked a cover story, and demonstrated attachment to his cover group by suggesting that he "represent[ed] the group of interpreters who [we]re students." He preferred to consider his relationship with MHS as "non-committal," even though—as a student—he may have repeatedly needed seasonal employment for several years. Another respondent similarly rejected full identification as an interpreter by distinguishing himself from others who might have considered the job a "career choice."[52] Ultimately, in preferring to engage in a consensual "non-committal" affair with the MHS, neither saw the value in engaging in collective resistance to change the conditions of their work sites.

The Caucus Responds to the Survey

Immediately following the survey results that were relayed in the November 1994 issue of the Caucus newsletter, editor Eric Ferguson argued against the tendency for some interpreters to uncritically accept being classified as temporary workers, especially in light of larger economic trends wherein temporary employment was being reproduced at rabbit speed. Drawing on Michael Kinsman's November 13, 1994, *Star Tribune* article, which sized up the situation for many temp employees as "temporary is permanent . . . but most are stuck without benefits,"[53] Ferguson made the case for why even students, and those who only think of the Fort as a "second income," should care about the Caucus's campaign to gain permanent status.[54]

Kinsman's article worked, in part, to point out the national trends in employment in the early 1990s that led Manpower Temporary Services to be the single largest employer in the United States. Ferguson found this alarming, not merely because 51 percent of temps earned less than $7 per hour, and 10 percent just a hair over $11 per hour, but also because of these "more worrisome" statistics: "19% of temps are under age 24, 48% under 34, 72% are women."[55] With these statistics in mind, along with those that suggested that employers in both the public and private sectors were going to increasingly rely on temporary workers, Ferguson urged all MHS seasonal interpreters to care about the issue of "permanent/seasonal" status:

> The group that has been least interested in this issue [of permanent status], and in Caucus membership, has been those interpreters who see this as a summer job while they are in school. However folks, you have more reason to be concerned than older interpreters. . . . Working as a temp is something all of us may have to fight the rest of our working lives, regardless of profession or employer. Younger workers are disproportionately affected. You students may not be temps all your life, but you're sure looking at a long delay in your career, and lack of pensions and medical care isn't something you can make up for later in life. . . .
>
> So, to put this in the starkest terms, all of us, particularly women and younger workers, face the prospect of being a temp much of our working lives. We can fight this now, or we can fight this later, perhaps when more of us have dependents and we don't know our co-workers. That is why all interpreters need to care about this issue—now.[56]

In urging all MHS interpreters to unite in the cause for automatic rehire—not simply out of solidarity with their fellow workers, but as a way to fight exploitative national employment trends that disproportionately affected younger workers and women—Ferguson highlighted the larger significance of the Caucus. As a workplace organization that technically represented the interests of a more broadly exploited workforce (temps), its import extended beyond the purview of the Minnesota Historical Society.

A year later, Ferguson continued to draw the connection between

MHS interpreters and the growing national temporary workforce in his editorial, "The Temping of America." This editorial was included in the September 1995 issue of the newsletter, so-timed because, as he wrote, "some of us are ending our seasons already, and the bulk of us face unemployment very shortly so this seems an appropriate moment to bring up again the issue of permanent status."[57] As he did similarly in his earlier editorial, Ferguson argues in "The Temping of America" that historic sites interpreters should consider joining in the fight against their temporary status by urging them to first identify themselves as members of the broader temporary workforce: "We receive the same benefits package as the typical temp, and when we reapply for our jobs (a phrase that sticks to the teeth) we technically have no more status than anybody who walks in off the street when applications are being taken. We can't even keep the employee handbooks at the end of the season. That, my friend, is a temp."[58]

Ferguson clearly recognized that if the Caucus were to succeed in its goals, it needed individuals to start understanding their workplace struggles as connected, more broadly, to those of others—not as issues that were peculiar to working as a historic interpreter for the MHS. His hope, no doubt, was that if more interpreters could take this view, more would feel compelled to join the "fight" for the issue of permanent status, regardless of whether or not they identified themselves as "career interpreters":

> So what to do? Fight it. Right here and now. Fight it because you don't have dependents yet, or because you do have dependents and don't want to be a temp all your life. Fight it because this isn't your career you're risking, or because it is your career and it's worth protecting. Fight it to protect the hard work you've already put into your program. Above all, fight it now so it doesn't plague you the rest of your working life. The day will come when management realizes that permanent status for seasonals makes sense, IF we never cease reminding them of this.[59]

While temporary and part-time work was nothing new in the 1990s, economist and labor scholar Chris Tilly reminds us that "what is new, or at least newer, is the long-term expansion of the involuntary workforce—part-time [and temporary] workers who would prefer full-time work."[60] The Caucus survey shows that while certainly not all MHS interpreters were part of the "involuntary" part-time workforce, many would have preferred to work full-time for the duration of the interpretive season. In the early 1990s, those in this latter category were in good company. According to Tilly, in 1993 (the year that the Caucus formed), "an average of 6.1 million Americans, or 5.5 percent of those at work, were working part-time involuntarily—a number comparable to the annual average of 6.5 million who were unemployed."[61]

MHS Administration Responds to the Caucus

A half year after the Caucus formed, on January 18, 1994, the MHS Historic Sites Division formed a "Strategic Planning Human Resources Subcommittee" in order "to identify and solve human resource related problems within the Historic Sites Department" and "to address one of six key goals identified by the core planning team" of historic sites.[62] The subcommittee—which consisted of several historic site managers, members of MHS education and human resources departments, and Rachel Tooker, the head of historic sites, stated its goal of "resolv[ing] identified human resource problems that are impacting our effectiveness and employee morale."[63] The issues the subcommittee was most concerned about were:

> Low morale among staff, part time staff
>
> Frustration from lack of input from Historic Sites into decision making
>
> Part time staff hiring policy
>
> Administration of pay and benefits for part time staff
>
> Benefits for part time staff, job stacking
>
> Permanent, part time status
>
> Performance review system
>
> Update present system
>
> Training for performance appraisals[64]

Notably, the list shows that members of the subcommittee were aware of the major workplace grievances that led to the diminished morale among historic site workers—especially with regard to hiring policy.

And yet, in a 1995 document noting the subcommittee's accomplishments for fiscal year 1994, it seems that the subcommittee's actions were little more than palliative. Of the three accomplishments listed, the first was the successful formation of subcommittee itself. The final two accomplishments for fiscal year 1994 were initiated to address communication issues between historic site staff and management: first, the subcommittee members created a "Historic Sites Welcome Letter" that was "distributed to all new and returning staff in the Spring," and they also implemented a "comment box system" called "Hey MHS," which allowed workers to address questions to "site managers or the Head of Historic Sites"—the latter possibly showing the subcommittee's desire to control the means by which workers communicated with MHS management: in other words, not through the Caucus.[65] Taken together, some employees might have understood the "Welcome Letter" and the "Hey MHS" comment boxes as smokescreens intended to cover the real issues at hand, like loss of sick time and hiring policies—not unlike the boss who throws an ice cream social for employees just after he's told them that they've been cut from the health plan.

The welcome letter begins by exclaiming: "Welcome to the employment with the Minnesota Historical Society!"—a welcome that may have rung hollow to those employees who had already been working at their respective historic sites for several seasons, and who had lost earned sick and vacation time the season prior to this hearty overture. The letter continues by impressing employees with the import of their jobs as employees of "the oldest institution in the State of Minnesota— a cultural resource admired nation wide for its excellent programs and record of public service. Since 1849 the Minnesota Historical Society has preserved and interpreted the history of Minnesota and its peoples. And beginning in 1970 [the MHS] has employed a dynamic staff of historic site interpreters to bring that past to life on sites around the state where history was made."[66]

After imbuing interpreters with a sense of their importance as employees of the MHS, the letter briefly describes what will be expected of them as MHS interpreters—expectations that focus predominately on the job's emotional requirements: "As an MHS interpreter you give historic sites visitors their first impression of the Minnesota Historical Society. The warmth, courtesy, and professionalism you project [are] important component[s] of your job and greatly valued by the Society, and its visitors. Further, the excitement and energy you bring to interpreting Minnesota history will have a positive influence on our visitors."

If anything, the welcome letter may have served to agitate employees' grievances about their status within the society, not so much because of the content of the letter itself, but because of content of the pages that accompanied it, which were intended to serve as a "brief introduction to [the] position and the benefits of employment."[67] These informational pages lend insight to how the MHS reckoned with the task of communicating with employees about charged, morale-related issues like benefits. In 1994, they dealt with those issues by obfuscating them.[68] To take one example of how real issues were clouded in these informational pages, let us look at how the issue of benefits was addressed.

The informational pages accompanying the welcome letter described three major benefits to MHS employment. The first benefit listed was an employee identification card "which may be used for free admission to any of the Society's historic sites and for a 25% employee discount at any of the Society's gift or book shops. When you visit the Minnesota History Center, your ID card may also be used for a 10% discounts [sic] in Café Minnesota or for a reduced fee at the copy center in the Research Center"—benefits that only rewarded employees if they shopped at the company store, if you will, by consuming MHS services and products.[69] The second benefit outlined "holiday benefits, which for most guide and clerk positions mean that when you work on an official designated holiday, you will be paid overtime (time-and-a-half) for the hours you work." Finally, the document notes that to earn vacation or sick leave, an employee must work "1044 hours or more in a year."[70] This last figure was set up as a statistical impossibility: forty hours a week for six months is only 1,040 hours. Thus, although sick and vacation pay was one of the Caucus members' major concerns, the above statement is not forthright about the likelihood for seasonal employees to be eligible for such benefits.

Although MHS administration was aware that the main issues affecting the morale of returning employees were cuts in benefits and their reclassification as "Project Employees," the informational pages accompanying the welcome letter do not explain why employees were reclassified, or why the benefits they previously had were stricken. It is clear from Caucus newsletters that not knowing exactly why they were reclassified only exacerbated the negative impact on morale. Management did not justify the reclassification until the February 1, 1994, according to the "Minutes for the Strategic Planning Human Resources Subcommittee," in which one member "retraced the discussion and process that led up to the new policies established in reclassifying the part-time and seasonal interpreters. The continuous employment issue was an important one but on-going appointments were not instituted mainly because it was cost prohibitive."[71]

Neither the welcome letter, nor the "Hey MHS" comment box garnered a mention in the MHS Interpreters Caucus monthly newsletters. Despite being listed as major accomplishments for the Human Resources Subcommittee in 1994, they were not seen as such from the Caucus's perspective. Taken together, the welcome letter and the comment box did not improve employee morale, did not improve communication between seasonal staff and the various levels of MHS management, and did not address the Caucus's desire for transparency about why seasonal workers were reclassified as temporary employees.

One Step Forward, Two Steps Back (1996)

Despite not having the unanimous support of MHS interpreters, the Caucus clearly impacted MHS management and administration. After the Human Resources Subcommittee's 1994 inaugural efforts (i.e., the welcome letter and the comment box), by 1995 the subcommittee moved to more directly address the concerns of the MHS Caucus members. A document listing the "1994–95–96 Key Goals" for the MHS Historic Sites Department included an "Action Plan" that was meant to address "human resource problems" for sites. The action plan included a "review of current departmental structure for managing part-time positions," as well as "focus group discussions (both site managers and interpreters) to review current MHS historic site structure."[72] By 1995, the subcommittee was more proactive about addressing issues that led to historic site interpreters' low morale, possibly because the Caucus did not go away in 1995. The organization rang in the New Year in its January 1995 newsletter by including a proposal for sick leave, which included several routes for addressing the Caucus's concerns. For example, the proposal suggests the "full restoration of sick leave benefits as they stood before fiscal year 1994" as one option, alongside another option that would allow workers to give their "accrued hours to the Sick Leave Fund so that someone in need may make use of hours that may otherwise go unused."[73]

Although MHS never redressed the issue of sick leave, management and administration did go forward with plans to research and reconsider "departmental structure for the managing part-time positions," undertaking the issue of automatic rehire. Focus group discussions served as a major component of this study. The Caucus acknowledged these discussions in its July 1995 newsletter, commending MHS for talking with interpreters face to face (i.e., not through a comment box) as they began their review of departments.[74] In addition to the focus group discussions, Eric Ferguson—editor of the Caucus newsletter—was invited to be part of an employee committee that served on a "one-day pilot" study about diversity training: "Yes, good things come to those who refuse to wait quietly. After a couple years of volunteering and insisting that seasonal and part-time employees should be included on employee committees just like 'real' employees, I finally got onto one."[75] Although the committee was not intended for the long-term, Ferguson saw it as a breakthrough, writing that he wanted "to publicly thank Craig [Cook, the Historic Sites program specialist] for taking a mere class C employee seriously and doing something about it. A minor barrier is broken, progress is possible, don't give up the ship, etc."[76]

The small but positive signs from MHS in 1995 kept the Caucus's sails billowing for the remainder of that year. In 1996, they were deflated as the small gains made were lost. For example, during its tenure (1993–1996) the Caucus had lobbied for the MHS to honor one of its hiring policies requiring that qualified seasonal employees be given interviews for other, permanent positions within the MHS.[77] In 1995, the MHS responded by honoring the policy, resulting in several seasonal employees getting interviews (though not necessarily being hired). The Caucus was proud of this small victory. But in 1996 the MHS revoked the policy striking it from the Employee Handbook.[78]

Cultural Workers Take a Seat at the Table

In 1989, as the construction of the Minnesota History Center was under-way, one of the Fort's "troopies," Erik J. Olsrud, penned a song called, "I'm a Troopie Named Stroopsiuskey." The song was sung to the tune of "I'm a Rover"—an old Scottish ballad that was popular at the time of the Fort's period of interpretation. While the Highland ditty narrates the plight of a "seldom sober" soldier, Olsrud's version relays the plight of a part-time seasonal interpreter at the Fort in the late 1980s.

In this song's chorus, we learn that Stroopsiuskey—a name that was "written on a bunk in the short barracks" at the Fort—has emotionally and intellectually invested in his seasonal job as an interpreter, but is distressed because the position offers no job security:

> Now I'm a troopie, named Stroopsiuskey
> I'm a troopie for the MHS,
> I work all summer, then I get fired,
> Though I always try to do my best.[79]

As an attempt to remedy his situation, Stroopsiuskey decides to make an appeal to the then director of the Minnesota Historical Society, Nina Archabal, by visiting her at the Minnesota History Center, or what Stroopsiuskey calls the "Taj-Ma-Nina."[80] In a word play that compares the History Center to a tomb for the dead, Stroopsiuskey not only places the building in opposition to a living history program, but also hints at the ire some interpreters felt because of the building's extravagance:

> He crepp-ed to her Taj-Ma-Nina
> Leaning gently upon a rock,
> He rapp-ed at her office window,
> "Nina dear, can we have a talk?
> *Chorus*
> She rose her head from mounds of paperwork,
> Reports and budgets filling her locale,
> "Who is that rapping at my Taj-Ma-Nina?
> Sounds like a seasonal with low morale."

Stroopsiuskey answers the director's call by identifying himself as part
of what Chris Tilly has called the "involuntary part-time workforce"—
those part-time, seasonal, and temporary workers "who would prefer
full-time work."[81]

> "Tis only me, a seasonal interpreter,
>   My wallet thin and my future bleak,
>   Could I please have my job all year round,
>   And work forty hours every week?"

The song continues, verse by verse, narrating how troopies who complain do not get rehired, how seasonals have lost their benefits, and
how—despite Nina's professed love for Stroopsiuskey, he must remain
part of the involuntary part-time workforce (although she does let him
know that he is welcome to "re-apply in the spring").

Interpreters first sang this song when "crowded into the blockhouse
at Prairie du Chien [in Wisconsin] on a hot night in June."[82] Prairie du
Chien was the site of an annual 1812 historic encampment and battle
reenactment that many interpreters attended on their own time because
they were passionate about living history. As such, the song is an example of Fort interpreters' unique workplace culture wherein those singing the song would have understood the references, and also would
have been familiar with the melody of the original song on which "I'm
a Troopie" was based.

Though unique to the Fort's work culture in the late 1980s, the song
raises concerns about labor conditions for "seasonals with low morale"
that remain relevant across a number of workplace contexts in the new
economy. These themes may be especially relevant for those who work
on the front lines of museums and public historical settings, as well
as for those who work in related arenas of the knowledge and service
economy. We might imagine for example, adjunct professors and graduate student employees finding a modicum of solidarity with this song's
seasonally employed troopie. Stroopsiuskey's plight draws our attention
to the gulf between those with unchecked power in the workplace and
those who experience the strain of involuntary contingent and part-
time employment, as well as to the emotional toll of investing in one's
work and the relatively low wages earned by many who ply their trade

in the marketplace of public history, the fringes of higher education, or in nonprofit arts, humanities, and cultural sectors.

With regard to public history, in recent years, Stroopsiuskey's plight has been playing out in the streets of Manhattan among per-diem workers at the Lower East Side Tenement Museum. Founded in 1988 by Ruth Abram and Anita Jacobson, the Lower East Side Tenement Museum interprets an 1863 tenement at 97 Orchard Street in Manhattan, with a mission to promote "tolerance and historical perspective through the presentation and interpretation of a variety of immigrant and migrant experiences on Manhattan's Lower East Side, a gateway to America."[83] The museum aims to accomplish this mission through outreach programs, and tours that take museum-goers into the museum's restored tenement apartments to focus on the lives of several immigrant families who lived at 97 Orchard Street during the late nineteenth and early twentieth centuries. Since 1988, the museum has enjoyed tremendous growth; the building itself was listed on the National Register of Historic Places in 1992, and in 1994 it was designated a National Historic Landmark. Two years later, in 1996, the museum formally acquired 97 Orchard Street, and increasingly garnered public attention, critical acclaim, and tourist dollars. Twenty years after its founding, the museum employed nearly one hundred staff, including thirteen managers, eight part-time maintenance workers, about forty full time staff, and roughly forty per-diem costumed interpreters, tour guides, and educators, who are responsible for conducting around 75 percent of all tours.[84]

These per-diem workers earn an average of $17 dollars per hour for the guides and educators, and $23 dollars per hour for the costumed interpreters, but they are not guaranteed hours, have no recourse if fired, and those who had worked at the museum for years did not see a raise until 2006—when they teamed up with United Auto Workers (UAW) Local 2110 to begin an organizing campaign with a platform centering on cost of living increases, health benefits, and job-security.[85] These concerns would also be at the center of a 2009 strike mounted by 420 frontline workers—including guides, hosts, and museum educators—at two Canadian museums: the Canadian Museum of Civilization and the War Museum in Ottawa. According to a news release on the Public Service Alliance of Canada's website, only six of these museums' fifty-five guides enjoyed permanent employment, and the majority of

these 420 workers were long-time workers, with only temporary contracts. The 420 workers who struck for eighty-six days did so on a platform of seeking fair wages and job security provisions (and notably, they
did so while continuing to occasionally provide programming *outside*
of the museum).[86] In Manhattan, in addition to those bread-and-butter
concerns, the Lower East Side Tenement Museum's per-diem workers
also have had complaints somewhat endemic to their tenement-house
working environment: docents and costumed interpreters who spend
much of their working hours in the tenements themselves have raised
concerns about working in cramped conditions with no air conditioning
in the summer, and inadequate heating in the winter.

By May 2007, a majority of Lower East Side Tenement Museum per-
diem workers had signed union cards and requested that a card count
take place—a process by which a neutral third party would verify
whether a majority of these employees had signed their union cards,
thereby affirming their wish to have UAW Local 2110 represent them as
their union. The museum pushed back; it maintained that the bargaining unit should include full-time employees, and under those conditions
demanded that the matter be settled in a National Labor Relations Board
(NLRB) election. Per-diem workers objected to the expansion of their
bargaining unit to include full-time staff, since by definition bargaining
units comprise employees that have a "clear and identifiable community
of interests."[87] By sending the matter to the NLRB and not allowing
for a card count, the museum's actions have been characterized in the
press as both anti-union and a bit ironic, especially considering that the
Lower East Side Tenement Museum is widely recognized for its efforts to
interpret labor history and workers' rights.[88] The museum has even hon-
ored the role that contemporary labor unions play in immigrants' lives.
UNITE!—a labor union that lends a major hand in organizing workers
in the garment industry—helped underwrite the museum's "Piecing it
Together" tour, which looks at sweatshop labor past and present. Also,
the featured honoree at one museum benefit was John Sweeney, who
was the president of the AFL-CIO at the time.[89]

Though not specifically addressing the situation for per-diem museum
guides in Manhattan, in a March 2010 blog posting, museum educator
and activist blogger Kat Hinkel asked her readers, "How can museums
be a medium for discussion of social fairness if they are operating just

like any huge, multi-national corporation instead of the nonprofits that they are?"[90] Hinkel and fellow blogger Kirsten Teasdale are working to redress this concern by building awareness about the conditions for museum workers in their blog, *Museos Unite!* Hinkel and Teasdale have appropriated the noun "Museo" and coined their own English definition for it to describe an individual "working in, volunteering in, or seeking work in a museum" who is also "interested in collaborating to change the way museums are run not only for the benefit of the public, but for the betterment of [the] Museos' situation in regard to pay, benefits, and professional development."[91] Under this definition, Lower East Side Tenement Museum's per-diem workers, Stroopsiuskey, and Caucus members could all be classified as "Museos"—and would likely find Hinkel and Teasdale's blog of interest.

Among the topics Hinkel and Teasdale have raised since they initiated their blog in August 2009 have been Museo job satisfaction, salary discrepancies, fair compensation, Museo solidarity, and the recent Museo strikes and walkouts in Canada, France, and England.[92] They have also put a fair amount of (virtual) ink toward combating the argument that if you love your nonprofit job in the cultural sector, that you should grin and bear the costs. Their rebuttal is, at its simplest: "Work is work. It should be fairly compensated regardless of its innate nobility or how much of a 'dream job' it is."[93]

The case study of the Minnesota Historical Society Interpreters Caucus shows that when workers invested themselves in a workplace, it may have garnered their consent to work, but it did not necessarily grant their complacency. Even so, in May 1996, Caucus membership voted to disband officially by the end of June. Reasons that the Caucus voted to disband were many, though all of them could be boiled down to the fact that the most active Caucus members were generally fatigued from expending a lot of effort and not seeing enough positive results to fuel them onward any longer. Still, the rationale that the Caucus provided its readership in its next-to-last issue is worth examining for what it reveals about how the Caucus framed its own demise.

The brief article from which I quote in this paragraph, called "We're Disbanding," begins by noting that Ferguson and the other officers in the Caucus found themselves being "pulled toward other projects."[94] Ferguson, for example, had been finding that editing the newsletter was conflicting "with writing projects that actually pay." And while Ferguson wrote that there was not a decrease in interest among the Caucus's membership, among those members there were no "other people ready to step up and do the work necessary to keep going." While Caucus leadership was pleased with the progress they had made with those things in their power—"organizing and communicating across sites, talking to management about our interests, improving our own skills, and educating our membership (and the many non-members who read the newsletter or attended a meeting) about workplace issues [and] making interpreters aware of the importance of their work and the skills they have developed, even if no one else is likewise aware"—"unfortunately," writes Ferguson, the Caucus did not have much "success with those things in management's control." Although the Caucus brought their concerns to management, they were discouraged by management's response: "Our concerns may be known, but they're on the back burner if they're even on the stove at all, and we don't get to help with the cooking." But while the Caucus felt that their concerns were not being addressed, Ferguson emphatically noted that their *goals haven't changed*—in particular, the issues of reapplying for interpretive positions every spring, the loss of accumulated sick time, and not being able to "buy into the MHS medical insurance pool, even at full price" remained unresolved but were of paramount importance to those interpreters who did not want to be regarded as "just a temp." "By forming the Caucus," concluded Ferguson, "we have taken our first steps. Next time we may well walk, and may we walk to our seat at the table where the decisions about us are made."

Despite the membership's decision to disband, Ferguson's message remains hopeful that a future generation of employees who choose to fight for a voice in the MHS might learn from the Caucus, and earn their seat at the table. In *The Next Upsurge: Labor and the New Social Movements,* sociologist and labor scholar Dan Clawson hopes that union campaigns of the late twentieth and early twenty-first centuries—successful or not—might one day be understood as having laid the "groundwork" for a future "explosion of labor action."[95] If Clawson's buoyancy is realized, the early union effort of interpreters at the MHS and its subsequent offspring—the MHS Interpreters Caucus—will be understood not as "insignificant historical oddities" but as "prehistory of the upsurge."[96]

While that future has not yet come to pass, the MHS Interpreters

Caucus was not insignificant. For one, although the Caucus has faded from the collective memory of Fort interpreters in the twenty-first century, its efforts have affected every employee since 2001, when seasonal interpreters won permanent status for their seasonal jobs and no longer had to reapply to work each season. Though the Caucus was not credited for this victory, that it continually and directly appealed to management to redress this issue from 1993 to 1996 no doubt heightened management's awareness that this issue negatively affected the morale of many of its employees—the majority of whom were rehired to work for multiple seasons. Certainly no management team wants a staff with low morale, especially if they are—as one Fort manager quipped—in the "customer service business."[97]

The MHS Interpreters Caucus is also important as an example of how workers who were labeled as "temporaries" acted proactively in a collective effort to self-identify as professionals and to appeal for improved working conditions. On the flip side of the coin, examining the Caucus complements insights offered by Jackie Rogers's study of temps who avoided collective action precisely because they wanted to resist identifying as temporary workers. Similarly, those who did not want to fully commit to the identity of a historic interpreter did not want to fight for improved working conditions on the job. While Rogers's study suggests that temporary workers rejected identifying as a temp because it offered no stable identity, I further argue that that instability is heightened by the assumption that we are all free agents who bear full responsibility for the contexts in which we find ourselves. Thus, if a job does not offer an individual all she would like, it is the individual's fault for having chosen the job in the first place. If Al Gini (a professor of business ethics) is right, that as Americans our work "not only provides us with an income, it literally names us, identifies us, to both ourselves and others" and that it "is the means by which we form our character and complete ourselves as persons," then clearly some MHS historical interpreters in the mid-1990s did not want this particular job to be a defining part of their selves—even while those supported the Caucus saw its grassroots efforts as a way to bring dignity into their work lives.[98]

Believing that they offered skilled emotional and intellectual labor, the Caucus members offer us an example of frontline interpreters who organized as a collective in order to resist the commodification of their specialized knowledge that they had accrued over time. Seeing as MHS Interpreters Caucus was born out of an earlier (failed) union attempt, this study complicates the only scholarly study of historic interpreters' relationship to organized labor. In their chapter, titled "Picket Lines," Richard Handler and Eric Gable examine how Colonial Williamsburg's managers and interpreters reacted to the 1990–91 contract dispute between the corporation's unionized hotel and restaurant workers, and management. The anthropologists found that management was antagonistic toward the unionized employees. They also found, more surprisingly, that "low-level" interpreters in the historic areas were similarly opposed to the hotel and restaurant workers' demands for pay increases and improved health benefits. They toed the corporate line, argued Handler and Gable, because they:

> imagined themselves to be very different from their counterparts in the hotels. Interpreters called themselves professionals. They likened themselves to a kind of in-house faculty. They did research; they taught. While they wore uniforms (in their case, costumes) marking them as service employees, their jobs allowed them, on occasion, to don the "suits" of the managerial class. As professionals, they thought of themselves as somehow superior to the workers in hotels and restaurants. . . . To preserve what they imagined were positions of tenuous privilege, they could not condone a labor disturbance, much less participate in one.[99]

By contrast, the MHS Interpreters Caucus shows that some interpreters could consider themselves "professionals" and not feel aligned with the interests of the managerial class. Certainly Caucus members recognized that they could identify as professionals all they wanted, but their employer nonetheless regarded them as temps—and the material conditions of their employment reflected that position: they had no job security, and no benefits.

Ultimately, even if participation for some Caucus members amounted to little more than paying the $5 in yearly dues, considering that the organization consistently maintained more than 30 members from every MHS historic site shows that MHS historical interpreters had broadly held concerns, and that, as a collective they were willing to exercise agency to improve conditions.

PART II

Historic Fort Snelling's
Front Line
(1996–2006)

CHAPTER 3
THE WAGES OF LIVING HISTORY
Rewards and Costs of Emotional Investment

O liver: *The first year at the Fort was the honeymoon year. I felt like nothing could go wrong; when things did go wrong, I was either naïve enough not to know it or I didn't care. I was just so grateful to be in a challenging, intellectually stimulating environment—certainly in comparison to retail—and the feedback I got from fellow interpreters and from the public was an amazing ego rush.*

During the second year, cracks started to appear in the veneer—the politics that come with any job: various staff members continually butting heads, and the limitations of the medium became much more apparent.

The honeymoon ended when I realized that no matter how much time I put into preparing to portray a particular character—or to do a particular vignette or demonstration, I was still primarily there to entertain. That's a bit of an overstatement, but I would feel that I wanted to pass on the knowledge I'd accumulated to every human being who came near me, but there was only so much I could do. First of all, I wasn't really from the past. Second, the visitors came with so many expectations that no matter how I would try to prepare for what we would be doing, the public would always throw it back in my face. Not that there weren't wonderful experiences, but I would sometimes feel that my expectations were too high for the public, or for fellow staff interpreters as well.

I guess my point is that the most interesting parts of my character's story never came up unless I rammed it down the public's throat, because they were not willing to sit there and listen to this character's thoughts, or life story, and it would be perfectly unnatural to do that; that's another one of the limitations of the medium.

What is most satisfying about the job? Positive visitor feedback. It's as simple as all that. I would not have known this until I started working at the Fort—but I seem to thrive on interaction with friends and strangers, in which I get an opportunity to show off what I can do: to perform, and then to have instantaneous positive feedback, sometimes in the form of something as simple as a smile; sometimes, a knowing wink or a nod from a parent of a child that I've just been interpreting to; sometimes just an outright compliment from visitors. Those are things I really enjoy. I don't get much enjoyment from doing something as simple and as obvious as firing a musket. Bang! There's a bit of smoke, and the children and everybody else clap their hands for moment. Big deal, right? But when I portray certain characters and I can see a visitor making a connection, those are great moments, and I feel like I've really earned my money.

There are days where I drag myself in, totally unenthused in the morning, but after the first one or two very positive interactions with visitors I'm flying high for the rest of the day, enough to buoy me up even though I'm physically exhausted by the time I'm ready to go home. In my mind, it justifies a lot of the extra time I put in researching characters or aspects of the nineteenth century.[1]

Like Oliver, many interpreters I encountered at the Fort were extraordinarily loyal and took seriously the work they performed, often at the expense of their personal lives out of costume. Throughout this chapter, I draw on interviews with Fort workers, and my own experiences as a worker there, in order to understand why and how some interpreters chose to invest emotionally in their place of work, and to understand as well the emotional costs of that investment. Ultimately I argue that interpreters at the Fort got an emotional return on investing in their jobs. However, despite the pleasure they derived from connecting with others through the medium of history, the experience also drained them and challenged them to negotiate their sense of self in the face of the many competing claims of the job.[2]

Hall of Fame / Wall of Shame

Thick, diamond-shaped stone walls surround the reconstructed and restored buildings of Fort Snelling. Flanking the northeast wall is the long wooden barracks, a white clapboard building whose main level contained badly wigged mannequins and static exhibits that detailed the life of the Fort's enlisted men during the nineteenth century. Beneath the wooden barracks was the nerve center for the site's living history program. There, one would find (1) the staff dayroom where meetings were held and breaks were taken; (2) several dressing and locker rooms where staff changed out of civilian clothes into their 1827 costumes; and (3) storage rooms for muskets and costumes. Spanning the length of this nerve center was a cool, damp, narrow corridor that seemed dimly lit even when its fluorescent lights were on. Still, it was not so dim that one could not read the words that were painted on the wall.

The wall was painted in 1991 as part of a twenty-year, all-staff reunion at the Fort. A shield painted on the concrete wall read "Roll Call of the Honorable Fifth," referring to the regiment of infantry interpreted at the Fort. As part of the commemoration, names and corresponding years of employment of those who had worked at least five seasons at Historic Fort Snelling were painted in a checkered pattern on white concrete blocks to honor those who had served a "full enlistment" in the interpretive ranks.[3] This tradition continued for nearly twenty years, until the wall was painted over as part of site renovations. Nearly a hundred names were on the wall, indicating the significant investment that workers had made in the Fort over the three decades it had operated as a living history site.

Some interpreters clearly felt conflicted about the honor of being recognized for having returned for multiple seasons to their part-time, seasonal jobs. This conflict expressed itself in the nickname that the wall earned over the years: "Wall of Shame"—a mocking play on "Hall of Fame" that betrayed the stigma some workers felt regarding having spent at least five years as a seasonal employee at the Fort. In *Stigma: Notes on the Management of a Spoiled Identity*, sociologist Erving Goffman describes the stigmatized individual as one who is somehow marked as discredited in the wider, "normal" society.[4] While physical deformities and mental defects may produce stigmatized effects, so might the "tribal stigma of race, nation, and religion" as well as perceived "blemishes of individual character."[5] One's chosen occupation, for example, could be perceived as a stigmatizing blot on one's character. As I discussed in Chapter 2, in order to avoid the perception that they have mismanaged their working lives, workers of potentially stigmatizing jobs may invoke cover stories in order to avoid being marked for having chosen to be employed in an occupation that may not be taken seriously as "a real job." Those I interviewed, rather than relying on cover stories to justify their jobs, fought against the stigma by redefining their work as a positive good that added value to society.

Reverberations of the social stigma of earning one's living through historical interpretive work echoed within the real stories that interpreters told about their working lives. Like the restaurant servers that Karla Erickson examined in her book *The Hungry Cowboy*, interpreters' stories often "reflect how much of their selves they invest in a job that, no matter how long they stay, others may not consider to be a real job."[6] Notably, Erickson also draws on Goffman's work of stigma to understand why the servers she interviewed described their jobs in terms of both pride and shame. But while Erickson sees the stigma of serving as paralleling a tribal stigma based on race, nation, and religion, I see the kind of stigmatization that historical interpreters experienced as closer to "blemishes of individual character" because workers wrestled with the fact that they alone were responsible for having made the choice to be employed in this line of work. But even so, as with Erickson's narrators, interpreters I interviewed took tremendous pleasure in their work. As a result, they went to great lengths to defend the honor of their job, in the wake of the stigmatizing shame of which they were nonetheless aware. In the words of Fort worker Elijah:

> I think that there's been far too much talk about "well, this isn't a real
> job," and "Oh, are you going to get a *real job* now?" Just because it's
> seasonal doesn't make it a "not-real" job, you know? I've heard so
> much of that talk that I've said, "No! I'm going to decide for myself
> how I feel about this job, and I'm going to conduct myself with
> the kind of professionalism I think I deserve." I've got a little more
> esteem now. You can tell me that I don't have a real job but I'm going
> to disagree with you.[7]

Here, Elijah acknowledged that his work as a historical interpreter carried with it the stigma of not being perceived by some as "real." Though this stigma apparently affected Elijah's self-esteem at one time, he took pains to reject the stigma by defining the value of his job on his own terms. Indeed, Elijah wished that interpreters who felt discouraged at times would hear the message that "you are an important employee. What you do here is important and you affect people's lives. Really. Whether you entertain them, or whether you teach them, or whether you show them a good time, you're an important person; you're not a mannequin behind glass and you're contributing to something that is unique in all the world."[8] Almost as if he had heard Elijah's message, Oliver described feeling proud of his labor when he was able to emotionally and intellectually engage with those visitors who saw his value as worth more than his capacity to produce a bit of smoke from his musket.[9]

While interpreters (myself included) would often be chided for working in a place that required them to dress in historic costume and talk "old timey,"[10] the perception that costumed historical interpretation was not a real job was also rooted in the conditions of employment: Interpreters had little opportunity to move up the ranks of their organization (the Minnesota Historical Society), the pay was low, and the work was seasonal. This tenuous economic position was not unique to interpreters at the Fort. Journalist Jean McNair's 1989 article for the *Washington Post* focused on how Colonial Williamsburg interpreters had difficulty making ends meet because of low wages. In the article, McNair quotes one interpreter "who was earning less than $8 an hour when he quit" as complaining that the wages at Williamsburg were " 'absolutely not commensurate with the cost of living in the area.' He said, 'We were going into the hole by $500 every month.' "[11] Over two decades later, in December 2011, the Colonial Williamsburg Foundation advertised a part-time, non-benefits-eligible position for a museum interpreter beginning at only $9.05 an hour.[12] Likewise, in 2004, Becky, an interpreter at Conner Prairie, told me that she could work at Taco Bell and start at a higher wage: "There is no chance for advancement, and no benefits," she informed me (when out of character), and then she quipped, "If I get injured I have to die immediately."[13]

As a point of comparison, in 2006, first-year Fort interpreters received a starting hourly wage of $11.46. While several dollars an hour higher than their interpretive counterparts at many other living history sites,[14] the part-time, seasonal employment available to interpreters at the Fort proved difficult for many to sustain in the long run. Paul, who had worked more than twelve years as a historic interpreter at various museums, made the difficult decision to leave his interpretive job at the Fort because he couldn't "live on 6 months' pay. And I knew that going in, and I knew it was only sort of a stepping stone."[15] But even while Paul knew that earning just six months' pay meant that he would not be able to prioritize his work as an interpreter indefinitely, he nonetheless "idolized Fort Snelling as an interpreter." As a native Minnesotan with a degree in history, Paul felt that working at the Fort was akin to playing "for the hometown team," and acknowledged that the job "sort of validated my experience as a Minnesota historian. It's like, 'Yes, you are qualified enough to get this job' and really, there aren't any other jobs, interpretively that I would ever want." Interpreters such as Paul rejected the stigma that could be attached to working as a costumed interpreter in favor of viewing the job as one within a well-respected cultural institution, the Minnesota Historical Society.[16] Researcher Julie Elmore, in her 2006 study of National Park Service (NPS) employee satisfaction, similarly found that the seasonal aspect of the job weighed heavily on many of the NPS interpretive rangers. Not unlike Paul, one NPS ranger noted in his interview his passion for the job, but the realities of needing to pay his bills and plan his future would inevitably lead him to find employment elsewhere: "I love this job. I love where I work. I love helping people, but inevitably I'll need more. . . . I have bills to pay. No one ever gives us any kind of warning at all about whether or not our position will be around next season. We don't get to know what's going on, and yet, I have to know so I can make plans."[17]

Ultimately, although there was a social stigma to working as a costumed historical interpreter, many of the interpreters I encountered strove to bring dignity to their work by articulating the cultural value of interpretation to the public, and by making a deep emotional investment in their jobs.

"Engage, inform, entertain, and stimulate"

In their study of Colonial Williamsburg, Handler and Gable described the interpreters they encountered as having a "divided consciousness" with regard to how they related to their workplace.[18] On the one hand, costumed workers at the restored colonial capital were only too willing to complain about the difficulty of making ends meet, the lack of benefits, the ineptness of management, and the frequent feeling of being hired merely to entertain the public. On the other hand, those same workers tended to love their jobs and felt great pride in wearing their historic costumes, which they viewed as "symbol[s] of a great corporation, Colonial Williamsburg."[19] Handler and Gable defined this divided consciousness as one wherein interpreters "recognized that their profession hardly lived up to the rhetorical expectations and that the corporate structure was at least in part to blame for their predicament, yet they continued to identify with the foundation as a lofty enterprise and to get considerable job satisfaction out of doing so. They were willing, as a result, to put up with or ignore or discount quite a bit of discomfort and claim that despite everything, they loved what they were doing."[20]

For this study, however, the term "divided consciousness" too tidily packages how names painted in the Fort's wooden barracks could trigger the interpreters' experience of both honor and shame from their jobs. The many years I spent working alongside Fort interpreters showed me that they did not merely "claim" they loved their jobs in spite of perceived problems. Rather, these skilled workers tended to experience real joy in connecting with others through the medium of history. True, these moments of joy compensated for the decisions the workers made to consent to the terms of their employment. But in the stories they told about their working lives, I saw their consciousness not so much divided as I saw workers eager to invest themselves in their work because they were proud of their interpretive skills, because they experienced genuine pleasure from exercising those skills, because investing themselves allowed them to see their work as having a social value, and to create a positive work identity for themselves.

In the larger literature about workers in the new economy, recent scholarship has probed the significance of workers' relative emotional investment or detachment to their places of work.[21] As sociologist Gideon Kunda has noted, much of the scholarship devoted to investment and detachment in the workplace focuses on seeing workers on a continuum.[22] On one end are workers who finds themselves totally committed to and emotionally aligned with the organization. These work individual sense of self may be significantly tied to their jobs. On the other end are the "alienated" workers who find themselves utterly detached and invested in their jobs only in so far as they provide a means to an end: payday. These workers are emotionally detached from the pleasures or pains that might otherwise accompany their jobs, and if better paying positions were to come along, these workers would experience no sense of loss from leaving their current jobs.

Overwhelmingly, Fort interpreters I interviewed and worked with could be described as emotionally invested in their jobs and were capable of experiencing both emotional highs and lows because of their attachment. As Oliver described in his narration, connecting with visitors could buoy an invested worker's spirits, while feeling unappreciated could send them plummeting. Only workers who did not feel alienated from the emotional labor they were hired to produce would experience genuine personal responses.[23]

After nine seasons of working at the site, in his interview Elijah frequently expressed displeasure with the site's management, with the politics between co-workers, and with how interpreters were treated as employees. But even considering those factors, Elijah was not a detached worker. To the contrary, because he was invested in his work, Elijah developed his own strategy for dealing with the emotional turmoil that he experienced as a worker at Fort Snelling in order to restore his personal sense of honor:

> I've figured out the only way to survive at that place, and I mean that literally—*survive* emotionally, physically, anything—is to not serve the site itself, and not serve yourself as much, and not serve the program, or the MHS. Forget about all that. Just serve the public. Serve the visitors. You *know*? You know? If you take care of them and you keep your attitudes and focus toward them in all the things you do, then everything else will just take care of itself on its own because it's a service job. It's not about *you*. It's not about *your* "thing," or your little playtime fantasy, or whatever.[24]

Here—even while Elijah distanced himself from the notion that he was serving the site, the program, or the MHS—he developed a personal strategy for surviving his work that was based on serving the public. Notably, in developing this philosophy of whole-heartedly serving the public and no one else, Elijah was clearly trying to negotiate his sense of self within a workplace that made many shifting claims on his identity.

As did Oliver and Elijah, other Fort interpreters tended to justify their emotional investment in their jobs by articulating the cultural value of their work. Overwhelmingly interpreters described their job's purpose as an effort to emotionally and intellectually engage visitors while trying to pass on knowledge about the past. Twenty-five-year-old Alyssa, for example, believed that good interpreters "have to be engaging with the visitors because you can't just spout facts at them, because if you just spout facts they won't be interested. To be [a good interpreter is to be] able to have that knowledge base and then to figure out a way to relate to people where they'll learn something but they'll also feel personally involved."[25] Achieving this goal was seen as adding a positive good to society. Donald, for example, stated his aims as follows: "I use my historic character and setting as a vehicle for meaningful conversations with visitors about history and its connections across time."[26] Paul, in another example, took care to distinguish his role as a historic interpreter from that of someone who merely practices living history. As an interpreter, Paul felt that his job was not to "try and live in [a former] time period," as reenactors often try to do, but to "translate the past into a vernacular."[27] In describing this work during his interview, Paul was animated, and proud to elaborate the high level of care he took in trying to translate the past for the public:

> Some things in the past aren't readily known to the public these days, because, well if you're talking about the early nineteenth century and you're talking about the toilet . . . sinks and the toilets have sort of changed in what they mean, and if you start using those words indiscriminately, how much is the public going to learn out of it?
>
> An interpreter translates things from the past into the present, just as an interpreter of languages doesn't translate literally, but translates into the vernacular. You know, the Hebrew expression for "angry" is "you've got a red nose." If you go around saying, "so and so has a red nose" it doesn't tell you that he's angry. So being able to translate as an *interpreter*: that's what I always considered myself to be.[28]

After sharing this philosophy of interpretation, Paul play-acted scenarios of how he put it into practice when working with the public. One scenario illustrated how he used his first-person interpretation as a nineteenth-century hospital steward to, quite literally, translate language common to his character into a vernacular that the contemporary public might understand. For example, he would explain what a bicarbonate of soda was by referencing a well-known Alka-Seltzer jingle (while staying in his period character). To wit, he might say: "When you *plop* a bicarbonate of soda in water, it *fizzes*, and oh what a relief it is." Explaining his interpretive choice in this instance, Paul said, "I doubt any hospital steward in 1827 ever said 'plop' . . . but it was something fun to say. I'm looking for how much bang for the buck. Every word has got to count when you're an interpreter, and not to say that each of us ever achieves that, but we look for it. A wise interpreter once said that if you're able to do that, it's like digging holes; eventually the public is going to fall into one and is going to have to ask for assistance out. So you keep the conversation going."[29] To get a visitor to fall into one of these "holes" meant that interpreters were successful in engaging visitors in conversations about history. Generally, interpreters who were invested in their jobs worked hard at the task of quickly sizing up visitors so as to gauge their interests, and to improve their chances of leading visitors into the proverbial hole.

Fort interpreters tended to describe the purpose of their jobs in ways that were consistent with each other, and also with the mainstream literature that theorizes the principles of interpretation, such as Freeman Tilden's *Interpreting Our Heritage* (which the Fort's 1970 *Interpretive Program* also quoted).[30] For Tilden, interpretation—whether practiced at a historic site, a museum, or a national park—would most ideally be carried out by those who feel passionate about the "art form" and who believe in the importance of their work, not unlike a religious disciple who feels called to spread the good news. Indeed, Tilden's tone often evokes a certain religiosity: "Thousands of naturalists, historians, archaeologists and other specialists are engaged in the work of revealing, to such visitors as desire the service, something of the beauty and wonder, the inspiration and spiritual meaning that lie behind what the visitor can with his senses perceive. This function of the custodians of our treasures is called Interpretation."[31] As such, Tilden saw interpreters as being called to reveal the "soul of things."[32]

While few of my interviewees were quite as effusive as Tilden when they described their aims and purposes as living history interpreters, Karl was perhaps the most Tilden-esque in his answer to my question, "What are your aims and purposes as an interpreter?" He even went so far as to reference Tilden in his response:

> My aims as a historic site guide are four. Not just aims, they're holy orders. They are sacrosanct. Engage the visitor. If you don't do that, you should be fired. Engage the visitor. Don't sit on your hands. You get up and go out and you reach out to people. If they're across the way and you see them, and there are no other interpreters around, you hail them. Secondly, inform them. That's your duty, to be informing them. You might argue education. Third, entertain them. You might argue acting, and that's wonderful. But that's [another] one: entertain. And finally, stimulate their thinking. One of the sages you have among your selected reference list, Tilden, uses the word "provoke." I don't like provoke, but *stimulate* their thinking.
>
> Engage, inform, entertain, and stimulate. Note: Study and research must undergird the informing and the stimulating. You've got to come prepared. You can't just wing it and say things you don't know are true—whatever truth *is* [chuckles]. Those four things guide me, day in and day out. And wear me out, too.[33]

In exercising this four-pronged philosophy of interpretation, Karl experienced great joy when he felt that he had connected with visitors. But alongside the pleasure of accomplishing his goals, he simultaneously experienced a "wearing out" that was both physical and emotional. A master at engaging visitors with history, Karl would sometimes enervate himself to the point of sickness, and said he frequently felt both physically tired and emotionally drained after a day's work. In my seven years as an interpreter at Fort Snelling, I observed (and experienced) this wearing out to be nearly ubiquitous among interpreters who, like Karl, considered themselves seriously invested in interpretation's educational function. And so, while interpreters took pride in and experienced a great amount of pleasure from their efforts to engage, inform, entertain, and stimulate the public, such an investment had costs—which were expressed both as emotional and physical exhaustion, as well as in a disjointed sense of self.

Shifting Emotional Gears

Interpreting the past to the public in an individuated manner carried with it the effect of taxing the emotional reservoirs of the workers. As Karl noted, "Teaching and acting at the same time is taxing, especially when you are moving about in the middle of your audience."[34] Specifically, Karl described what it felt like to be exhausted from constantly adjusting his self-presentation to the public in an effort to best meet their various needs and desires:

> Each visitor has a different personality and interest. I strive to accurately read those and shift my mental and emotional gears constantly to effectively relate to them with courtesy and sensitivity. Consequently, I'm emotionally drained at the end of the day. Just exhausted. And I'm not alone. Talk to interpreter after interpreter—just bushed, whipped, wiped out at the end of the day. And it's not just physical alone, it's this shifting gears, shifting gears. At least the good interpreters. There are some interpreters who don't stick around real long, who just sit on their fannies and are annoyed if they're asked a question—that's too bad.[35]

Here, Karl describes how the interpreter's first task was not to interpret history, but to interpret clues (eye contact, follow-up questions, listening to noises, etc.) that might indicate the visitor's interests, both regarding content and presentation style. If an interpreter gleaned that someone might be most interested in a quiet conversation rather than a boisterous presentation, the ideal interpreter would shift gears and adjust accordingly.

With all this shifting of gears, interpreters not only experienced emotional exhaustion, but also often had difficulty locating their sense of self. Sociologist Arlie Hochschild's 1983 study of flight attendants found that many of her respondents felt inauthentic as a result of adhering to the emotional demands of their job, which demanded that they work to meet customers' requests while remaining emotionally calm and pleasant.[36] Workers wanting to avoid feelings of inauthenticity often elected to invest themselves in their emotional displays and integrated those emotions into their "actual" personalities. Hochschild identified this investment as a kind of "deep acting" wherein the workers would exhibit emotions appropriate to the job and feel sincere in doing so, whereas in "surface acting" the worker would exhibit the required emotions, but without necessarily investing themselves in the display.[37]

In her response to my question about the emotional demands of her job as a historic interpreter, Maggie, who worked as a public school teacher most of the year, highlighted the difference between surface acting (when you are just "putting it on") and deep acting (when you believe it):

> There are many times when I go home much more tired [from the Fort] than even from teaching, which is a pretty physically demanding job. But in a way, it's like teaching; you have to be "up" for the visitors who are the students. You have to be upbeat. You can't—well some people get away with it, but I can't—you have to put on a façade whether you feel like it or not. You just learn to be "up" and put on this façade and after a while you begin to believe it, and you know, you end up with a fairly upbeat personality. Either that, or you get beaten down by it.[38]

Here Maggie suggests that her service jobs have conditioned her personality so that both in the classroom and at the Fort she is able to be "upbeat" for others. In describing the process of developing such a personality, she confesses that it begins by putting "on this façade and after awhile you begin to believe it." This points to one of the effects of deep acting: the workers' sense of self—personality, character, essence—changes as a result of the performance or personality that is expected at their place of work.

Returning to Karl's notion of shifting gears, wherein interpreters were expected to adjust their performance according to what cues they received from customers, interpreters knew that an upbeat personality was not necessarily what was called for in all interactions. Communications scholar and former museum educator Lois H. Silverman's fascinating research on the therapeutic potential of museums shows how artifacts at museums have the capacity to elicit powerful emotional responses from visitors, often inspiring them to share memories and personal stories that may relate very little to the intended pedagogical functions that led to the object's display.[39] At the Fort, some interpreters found themselves in the role of de facto therapist when visitors were moved to share personal—and sometimes painful—memories with interpreters because of their encounter with objects or buildings at the site. Maggie experienced this when she was stationed in the "the commanding officer's house dressed up as Mrs. Snelling" and "many times" found herself "listening to men tell their stories about being in Europe in World War II, with tears streaming down their faces."[40]

In such scenarios when interpreters were confronted with visitors who were strongly affected by their trip to the historic site, workers often chose to break out of character in order to better emotionally meet the visitors' needs. Maggie explained that in these situations, she respectfully listened to the veterans' stories, and when "they say, 'I don't know why I'm telling you this right now,'" she comforted them, explaining, "It's the place; it has a lot to do with it."[41] Scholars such as Karla Erickson, Hyun Jeong Kim, and Genevieve Lovell have argued that workers in the hospitality industry who perform deep acting often find themselves feeling emotional rewards. The same was also true for interpreters I encountered at the Fort.[42] Maggie, for example, described feeling personally gratified in being able to offer the service of comfort: "I love those experiences, those are really wonderful." While Maggie was being called on to emotionally adjust to suit the visitor's needs, she did not experience this gear shifting negatively.[43]

Upbeat one moment, empathic the next, interpreters were constantly shifting gears to meet customers' emotional needs and frequently described their emotional reservoir as quite low after a day of interacting with the public. Oliver, for instance, said in his interview that he often felt "like a zombie" at the close of most workdays at the Fort. He found that this sense of tuning out and feeling "absolutely wasted" would come over him the instant the last tourist had left the Fort, suggesting the extent to which he had been performing emotional labor during the workday. During the interview, Oliver described this performance as carrying with it "a great and somewhat unpleasant irony," because in giving so much to the public he found that he tended to lose his desire to interact with his own family after work:

> I can spend an entire day talking to complete strangers and no matter how tired I am I will almost always find a way to seem fresh and alert to them or at least have a sense of humor, and try to be "up" and "on," but in that 10- or 15-minute drive home, I'm done for and I find

it difficult to engage in more than just simple conversation at home, and in fact, sometimes find it annoying, because I'm simply tired of being pleasant, and it's not that anybody at home does anything wrong, I just simply have had it with people, with interactions with other people, with other living creatures. [All I want is] a nice cold drink, a book, a movie, something that involves as little as possible interaction with myself.[44]

Henry echoed Oliver's experience. In response to my question about the emotional demands of the job, Henry noted that his emotional output at the Fort ultimately put stress on his relationship with his fiancée:

I go home, and I'm just utterly physically and emotionally exhausted. And I've had fights with my fiancée because she's wanted to go do things and I'm like, "I need a couple of hours to pull myself back together." And I've felt like I've needed time to rejoin the correct century sometimes. Just step out of it and be like, "okay, it's not 1827 anymore, it's 2002." I need to take some time and figure that out. And Emily's wanted to go do things, and she's been angry with me because I have not been interactive with her because I've spent all day interacting with other people that I just don't have it in me to be social with her any more.[45]

Here Henry described how interacting with the public all day made him less eager to spend social time with others after work, either with his fiancée or in any other situation that might require him "to be performing."[46] Significantly, rather than choosing to give less to his job so that he might have been able to give more to his nonworking life, Henry and his fiancée chose to resolve the problem by limiting the activities they would engage in on work nights.

In narrating his experiences, Henry described noticeable differences between the emotional demands made on him at the Fort (where he had to emotionally shift gears and engaged in deep acting), and the emotional demands made on him at his second job (wherein he was not required to interact with the public). Notably, almost as though he was trying to distinguish his true self from the roles he portrayed at the Fort, during this section of the interview, Henry referred to himself in the third person:

> I wander into [my other job] and I'm just Henry and Henry doesn't
> have to be a lance corporal, Henry doesn't have to be a blacksmith,
> Henry doesn't have to make sure he doesn't say, "okay" or "hello."
> He can say whatever he wants to say. And Henry can actually shut
> down from [his other job] periodically. I can walk into my office
> where I primarily work out of and sit down in one of the chairs
> and take five minutes and tune out the fact that I've just spent the
> last hour sharpening lawn mower blades—which is horribly mind-
> numbing work but they pay me to do it, that's why I do it—and I
> can sit and take five, ten minutes and just regroup and go back. I just
> don't feel like I get that opportunity [as an interpreter at the Fort].
> I always need to be on call, always need to be ready to respond to
> something, always need to be ready to deal with someone coming
> and having to interact with them.[47]

In having to be constantly at the ready at the Fort, Henry felt that
demands on his sense of self were considerable. At his other job, Henry
felt like he had opportunities to "regroup" and locate his sense of self—
but at the Fort he continually felt like he had to be "on call" and play
roles outside of his self (lance corporal, blacksmith, etc.).

Such conflicting demands on the self helped to foster a kind of ambiv-
alent worker—that is, one that Gideon Kunda described as confused
between the "seductiveness of increased involvement [with one's place
of work] and the desire to maintain personal autonomy."[48] For many Fort
workers this confusion was exacerbated by one of the demands of the
job, which required workers to perform as people other than themselves
for much of the day—a job requirement that both attracted people to the
job, and yet could also contribute to emotional stress.

The Emotional Toll of Time Traveling

As Henry's dilemma suggests, portraying figures from the past while also
working as service workers and educators very obviously affected how
interpreters reacted to the world when they clocked out of the past and
returned to the present. When I asked Brynn, who had worked eight
consecutive years at the Fort, about the emotional demands of working
as a historic interpreter she noted that it was "emotionally exhausting

just to mentally time travel."[49] "I've had days when I've been three different characters, three different people, including myself in one day," said Brynn, "and by the end of the day, I'm not sure what century I'm in, and who I am."[50] Besides the effort demanded of these time travelers as they switched between portraying people of the past and themselves, Brynn believed that the level of emotional exhaustion that interpreters experience "depends a lot on which role you're playing, because some roles carry a lot of emotional factors with them." When Brynn portrayed the commandant's wife, Abigail Snelling, for example, she described it as being very "straining" to tell her stories "about losing her children, or talking about her experiences as a prisoner of war, or her experiences standing in a room with a cannon shot coming through the room and killing somebody in the next room, because she lived through all of that."[51] While she wondered if "some of those things hit [her] harder because" of parallel stories in her own family background, she also believed that because interpreters were "living and reliving the joys and sorrows of previous people, you also can't keep your own perspective out of it."[52] Despite the emotional strain that Brynn experienced when she invested in the "joys and sorrows" of her characters, Brynn, who had a background in performance, described the strain as potentially "rewarding" because of the times when her efforts would lead the public to validate her performances as realistic, or when she felt emotional connections with visitors:

> It's much more rewarding when I have people tell me, as I have had visitors tell me, that they almost believed I really was the person. When I'm telling a story and I can see tears come into somebody's eye, or I can see them sharing the joy of it, it's the same kind of high I get . . . when I hear the reactions from an audience to what I'm doing and I feel they've gotten into what is happening on the stage. You draw as a performer. I draw energy from that; I always have. It's been one of my joys as a performer because I feel like if I have somehow touched something in the person, in somebody in my audience, then on some human level, we have connected in an emotional way. Now, I can be completely exhausted, hardly able to stand up, and if something like that happens, it will give me the energy to go on and to keep doing it.[53]

In this spirit, moments when workers felt they experienced an emotional or intellectual connection with the public would be treasured as moments that helped them justify their choice of job.

The importance of connecting to the public brings to mind the comments of Oliver, who found that even on "days where [he] would drag [him]self in, totally unenthused in the morning, after the first one or two very positive interactions with visitors, [he could be] flying high for the rest of the day, enough to buoy [him] up even though [he could be] physically exhausted by the time [he was] ready to go home."[54] For Oliver, as for Brynn, this visitor affirmation could be "an amazing ego rush, and in [Oliver's] mind, justif[ied] a lot of the extra time [he] put in, researching characters or aspects of the nineteenth century."[55] Likewise, Martin noted that he especially enjoyed working at the Fort when he got to work with "good interpreters" or when he encountered visitors who wanted to "participate in the interpretive experience. . . . Those are the times," said Martin, "when you're talking to people, and a half hour or hour later, you realize you've missed your break, and you're not getting one for another two or three hours and you don't care, because everything is going well, you know? So that's when I get excited."[56] In this manner, when workers experienced emotional fulfillment either from the interpretive encounter, or from feeling connected with their historic characters, more emotional labor could be extracted out of the worker.

Again echoing Lois Silverman's work regarding the therapeutic potential of museums, interpreters were no less prone than visitors to respond emotionally to the history, buildings, and objects at the museum.[57] Not unlike Brynn, who was emotionally impacted by interpreting Mrs. Abigail Snelling's stories about the War of 1812, Alyssa felt strong emotions of sadness when she portrayed Mrs. Amelia Green, one of the few officers' wives at the Fort in 1827. Historically, we know little about Mrs. Green, but one key detail about her life was the death of her only child, a five-year-old son, Melanchton Smith Green, the year prior, in 1826. When asked about the emotional demands of the job, Alyssa mentioned the challenge of playing Mrs. Green, specifically: "This is strange but when I was Mrs. Green I would identify with her, by playing her all day, and I'd start to get sad. You know, my child had died and my husband was gone. And it almost would carry over a little bit at the end of the day where you're not really sad—but a little reflective, thinking what it must have been like to be somebody like that and to be so alone."[58] Like Henry and many other interpreters, Alyssa could not simply clock out from work. Instead, she continued to feel the weight of her emotional work even after the end of her workday. In this case, she cited her empathy for the historical characters that she would portray as one source of this emotional strain.

Another source of emotional strain for Alyssa lay in the borderlands between the historical portrayals demanded of her, and her conception of her contemporary self. At one point in our interview, Alyssa described a scenario that occurred during the first few months of her employment at Historic Fort Snelling. In this situation, Alyssa was portraying the cook in the Commanding Officer's House when one of her coworkers, who was portraying a soldier, came through and took a piece of leftover cornbread that she had served at "dinner" earlier in the day. She said she "didn't think anything of it" because she hardly thought it was "against the management's rules," only the "rules of 1827." She explained that she knew that a soldier would not have been welcome in the commanding officer's kitchen, but she "figured that he would eat it right away and nobody would be the wiser." Unfortunately, "he chose to be very blatant about eating it as he went across the parade ground."[59]

What happened next shows the complexities of (and raises several questions about) the dynamics between interpreters' role playing from and across different social-class and gender perspectives. As Alyssa explained it, the woman portraying Mrs. Snelling came into the kitchen and, in character, addressed Alyssa (in character as the cook). She asked if Alyssa's husband (meaning the enlisted man whom the cook was interpreted as being married to) had stopped in. When Alyssa said no, "Mrs. Snelling" chastised her (without a direct accusation) for giving food to the soldier, who was now eating cornbread from "her" kitchen in plain view of the public. The scene implied—certainly to me as I listened to Alyssa recount it—that if the cook had slipped a piece of cornbread to her husband, who then had passed it on to the soldier, the offence would have carried less weight. As Alyssa continued: "I don't remember *exactly* what she said, but I felt so bad. I felt like I was going to be fired from the position as cook [small laugh] and I didn't like being treated that way even though she didn't raise her voice or anything. But it was still that upper class to lower class exchange where I had no defense."[60] By "having no defense" Alyssa meant that her character—a domestic employed by the Snelling family—would be expected to show deference to her employers; at that moment Alyssa was choosing to enact that deference:

> I couldn't say that "he didn't mean any harm" or "I didn't mean any harm." I felt really bad for the rest of the day just because I had no way of defending myself against that class attack even though we were technically co-workers. But playing the role you can't be the same, and I think I hadn't internalized my role enough. I think that was toward the beginning of my time there, and that I hadn't internalized it enough to realize that giving the cornbread was against the rules because I was looking at the guy who came in as a co-worker and thought that there was nothing wrong with giving a co-worker a little bit of that left-over food. But [the woman portraying] Mrs. Snelling had worked there for several seasons and had internalized her role and class, and she saw [the cornbread incident] as something she could use in interpretation, whereas I hadn't thought of it that way. . . . I was thinking of him as a co-worker and her as a co-worker.[61]

A short time later in the interview, Alyssa reflected on why the experience upset her so much. She explained that even though she knew the woman playing Mrs. Snelling had chosen to improvise the scenario in order to demonstrate class differentiation for the two visitors present at the time, Alyssa didn't feel that the humiliation "was worth the education of these two people in terms of the class issues." In a moment of self-analysis, Alyssa said, "I think for a person who's just a regular college-educated girl, to be treated that way is so outside of your normal experience. For me it was hard to deal with being treated that way, even though I knew [that my co-worker] was not treating *me* that way."[62]

As difficult as it might have been for some interpreters to be on the receiving end of interpretive moments whose purpose was to demonstrate power relations, Henry reported feeling a stress of a similar nature the first time he was assigned to play the role of drill sergeant, whose job would be, in part, to discipline the soldiers. Henry, who was known among co-workers to be an easy-going, affable fellow, felt uncomfortable interpreting a historical hierarchy, which required his character to assert authority over others. He described his inaugural experience of portraying a sergeant as one that sent him home exhausted, attributing that fatigue to negotiating the difference between how a drill sergeant would have been expected to relate to the privates (wherein his character's rank warranted him considerable power) versus the sense of comradeship he felt with his co-workers (even though his character was expected to demonstrate power over them):

> You know how hard it is to yell at people even though they know you're just kidding and you know you're just kidding, but to actually scream at people that you respect and you don't really have anything against them, but your character is screaming at them? It's kind of weird, just to haul off and start laying into someone about doing something wrong even though if you were in that role, you'd still be doing the same thing wrong that they're doing.[63]

Even though Henry felt that all parties involved understood that role-playing scenarios wherein Henry's character was expected to scream at the soldiers were not intended to reflect his actual attitude toward his co-workers, he nonetheless felt compelled to apologize to his co-workers at the end of the day: "I actually apologized in the locker room, I'm like, 'I'm sorry I screamed at you guys, it's just not part of who I am' and they're like, 'it's part of the job,'—'but I just didn't feel right screaming at you guys for being out of step because I'm always out of step, or yelling at you for not having your uniform buttoned up right because mine's never buttoned up right.' So it was just really odd doing that the first time I played sergeant."[64]

Both Alyssa and Henry attributed the emotional difficulties they experienced when playing roles with which they did not personally identify as a matter of not having had enough practice at separating their conceptions of their authentic selves from their perceptions and portrayals of their historic characters. In essence, they were taking their work personally. However, because Henry took care to mention that playing sergeant for the first time was exhausting, we may assume that subsequent times were not quite as difficult for him, and that he was ultimately able to internalize his performance of a stereotypically masculine character (aggressive, dominating). Such internalization was a sign that Henry was "improving" his ability to deliver the service of living history for the public, and, seen more cynically perhaps, that his emotional labor was being more easily extracted.[65]

Though not all of my interviewees brought up corresponding anec-
dotes, during my own time as an interpreter at HFS, many interpreters frequently took interactions personally between co-workers who
were technically "in character" regardless of how much practice they
had had at performing their roles. Ennis, who worked at the Fort for
just one season, decided not to return because, in part, he was tired of
being razzed by his co-workers for being a Catholic—a "Papist." "As
weird as it sounds," he told me, "I couldn't tell when they were serious
and when they weren't—especially since some of them would continue
harassing me about it even out of costume."[66] In this case, this worker
was Catholic, and he was troubled because he did not know when and
if other interpreters were drawing the line between his "real" Catholic
self or his character's. Another former employee at Historic Fort Snelling, Sean, who likewise was a "real" Catholic of Irish descent, told me
a similar tale, and resented the anti-Catholic jousting he experienced
while working at the site; he felt it went too far, both in front of the
public and behind the scenes.[67]

An interpreter named Todd, one of those who teased Sean for being
Catholic, brought up the subject in our interview: "We might make
a comment just by calling him 'Irish,' or saying certain derogatory
phrases about the character because that's the way it was in the nineteenth century."[68] Whereas Sean tired of and even resented the derogatory remarks made about his own and his "character's" Irish Catholic
identity, Todd assumed that Sean was "very up on it and [was] one of the
fellows who receives it very well." Todd was careful to note that these
derogatory remarks were only made in good fun to demonstrate a historical fact regarding anti-Irish nativism. He also wanted to distinguish his
Irish-hating character from his "real" self. Although Todd's character
may have hated the Irish, Todd was careful to note that he had "several
Catholic friends and this fellow [was] probably one of [his] closer friends
up here" and that he was "happy to call him [Sean] a friend." Even so,
betraying how much Todd had internalized the role-playing customs at
his worksite, Todd also initially misremembered his close friend Sean's
first name during the interview. He did correct it, and apologized for
the memory lapse, saying, "Excuse me—you never know them by their
first names. We call everyone by the last names which is the way it was

done historically in the military."[69] In any case, despite his character's remarks about Irish Catholics, the "real" Todd claimed not to have any real feelings of hostility against them.

That the borders between their selves and their characters were sometimes porous and indistinct seemed endemic to this living history worksite. As the job required, interpreters were not only deep acting so as to feel "genuinely" upbeat for visitors as service workers, interpreters really were cooking over an open fire, trying to march in step, mending patches in clothes, forging iron in the blacksmith's shop, firing cannons, selling items in the sutler's store, and skinning and tanning the hides of animals. Since these activities would continue even when the public was not around, it is no wonder that boundaries sometimes blurred.

Speaking to this boundary blurring is freelance writer and second-season Fort interpreter Jon Keljik's 2006 article in the Minneapolis publication *The Rake*.[70] In this "Rakish Angle" feature story, Keljik described how interpreters' performances of the past mingled with the workers' identities in their present—a "paradox that was sometimes difficult to grasp."[71]

> It didn't help that all the chores and daily routines from our 1827 show would go on with or without twenty-first-century onlookers. Usually, by the time the Fort would close for the day, the last visitors had already returned to the world of microwave burritos and Internet shopping. Yet we soldiers faithfully conducted the retreat ceremony—an inspection of the men, followed by a saluting of the flag as it's lowered—with no one looking on except for others in period dress. An officer would stroll past us men in line, remarking on unpolished brass or stained trousers, doing so in such hushed tones that anyone who had been watching this elaborate ritual would have been somewhat mystified. If it served any conceivable purpose, it was to bring us interpreters closer to believing what we were doing wasn't just for play, but was real.
>
> Many things were both. For the sake of the fictional Private Kelly, I shaved my red beard into the thick muttonchops that went out of style after Martin Van Buren. Yet, hanging out at bars on the weekends or with friends who hadn't seen me in a while, I got a few odd

glances and many questions. Though the side-whiskers looked out of
place without their accompanying high-collared shirt and a pocket
watch, I couldn't exactly say, "These mutton chops aren't mine."[72]

Keljik's observations about the interpreter's quandary in locating one's
"self" run parallel with mine. Often it was jarring when we became
self-conscious that our identities had been so dramatically shaped by
our place of employment, and that our prior senses of self were decisively fused with the masks we were encouraged and required to wear
at our place of work. Where did our characters end and our "real" selves
begin?

To draw on my own experience, I noticed that particularly when my
work schedule approached full-time at the Fort, even when I clocked
out, my ordinary speech patterns, habits, and mannerisms were awk-
wardly altered. Frequently, I would go out to restaurants and unwit-
tingly begin eating with my knife rather than my fork, as was custom
during the Fort's period of interpretation. Not only would I greet strangers on the street with a "good day," but after a day of playing an officer's
wife my general manner of speaking conjured more of an American version of Eliza Bennett in Jane Austen's *Pride and Prejudice*, rather than
the colloquial tone of a twenty-something female in the twenty-first
century. I was not alone. Day after day, especially immediately following the end of the work day, when out of costume and walking to our
cars, interpreters often continued to smile at and greet the public—that
is, anyone who may have been walking outside the walls of the Fort,
perhaps just for a closer view, or perhaps on their way to the nature
trails at the Fort's adjacent state park. These folks often appeared right-
fully confused as to why individuals trailing out of the Fort dressed in
contemporary clothes were so keenly smiling at them—sometimes even
greeting them with a deferential nod and a "how do you do?"

Furthermore, after working hours when my hands were idle—
strange though it is to confess—I found that I longed to sew, since I did
so much hand sewing while working at the Fort. When I attended the
Midwest Open Air Museums Coordinating Council's (MOMCC) annual
meeting in spring 2003, I was struck by how a large number of female
interpreter-attendees knitted and sewed throughout the presentations
and sessions.[73] Had I not worked as a living history interpreter myself,

I may have considered this rude because of my experiences with the normative behavior at academic conferences. At this particular conference, interpreters were in a space with others "like them"—people whose after-work-hours life was profoundly shaped by the activities of their work life—and in that space, they would not have to be self conscious about that; they would not have to, as Henry put it, "rejoin the correct century."[74] For those of us whose social circles outside of work (roommates, friends, spouses, partners) did not include others who were involved in living history, this work-related residue took an emotional toll, as it was somewhat difficult to locate one's own sense of self. In his ethnography of Plimoth Plantation, Stephen Eddy Snow similarly noted how "after many seasons of playing the role of a Pilgrim, an interpreter may undergo some partial transformation, coming to a point at which it is not always easy to distinguish the boundaries between the self and the role."[75] Thus for Snow's Pilgrims, and for the Fort's interpreters, these places of employment made claims to parts of the interpreter's selves.

For me, the quandary over where our characters ended and our "real" selves began found its most potent articulation in October 2005. At this time, the Fort had staged the death and mock funeral of one of the "privates" of the Fifth Regiment, an event for which the male interpreters had practiced how to authentically march—as well as how to appropriately handle and fire their muskets. For this mock funeral, thirty-two-year old Robert—a former college football player turned history teacher and the biggest and strongest of all the Fort's "troopies"—dug the grave.[76] By several accounts, this dramatic ceremony moved many visitors and interpreters alike to tears.

Two weeks later, Robert shot himself at his home and died. I had known Robert as a smart, quiet man with a wry (and sometimes cutting) sense of humor. But despite knowing him for six years as my co-worker, I was not close enough to Robert to know the extent of his circumstances when he took his life. I had known only that times were tough for Robert at the time of his death, and later heard that in the note he left behind, he stated he was going to Valhalla—the hallowed hall in Norse mythology wherein soldiers who were martyred in battle would eternally feast with their creator. Of course, Robert had only ever been a soldier in a reenacted army. If the Valhalla reference were true, it would seem that Robert's sense of self was enmeshed with living history to the end.

At his memorial service many men who had reenacted and interpreted with Robert throughout the years paid their respects by dressing in army costumes from various historical time periods and solemnly
marched together, in line and in step, to the Fort Snelling chapel, rifles
and muskets in hand. The spectacle of these men marching in the funeral
procession, and the attendant musket and rifle salute, disturbed me to
the extreme. The familiarity of the funeral procession made me uneasy
because it made no distinction between our performances inside the
Fort's walls, and our performances outside. Even the secular hymn that
was chosen for us to sing at the funeral was a song that we frequently
sang inside Fort walls. On this count, I could not bring myself to join the
congregation in song. I was not stifled by tears, but by my own desire
to police the boundaries between my sense of self and the performances
I delivered as an interpreter at my place of work. Perhaps Mrs. Tyson,
Mrs. Snelling, or the other characters I portrayed at the Fort could sing
"The minstrel boy to war has gone / In the ranks of death of death you
will find him," but I could not. At the time, I needed desperately to
distinguish between the mock funeral that so recently had been performed, and the real funeral that was taking place. Sitting there in the
chapel, amidst my living history colleagues—some in costume—and
others from Robert's other social circles in the "real" world, I found
myself thinking: *Couldn't we interpreters just this once, be normal?*
Like everyone there, I was distressed by Robert's death and its surrounding circumstances. But I also felt another emotion because of my connection to those in costume, something distinctly different. Something
akin to embarrassment—akin to shame. I was not alone. The "honor
guard" was organized at the request of Robert's family, but those who
agreed to take part were under the impression the guard was to be part
of a simple memorial service, not the actual funeral. As one interpreter
noted to me, "I think we all felt ashamed when we were sitting in there,
dressed up and realizing we were in an actual funeral; it was very, very
messed up."[77]

Returning again to Goffman's notion of the "stigmatized self"—the
shame that a stigmatized individual experiences is especially reinforced in the "the immediate presence of [non-stigmatized] normals."[78]
At the memorial service, as I was in the "immediate presence of normals"—meaning those not immersed in the world of living history—I

experienced the emotion of shame because, by the standards of the wider society, living history theatrics had their time and place. When one of us let that world bleed over into the world of the normals, it often was to a mild but nonetheless stigmatizing effect—a stigma that interpreters worked so hard to resist when they articulated the social value of their work in their self narrations. As Jon Keljik noted, at staff parties it was well and good when "conversations often turned to different types of gun powder or how best to hand-stitch a dress," but here were my co-workers at someone's actual funeral, dressed in historic costumes and performing the same rituals they had rehearsed for a museum-orchestrated vignette. I keenly felt both the degree to which the lines between present and past bled into one another in the lives of myself and my co-workers, and the potential stigma of having one's name written on the "wall of shame"; there seemed to be some question of whether some or all of us had lost (or were losing) our footing in reality. How long could we hold out?

The Wages of Living History

Having a workforce whose members view their jobs as meaningful benefits any organization, and certainly management at the Fort encouraged workers to invest in the organization in myriad ways—whether hosting off-the-clock morning training sessions where workers could learn to sing the songs of the voyageurs (French fur traders), inspiring them to be customer service superstars at on-the-clock training sessions (as I describe in the introduction), and even by hosting after-hours parties where workers danced reels and roasted pigs on a spit. And while management encouraged interpreters to invest in their jobs, top-down efforts to encourage worker investment only reinforced what interpreters I encountered believed even before they applied to work at the site: that this kind of work mattered.

While Handler and Gable's analysis of interpreters at Colonial Williamsburg tended to view workers who professed to enjoy their jobs as having been strongly influenced by the Colonial Williamsburg Foundation's top-down control efforts, my observations and experience gest that the powerful drive to establish a positive work identit their work as interpreters came from below—from a self-selectir

of people who sought out jobs on public history's front line because
they saw it as a unique way to connect with others through their shared
passion of history. Here, my conclusions support Cathy Stanton's symbolic analysis of why public historians and frontline rangers at Lowell
National Historic Park were driven to their work. As Stanton ultimately
argues: "Their choice to take jobs in public history is a comment—
sometimes direct, sometimes more veiled—on their frustration with the
kinds of human interactions and experiences that many have experienced in other areas of the postindustrial economy. Their solution to
this dilemma has been to find work in the public history field, where
they feel they are doing socially valuable work and experiencing genuine encounters with other human beings."[79] Although Stanton saw a
particular drive from her informants to use the history at Lowell to
connect to their "working class forbears" in ways that I did not at the
Fort, frontline workers at both of our respective sites were predisposed
to find pleasure in the work of connecting with others through history,
and to see the work of interpretation as having social value.[80]

Workers at Fort Snelling, however, at times found it a challenge to
feel proud of their labor in the wake of a prevailing social stigma, that
to work as a costumed historical interpreter was not "a real job." In
their efforts to construct a positive work identity, interpreters often
threw themselves into the work of serving the public. While they experienced great joy from connecting with visitors, they also experienced
emotional exhaustion through their efforts to shift their emotional gears
to meet visitors' needs. They also experienced emotional exhaustion
through the unique job requirement of acting much of the day as though
they were someone from the past. This time traveling was emotionally
taxing not only because interpreters had to negotiate the borderlands
between their sense of their "real" selves and their "pretend" selves, but
also because it was often awkward and sometimes stigmatizing when
those boundaries between selves blurred, especially in the presence of
non-co-workers.

Ultimately, for interpreters at the Fort, the benefits of the job were
often emotional in nature. Interpreters took great joy in connecting
with visitors, in treasured moments that would confirm their efforts
were worthwhile, and in the feeling that their jobs were legitimate
and respectable. In Brynn's words, interpreters could "be completely

exhausted, hardly able to stand up, and if something like that [kind of connection] happens, it will give [them] the energy to go on and to keep doing it."[81] Interpreters who developed an emotional attachment to their work tended to invest in their jobs, both spending and reaping the wages of living history, above and beyond what otherwise might have been required. Not unlike the restaurant servers and flight attendants that have been the subjects of other studies, interpreters experienced the joys of connecting with co-workers and the public alongside the pitfalls of the loss of personal identity. But the wages of living history go even farther into the depths of what it means to perform emotional labor. On the one hand, as boundaries blurred between past and present, the most invested workers lost their "selves" (almost entirely) to their jobs. And yet: In the process of such investment, they gained a new "self," and found a new place of belonging, among others whose names would also be found on the wall of shame/fame.

CHAPTER 4
PURSUING AUTHENTICITY
Creative Autonomy and Workplace Games

Martin: *When I was younger and I went to play with my friends, we would play army and run around in the woods. And sometimes I feel like if we would run around a little bit more at the Fort, that's what we would be doing, you know? We have schedules we have to follow during our game of army, but it's the same thing. I think that this is a key part of it: if you get to work with other people who are good interpreters and visitors who want to participate in the interpretive experience, those are the times when you're talking to people, and a half hour or hour later, you realize you've missed your break, and you're not getting one for another two or three hours and you don't care, because everything is going well, you know? So that's when I get excited.*

Sociologists Michael Burawoy and Rachel Sherman have shown for manufacturing and interactive service worksites (respectively), that workplace "games" allow workers to "pass the time, reduce fatigue, and establish skill," and give them creative autonomy over the "raw material" of their sites.[1] In this manner, Burawoy's factory workers slowed down or sped up the pace of their piece-rate games, while Sherman's luxury hotel workers made a game out of correctly predicting guest demands, which had emotional and financial benefits. At the Fort, the raw material over which interpreters had creative control was the site's history, and at times they enjoyed considerable autonomy while digging their interpretative holes (i.e., in deciding the degree and manner in

which they would engage with visitors about that history).[2] The extent
to which interpreters experienced this autonomy led them to—in Burawoy's phrasing—consent to labor, and to abide by the rules of the organization so that they could continue to play their workplace games.[3]

In the work context of the Fort, using the raw material of history,
workers constructed games relating to authenticity. These "games of
authenticity" rested on the extra efforts that interpreters would put
into their jobs to get as close as possible to the time period they were
portraying, often through acquiring knowledge and perfecting period
skills such as blacksmithing, carpentry, musket firing, hearth cooking,
knitting, hand sewing, or tatting.[4] These work displays served as the
primary icebreakers interpreters could use to engage with tourists, who
expressed delight, awe, and sometimes incredulity. Behind the scenes,
interpreters would sometimes make fun of visitors who questioned the
authenticity of one's physical work display,[5] as when visitors asked if
that was "real fire" they were cooking over. Likewise, interpreters took
great pride when they could verify to visitors that one's work displays
were "the real thing," and their skills "authentic."[6]

Experts in the literature have identified a preoccupation with authenticity as a pervasive part of the workplace cultures of living history
museums since first-person interpretation launched onto the museum
scene at spaces such as Plimoth Plantation, Colonial Williamsburg, and
Historic Fort Snelling in the late 1960s and early 1970s.[7] At the Fort,
interpreters who were invested in their jobs expended a great amount
of energy in trying to achieve authentic appearances and authentic
domestic, military, or craft skills. Over the years, the Fort's interpretive
staff learned to sing popular songs of the early republic; to play musical
instruments such as the fife, flute, and drum; to repair cast iron skil-
lets; to start fires from flint, steel, and char cloth; and to roast chickens
in the tin kitchen. While I never became too interested in developing
my cooking skills (a co-worker once chipped her tooth on my overworked, overbaked gingerbread), I took pleasure in fire starting (which
might explain the gingerbread). Also, after a supervisor told me that
my sewing stitches would be considered proficient for a young lady of
about twelve years (in essence, a critique that my sewing skills were
not authentic), I took it upon myself to develop some expertise with
a needle. By the time I left the job in 2006, I had hand sewn two of

my own dresses (one of which I wore regularly at the Fort), as well as two men's shirts (which two co-workers wore regularly at the Fort). For me, achieving the authentic skills of sewing—and to some extent, knitting—became enjoyable ways to "pass the time, reduce fatigue, and establish skill" that served to pique the interest of visitors who encountered me in the midst of working at my authentic craft.[8]

Most importantly, honing these skills also instilled me with a great sense of pride, and, like my co-workers, I spent considerable time off the clock developing my period skills to the benefit of visitors and management—and also myself in so far as performing an authentic craft provided me with a positive work identity. But assigning authenticity a cultural value is, as sociologist E. Doyle McCarthy has argued, coterminous with the rise of individualism (that is, the "notion that the human person . . . is an autonomous agent directing its own action by its own will"), and games of authenticity played into a deep yearning not only to be part of something bigger than ourselves (i.e., history), but to be perceived as unique, and to be valued at work for our creative contributions.[9] As I described in Chapter 3, interpreters at the Fort deeply prized moments when they felt as though they were being valued for, in Elijah's words, being individuals who were contributing to something "unique in all the world."[10]

But while interpreters could use games of authenticity as fun ways to instill self-pride and to create community with visitors and co-workers, these games could cut both ways. Because the Fort's organizational structure fostered a culture of surveillance, some turned games of authenticity into ways to police others for evidence of authenticity. By demonstrating one's commitment to the game of historical authenticity in this way, I argue that these individuals were trying to gain status among one's co-workers as part of an "in group" of authentic interpreters. My case study shows that while the experience of this policing for authenticity differentiated by gender, both male and female interpreters who felt they were being policed resented attempts to interfere with their own sense of creative autonomy.[11] When games turned into competitive power plays, infighting resulted, which had negative effects on the workplace culture and limited frontline interpreters from reaching their greatest potential.

Autonomy and Oversight

Sociologists Linda Fuller and Vicki Smith discuss how feeling autonomous is important for interactive service workers who experience direct
and constant managerial supervision as "intrusive or overtly antagonistic."[12] Interactive service workers, insofar as they are required to make
snap judgments with regard to what kind of service delivery would best
suit each individual customer, perform better when they are freed from
top-down managerial control structures and are trusted to "make the
skilled judgments necessary to provide quality customer service under
fluctuating circumstances."[13] Workers in environments where they feel
trusted, also feel freer to express themselves and innovate on the job,
which benefits management, clients, and themselves.

In many ways, Fort Snelling offered interpreters an amount of autonomy to play workplace games and make interpretive decisions without
the burden of constant managerial oversight. Fort interpreter Alyssa
observed that relative autonomy was standard at the Fort when she
worked there in 1999: "The thing that is unique about working at the
Fort is that they really can't control the workers in any large way. . . .
In the morning you get into your costume and you head out in twenty
different directions, and I think that each interpreter goes their own
direction with their own view of what is most important."[14] This sense
of having a degree of freedom away from managerial control appealed
to interpreters' desires for autonomy, and they resented when this freedom was encroached upon. The general manager for guest experiences
at Conner Prairie Interactive History Park, Aili McGill, similarly found
that interpreters there were protective of their relative autonomy during
day-to-day operations.[15]

In his interview, Fort interpreter Todd recalled an incident where
he felt that management squelched his creative autonomy. The incident
centered on a game of authenticity that he and his co-workers were
playing that involved a rooster. One of Todd's colleagues, another male
interpreter, had brought this rooster to the Fort because he and his co-
workers had found "documentation that there was some sort of poultry
and small amounts of livestock" at the Fort:

> It was a very docile animal, and it was very old, so we weren't wor-
> ried about it attacking anyone. We had kept it tethered and we always

> made sure people didn't get close to it. And yet, that was a situation
> where [management] thought, "No this is a liability." And yet later in
> that same season we have [volunteers for a Civil War weekend event]
> bringing dogs, horses, and oxen out, and those aren't liabilities? The
> dog is over jumping on people, and the oxen—granted this was only
> a two-year-old ox—but it was still, easily 1,200 pounds; all he has
> to do is step on a foot and you've busted toes. Whereas this rooster
> that doesn't do anything, was considered a liability. Many of us were
> upset because of that.

In this recollection, Todd significantly notes that an on-site rooster
could be justified because they had found historic documentation (i.e.,
proof of authenticity). He also identified site management as responsible
for thwarting his and his co-workers' efforts to provide an "authentic"
atmosphere for guests via the rooster, thus interrupting their games of
authenticity and their creative autonomy.

But who held the power to enforce the rules of this worksite's unique
games of authenticity was part of an ever-changing power dynamic
that sociologist Robin Leidner has identified as a shifting "three-way
dynamic of control" at service economy worksites.[16] In this three-way
dynamic of control, power is dispersed—among visitors, co-workers,
and management, with each at times having the power to control or
affect the behavior of the other parties. In a worksite where workers
prized creative autonomy, they felt resentful when they experienced
efforts to control them as too heavy-handed. Interpreters' narratives
revealed resentment directed at two components of this triadic labor
model: the testing procedures that management employed, and co-
workers who policed for authenticity—especially when that policing
was related to how interpreters performed prescribed gendered roles of
the past and present.

Testing Authenticity

Although management did not often supervise interpreters directly, the
quality control structures in place while I worked there were largely
aimed at managing, rather than cultivating, interpreters. To those ends,
tests were instituted to document that interpreters had learned certain
information, while the lion's share of direct supervision was spread out

laterally among co-workers. Both of these measures encouraged a competitive environment, which made for a divided workforce.

At the beginning of the season, everyone was required to read the "Guide Staff Training Manual" and, on paid time, to take the corresponding, beginning-of-season general test on the manual. While I worked at the site, the manual's contents varied from year to year, but consistently contained the "MHS Mission Statement," the "Staff Administrative Handbook," "School Tour Program Notes" and "Army Life in the Early 19th Century"—a history first penned in 1977 (and whose first revision and update took place in 2004). Thus, although Alyssa noted "each interpreter goes their own direction, with . . . what they view as most important," the information contained in the various components of the Fort's training manual was intended to serve as the basis for interpretation, from which interpreters were expected to draw in their authentic presentations and interpretations of the past.

"Army Life in the Early 19th Century" was arranged in a question-and-answer format and "organized to make clear what we believe should be emphasized"; it was designed "to enable you to think for yourself, and convey your knowledge in your own words."[17] Although individual thinking and interpretation was ostensibly encouraged, neither "Army Life" nor the other parts of the composite training manual issued to interpreters at the start of each season included primary sources so that interpreters could draw their own historical conclusions.[18] Thus, "Army Life in the Early 19th Century"—a secondary source—was presented as not an interpretation in and of itself—but as a collection of incontrovertible facts. Handler and Gable similarly noted that the practice of packaging interpretive material as unmediated representations of the past was a training strategy for guides at Colonial Williamsburg.[19]

The general knowledge test administered at the beginning of the season did not test one's ability to convey information effectively or to interpret the past in a meaningful or engaging way; it tested for fact retention. For example, one test question asked about the reasons the Fort was built. To answer the question correctly, interpreters would need to have committed the following John C. Calhoun (1782–1850) quotation to memory: "The military movement which has been made up the Mississippi . . . was ordered for the establishment of posts to effect two great objects—the enlargement and protection of the fur trade, and permanent peace of our North Western frontier by securing a decided control over the various tribes of Indians in that quarter."[20] For testing purposes, workers had to write the quote—or parts of it—verbatim.[21] Although on the one hand this allowed management to test for a baseline knowledge of the military's rationale for establishing the post in the 1820s, on the other hand such rote memorization did not allow management to evaluate interpreters' ability to interpret history, or to place facts in their historic context—skills they would need to do the creative work of interpretation that they enjoyed at this worksite. This testing procedure not only stunted creative thinking, it encouraged the cult of authenticity among interpretive staff wherein historic details were policed as being either right or wrong—authentic or inauthentic.

Tara, who was in her second year of employment at the site, had a "pretty strong feeling about the tests" and felt particularly vexed about the kind of rote memorization that was required of workers in order to pass them:

> The time that it takes to study all that material, and I have voiced this—I think that it takes time away from reading [other] manuals about the stations, whereas I have to worry about the exam coming up where I have to know quotes. For me that takes away the time that I would rather be using learning my station and learning, "How do I talk to Mrs. Snelling?" "How would the soldier talk to me?" and "How would I talk to the soldier?" This is the day-to-day stuff that I need down the road down at the Fort . . . not the quote from something that I'm going to forget five minutes after I walk out of my exam. I know I've got to know it because I did last year and I don't remember it, and I'll have to memorize it again. So I think the tests are not a good idea.[22]

Although Tara recognized the need for management "to evaluate whether people are reading that manual," she did not feel that tests with right or wrong answers helped train her for the creative work of digging interpretive holes with the public.[23] In fact, Tara strongly felt that workers who were invested in their jobs would certainly be reading their manuals anyhow, in order not to be perceived as inadequate in front of the public:

> I think it's really clear if people have read their material when they
> start down at the fort. It's really clear who knows what's going on
> and who doesn't. It's a lot of time spent outside of here that could
> be spent differently. The bottom line is that nobody wants to come
> across as being inadequate. Nobody. So the way you do that is to read
> the manual. I don't think I need the threat of a test to make sure that I
> don't come across and look stupid in front of the public. I think that
> in itself is enough of a threat for most people. I find it really kind of
> third grade and I've voiced it.[24]

Because Tara self-policed to ensure that she knew the relevant material
in her manual, she resented top-down imposed testing procedures that,
she felt, did not support her ability to interpret history with the public.

In addition to taking the general test at the beginning of the season,
interpreters were also required to take specialty area tests on various
aspects of Fort history (first-year employees were required to take one
specialty test, while second-year employees were required to take two).
Interpreters who didn't take the additional tests were technically only
supposed to portray the roles of working-class men and women who
would have predominated at the frontier outpost in the 1820s: privates
in the army (for males) or laundresses or domestics (for females). As
with the general test, interpreters were expected either to study for
these additional tests off the clock, or to study during their workdays
when the public was not around. The incentive for this extra effort was
a kind of upward mobility at the Fort, given that passing tests both bolstered performance review scores and qualified individuals to interpret
additional roles and to be assigned a wider range of stations at the post.

Generally, gender governed what specialty tests one would take. The
"House Basic Test" covered the history of the Commanding Officer's
House at Fort Snelling, including both its architectural details and the
history of the Snelling family. While this test was intended to qualify
individuals to interpret more than just domestic roles in the Commanding Officer's House, usually only women were assigned to interpret in
the house, most often as Mrs. Snelling or as one of the other officer's
wives; male interpreters who wished to portray officers, whether inside
or outside of the Commanding Officer's House, were required to pass
the "Officer's Test." Similarly, the "Shops Test" theoretically qualified

individuals to interpret in the blacksmith and carpenter's shops, but women who took and passed the test (including myself) were never scheduled to interpret in that station.[25]

Many interpreters found fault in the testing process because they felt that such top-down methods of control did little to encourage their intrinsically motivated efforts to improve their skills or to acquire specialized knowledge. Jacob, for one, felt that the tests did not adequately reflect the work-related, creative efforts of employees, which often were considerable:

> Well, the problem is that they suggest that you take a test in an area of interest but Todd, for example, spends so much time reading every [army] field manual—you know, he's read Napoleon's and Winfield Scott's [field manuals] and he reads all of those because he's interested in the drill manual—but there's no test there. Whereas I can take the Keel Boat Test and the Fur Trade Test and the Sutler's Test and you know, do fine, but he doesn't have an option there [because those don't interest him]. And I think if they're going to have tests they should have some other option. He could craft an essay or something on what he did just to show that there was some outside effort, which is what the tests are for. And it has definitely enhanced his job. It's beneficial to us all . . . I get to learn the marching techniques that he's gotten by reading through those field manuals. But then again, when it comes to his performance review, he gets no credit for doing that . . . the outside effort.[26]

Jacob observed that even while Todd's interests did not correspond to available area tests, he put considerable effort into bolstering his knowledge and authentic portrayals of the military aspects of the job. But these efforts would not necessarily be recognized in Todd's annual performance review.[27] In such a scenario, an opportunity to harness Todd's passions in ways that could contribute to the larger organization was potentially lost because the organizational structure limited the rewards and support workers like Todd received, despite their intrinsic motivations.

How interpreters responded to testing requirements varied considerably. Some took the testing process very seriously, and considered tests valid markers of achievement. These workers tended to treat taking and passing tests as a game where tests passed represented points earned

toward the worker's claims of authenticity. Some interpreters took ownership of the testing process by developing tests in their areas of expertise,
as was the case for various interpretive area tests such as the Shops Test
(carpentry, blacksmithing, etc.), the Sutler's Store Test, and the Hospital
Test. Those tests provided ways to support the organization while also
empowering interpreters as creative agents who, through test taking, also
were able to demonstrate their authority on historical subjects. Still other
interpreters resisted the tests because they perceived the tests as removing them from the more game-like aspects of the job. To these workers,
the imperative to take tests squelched the freedom to explore one's interpretive interests, and represented less degree of freedom from managerial
control and less autonomy that Fuller and Smith argued were so important
to the workplace satisfaction of interactive service workers.[28]

"The whole thing's a joke; everybody cheats"
My experience in the field gave me the impression that most of the
interpreters who resented the testing procedures at the Fort took what
tests they needed to take in order not to be evaluated negatively on their
performance reviews, but they did not perceive the tests as legitimate
markers of one's ability to effectively interpret history. For many of these
workers, it was standard procedure to take the area tests "open book"
even though management expected them to know the answers by rote.
Craig, who had an advanced degree in history, had a less than positive
assessment of the testing process at the Fort:

> The whole thing's a joke; everybody cheats. They have the test, [we]
> ask for the test . . . and then we go up and write down the answers
> from last year. And that's fine, I suppose. But it's a big joke. Why not
> just get rid of the whole thing? They know we're cheating. We know
> we're cheating. But they do it to cover their butts. And then . . . if
> some poor unfortunate souls decide to be honest and they don't do
> well on the test, here's [one of the managers], making fun of them.
> . . . I think that's a problem out there. They don't know how to do
> it. They don't know what to do. It's my belief that they allow that
> whole test thing to go on because it makes everybody happy: every-
> body passes. They have the answers, and they can cover their butts
> by showing people downtown, "Look! They all passed the test!"[29]

Like Tara, Craig did not feel that tests adequately measured one's knowledge of the material, in part because site management did not consistently monitor or enforce testing procedures. Cheating on the tests in order to pass also might have been inadvertently encouraged by one of the managers who sometimes publicly chided employees who did not pass the test. Other employees claimed to take the tests "open book" because management did not give them the test until last the last few minutes of their workday.[30] But the pervasive cheating on the tests also represents a disgruntled workforce who would have preferred that management spent less time on measuring knowledge and more time offering workers opportunities to express their intrinsic desires to learn new information and skills that would benefit themselves, their organization, and visitors.

"They're not qualified to play those parts"

At times, management may have undermined the significance of tests as markers of achievement. In some instances, for example, management asked individuals to play roles that they had not tested into, as was the case when management asked two new female staffers to play officer's wives for a short play that was to debut on Memorial Day weekend in 1999; I was one of newcomers asked to portray an officer's wife in this play. As Alyssa recalled, this occurred during our first month of employment at the site. The rub was that one of the managers asked us to portray these roles before we had passed the House Basic Test, the test that was designated as the entrance exam for female interpreters to portray officer's wives and to interpret "upper class" characters in either the Officer's Quarters or the Commanding Officer's Quarters. When management asked us to portray the parts of Mrs. Amelia Green (wife of a lieutenant) and Mrs. Abigail Snelling (wife of the commanding officer Colonel Snelling) management ignored their own protocol regarding testing procedures. This breach upset some of the female "lead guides" (that is, interpreters hired to take on extra duties with some pay incentive but without managerial titles and/or supervisory authority) who viewed the two of us as not having earned the right to play the lead characters in this particular workplace game of upper class ladies.

Alyssa, who was asked to portray Mrs. Green, recalled the reaction from a few of the female lead guides.

[They] were really mad about the fact we were given these parts
when we weren't even technically supposed to be given upper class
roles because we hadn't taken the test yet to be upper class, and there
was some talking behind backs going on. And we were just doing
what we were told. Our management told us: "You're to play these
parts." But then the other workers were like, "Well, they're not qualified to play those parts. Why are they being given those parts?"[31]

Alyssa acknowledged that most other interpreters did not seem to care
whether new interpreters played parts they had not tested into, but she
did recall the two veteran female interpreters who were quite vocal in
their objections. Over their years of experience working in the site, both
of these women had a good deal of knowledge about the site's history,
and Alyssa and I might have learned much from such knowledgeable co-
workers if the Fort's organizational structure had been set up to nurture
rather than discipline its workers.

Unfortunately, instead of everyone working together as a team, and
feeling successful in the organization's overall goal of presenting a play
about women's experiences during wartime, Alyssa and I felt confused
about why we were being subjected to scrutiny and ire. Notably, one
of the lead guides angry with management for asking us to play these
parts had frequently portrayed Mrs. Snelling, the role that management
had asked me—a newcomer—to play. My playing Mrs. Snelling after
one month on the job without having tested into the role seemed to be a
personal affront to her. But the affront wasn't personal; it was structural.

At this time, in 1999, the role of Colonel Snelling was not interchangeable between all male staff members, and for many years management approved only the smallest handful of male interpreters to play
Colonel Snelling.[32] Asking a newcomer like myself to portray Mrs. Snelling suggested that the upper-class roles for women really demanded no
great amount of expertise and were easily filled by any woman on staff,
regardless of experience. By contrast, specialized male roles such as Colonel Snelling, Doctor MacMahon, and the Fort's sutler, Captain Leonard
(a War of 1812 veteran who retained his military title while serving
the Fifth Infantry in a civilian capacity), were next to sacrosanct; only
one or two male members of the staff were ever permitted to portray

them. This may help contextualize why some female lead guides reacted so strongly to management's breach of protocol, as the transgression undermined the meaning of achievement to those who valued that kind of recognition. If tests lost their authoritative power to differentiate the authentically qualified staff from the unqualified staff—some female lead guides no doubt felt that their precarious positions would find a similar fate. This might also help explain why these same lead guides tended to micromanage their co-workers, using notions of authenticity to strengthen their own rocky sense of prestige within the Fort's organizational hierarchy.

Overseeing Authenticity: *Lead Guides as "Eyes and Ears of Management"*

While I worked at the Fort, the interpretive staff consisted of roughly fifty part-time guides, so that during most days in the peak tourist season of June, July, and August no more than thirty were generally scheduled to work (and roughly fifteen were generally scheduled to work during spring and fall school tours seasons). Of the total number of hired guides, anywhere from six to eight individuals would be designated as "lead guides."

The lead guide position carried with it a considerable amount of increased responsibility with little monetary remuneration. In 2001, for instance, lead guides earned only 43 cents an hour more than other staff members. Remuneration for lead guides was the honor of being differentiated from "regular guides" and from satisfaction derived from a job well done.

As part of their increased responsibility, lead guides were expected to conduct specialty seminars on interpretation or Fort history, run special events, assist with scheduling, survey the work performance of their co-workers, and contribute to co-workers' pre-performance reviews, and performance reviews (PRs). Paul, who served as a lead guide for three of his four seasons at the Fort, felt that management heavily relied on the lead guides in doing these performance reviews: "Lead guides spend an awful lot of time [on PRs]. We work hand in hand with each and every interpreter. At least we've tried."[33] Although lead guides had significant additional responsibilities compared to other staff, most guides I interviewed did not think taking the position as a lead guide would have been worth it, and a few did not see the function of the position at all, as Craig articulated:

> There's no distinction between lead guides and anybody else. What's-His-Name told me once that most people turn down the lead guide; he didn't want to be a lead guide. And [another guide] quit being a lead guide. Nobody wants to do it cause all it is, is you do a little bit extra work: locking and opening and nobody wants to do it for the extra 30 cents an hour, so I would guess. I don't know why anybody would want to do it. It's stupid.[34]

Craig also took issue with lead guides having the responsibility of contributing to one's PR, saying that he just didn't "understand that whole lead guide thing. I mean they do these evaluations and I never see most of these people. I never work with most these people, but they evaluate, so I don't take it very seriously."[35]

This endemic attitude, which didn't take the managerial authority of the lead guide position seriously, would cause trouble on multiple fronts, leading to the position's demise in 2004. Brynn, who proudly served as a lead guide for several years before the position was eliminated, felt that one of its "anomalies" was that lead guides had all "the responsibility without having the authority" because, while they were expected to evaluate their co-workers, their positions were not technically supervisory. Nonetheless, some lead guides were critical of how their co-workers played games of authenticity at the worksite, and were highly critical of how their co-workers performed the tasks and personae of the past, frequently voicing their appraisals on how authentically their co-workers, say, split wood, baked gingerbread, or polished furniture. Interpreters tended to resent these critiques. Indeed, interpreters were consenting to this type of labor precisely because they valued the possibility of creative expression at the worksite, and the micromanagement inherent in these appraisals, as they experienced them, reduced a worker's relative autonomy and squelched the delight in engaging in worksite games.

When I interviewed her, Kathleen had served as a lead guide for two of her eight seasons on staff. After her second season in that so-called authority, she decided to reapply only as a regular guide, because she had become disenchanted with the position. She felt not only that management exploited lead guides, but also that the position was not meeting her hopes for helping to create a nurturing work environment. In her ideal conception of what lead guides could do, Kathleen saw them "as being a resource for the other guides":

> I see them as being able to help facilitate the development of skills that they see in somebody that has possibility, to encourage that, to be of service. Encouragement. If they see a situation that is incorrect and shouldn't be happening then I see it totally their job to take that person aside, away from other people, and just say, "You know, I have a better way of doing it," or "I think you might want to look at what you're doing," or "the site frowns on it being done this way, let me help you so you don't get in any further trouble."

In this statement Kathleen describes her ideal for what the position could be. While allowing room for lead guides to offer constructive feedback to their co-workers, she stressed that in principle lead guides should serve to encourage and support the grassroots efforts of the frontline interpreters. When Kathleen described her perception of how the lead guide position was actually functioning, however, she portrayed a top-down management structure wherein lead guides overstepped their bounds with regard to their surveillance and policing of co-workers:

> I see that [encouragement] not happening. I see lead guides using their position as one of authority to kind of play God and to make people feel bad. I see a lot of times that they're pointing out the bad things and not the good things, and then I don't think if you talk to somebody about something that they're having difficulty in, that that should show up on their performance review. . . .
>
> I've been hearing this a lot . . . that the lead guides are the eyes and the ears of management. And I think, yeah, they are, because they write the PRs, but people do that in a bad way. It's like we're bad children being watched; they're like babysitters reporting to Mom and Dad, and I don't think that's what a lead guide should do.[36]

For workers like Kathleen, being too closely monitored rather than supported, fostered resentment, and this was especially true when lead guides policed or critiqued workplace games of authenticity, or threatened another interpreter's own sense of creative autonomy.

In my field notes from August 3, 2002, I registered my own frustration with one lead guide who, in a locker room exchange, remarked to me about a photograph she had seen of me in the staff meeting room. In the photograph, I am portraying a domestic serving dinner to one of the interpreters portraying an officer on the veranda; the issue was that in the photograph I had no shoes on—a clear violation of the dress code for a domestic serving dinner at table to an officer. To provide some context, prior to the taking of the photograph, I had cooked the meal downstairs in the officer's basement kitchen, where I was also supposed to pretend that I was quartered with my family. Upstairs a co-worker was portraying Lieutenant Platte Rogers Green, for whom I was to pretend that my character, Mrs. Tyson, worked. Downstairs in the kitchen, my character did not need to follow any particular dress code, but when serving at the dinner table she needed to have a neater appearance, complete with shoes.

After cooking the meal barefoot, I prepared to bring the meal upstairs. A group of visitors, who had watched me cook the meal in front of the hearth, followed me upstairs to see the next step in the process—serving the meal. As I gingerly balanced the china on my tray, about halfway up the staircase to the lieutenant's quarters, I announced to the visitors that I'd forgotten to put my shoes on (in fact, I had left them off deliberately to open the possibility for an unscripted scenario). I explained that while I didn't need to mind how I dressed so much downstairs where I did the cooking, I was supposed to be dressed appropriately in the presence of my employer, which included the wearing of shoes. Rather than going all the way back downstairs to put my shoes on, my character decided to risk it and shared the following exclamation with the visitors: "Hopefully Lieutenant Green won't notice this once!" In so doing, I was exercising the creative autonomy that I had come to value at this job by playing a workplace game with an unpredictable outcome. The Fort's visitors had fallen into my interpretive hole and were eagerly watching this situation unfold. Had the man playing the lieutenant noticed that I was violating the dress code, he might have improvised any number of scenarios, from sending me back downstairs to dress appropriately, to threatening my job. "Lieutenant Green" did not notice, and I quickly and quietly served him his plate of fish, poured his tea, and took my leave, visibly relieved that I avoided reproach—either to the relief or the disappointment of the visitors.

As it happened, one of those visitors (a weekly regular at the Fort) snapped a photograph during the brief moment when I was serving dinner to the lieutenant in my bare feet. This photograph made its way down to the staff meeting room. At the end of a work day, as we women stood changing into our civilian clothes in the locker room, without asking or knowing the context for this photograph, one of the lead guides remarked that while it was "such a good picture," I was not authentically portraying the role of an "upper-class domestic" because of my bare feet and ankles. Like Stephen Eddy Snow's Pilgrim interpreters who would sometimes "get inspired and want to do a little historical playwriting of their own" by enacting scenarios that could have conceivably happened but were not historically documented, when I made the choice not to wear my shoes I was playing my own game of authenticity, operating under the assumption that even while there were—and continue to be—established codes of behavior for women and domestics, those boundaries were rigidly policed because sometimes they were crossed.[37] Meanwhile, this lead guide was also using notions of authenticity in order to defend her claims about the inappropriateness of my bodily display. Although I felt confident in my interpretive choice, I nonetheless reacted to the locker room comment by feeling ashamed for having given the impression that I was wantonly exhibiting my body—even if it was just my feet—for public consumption.[38] Although being subject to this kind of surveillance was upsetting in and of itself, what was especially upsetting to me was that I was made to feel alienated for doing something that I had felt was a minor but nonetheless thoughtful contribution to the larger organizational goal of breathing life into our performance of "the past."

If this had been an isolated situation, I may not have taken the comment about the photograph much to heart. But policing tends to lead to more policing and less trust in an organizational culture, and that season I was not alone in feeling that I could not escape the critical gazes of certain female lead guides no matter what I did. At times it seemed as though any remark made by these female lead guides would meet the gritted teeth, rolled eyes, and sighs of exasperation from interpreters who collectively felt micromanaged—their sense of creative autonomy squelched amid waves of critiques about how authentically we baked, sewed, knitted, chopped firewood, or even talked. Even male co-workers openly complained to me that they, too, were on the receiving end of lead guides' criticism about the authenticity of their interpretive choices.

What could be described as a heated work environment reached a boiling point one day in July 2002, even before the first visitor had walked through the gates.[39] As the female guides were changing into costume, one lead guide remarked that it was "inauthentic" for one of the women to portray Mrs. Snelling because the interpreter was too old. While the "real" Mrs. Snelling in 1827 was thirty years old, this interpreter was in her late forties, and was changing into costume with the rest of us when the comment was made. Her feelings were clearly hurt, and she was visibly holding back tears. After she left for her post, another co-worker—Elizabeth—and I went to see if she was all right.[40] At this point, she did cry and said that this comment was "just the tip of the iceberg," that she was tired of being criticized at every turn, so now that even her age was considered inauthentic.

Shortly after the three of us had talked over what had transpired that morning, I took my place downstairs in the kitchen where I was assigned to work that day and began sorting coals from the ash in preparation to cook. Although Elizabeth's schedule dictated that she was supposed to be cleaning the static exhibits in the Long Barracks (a task that rarely required the full thirty minutes that our schedules allotted—often interpreters would read the exhibit displays to stretch the time), on this occasion, she quickly finished cleaning the Plexiglas display cases so that she could talk with me about what had happened in the locker room that morning. Although no one from the public had yet arrived to visit the site that morning, as we crouched by the hearth sorting coals and talking about the morning's events, another lead guide approached us, shook her finger at us, and warned that the two of us needed to "be very cautious," that "everyone from lead guides on down" had been talking about the two of us, that "it was suspected that we had been arranging our schedules to see each other," that we had been "jeopardizing our stations," and finally, that we had been seen on several occasions walking arm-in-arm together on the parade grounds (which, incidentally, would not have been historically inappropriate for women of the same social status but in this instance was claimed to be "inauthentic").[41]

For my own part, I had sensed that some lead guides disapproved of those of us who tended to break character and joke when the public was not around, but I was confident that my station had never been jeopardized, nor did I feel I had ever compromised my living history impressions at the public's expense. I felt micromanaged, to be sure, but I also felt that although Elizabeth and I were only friends, this lead guide was insinuating that we were carrying out a relationship of another sort. As a way to claim control over us as workers, she chastised us for the apparent "inauthenticity" of walking arm-in-arm—even while historians such as Carroll Smith-Rosenberg, in her article "The Female World of Love and Ritual: Relations Between Women in Nineteenth-Century America," have persuasively argued that such a gesture was not likely to have turned heads.[42] In response, Elizabeth and I used our own understanding of historical "authenticity" to defend ourselves against this lead guide and her critiques.

But why did some lead guides resort to intrusive supervision of their colleagues? In journalist Carol Hymowitz's *Wall Street Journal* editorial on micromanagement, top business executive David D'Alessandro—the former president of John Hancock's insurance division—offered his opinion that micromanagement is "a sign of insecurity."[43] In another *Wall Street Journal* editorial, former CEO Joe Esposito offered a similar conclusion, noting that because "managers frequently have to serve the interests of constituencies that are unknown to their staff members" they might resort to micromanagement as "a response to outside pressures."[44] Citing one specific example of a micromanager, Esposito said: "He was doing what he was doing in order to make it appear he had greater control than he had." Esposito added that what no one suspected was that in reality "he was feeling desperate himself."[45]

The female lead guides at the Fort may have resorted to micromanaging because the extent to which they had legitimate control was, in fact, rather limited. As Brynn explained, "Going from guide to lead guide, you enter a rather nebulous state. . . . We are expected to plan and organize parts of the program, we are expected to do work assignments for people, we are expected to give input on people's evaluations; and yet we are not given any kind of supervisory title."[46] Lead guides may have micromanaged as a way to try to exercise authority within the limited structure provided them, while building their own positive work identities as being "in control," and more able than their fellow co-workers.

In the following, for example, note not only that Brynn felt defeated by the working conditions set up for the lead guides, but also that she conceived of herself as more knowledgeable than her co-workers:

> One of the anomalies of the lead guide position [is] about having the responsibility without having the authority. . . . You cannot do what is expected of a lead guide, as far as I'm concerned, to the very best that it can be done, within the current structure, unless you are willing to give time off the clock. It physically cannot be done properly because as lead guides, we also have a responsibility to be out there in front of the public as much as the other guides, and to spend that time with the public. . . . We are some of the most knowledgeable and informed and broad, as far as what we're capable of doing. The vast majority of the lead guides are qualified in anywhere from eight to all eleven areas of the fort. We may not always work in all of them, but we are qualified in them. So we are the ones—if there is nobody else there who can answer the question, one of us ought to be able to, and because of that we have to stay out in front of the public.[47]

As with the low-level temporary workers that Vicki Smith studied, when "given an opportunity to prove themselves" some lead guides "intensified their efforts to do so" even though it meant little external enticement.[48] Significantly, Brynn frequently worked off the clock in order to excel in the position of lead guide, even though she did not feel like she received adequate support and recognition for her efforts.

Like Brynn, Paul took the role of the lead guide seriously, even while he felt defeated by the structure of the organization and its prescribed positions. Understaffed as the Fort often was, lead guides found little opportunity to properly observe the co-workers whom they were supposed to be evaluating for staff performance reviews. Addressing me in the interview Paul said:

> I literally did not hear you interpret until like the end of July or early August, and how was I supposed to get any sort of feedback for you if I had no idea who you were. . . . I know [you're] cooking down in the kitchen today but doggone it we're short on duty squad again and that means the old sergeant has to sit around and mind the barracks while the guys take their break. . . . [Lead guides] just

> aren't able to do those sorts of things. When they had bigger staffs
> it was not a problem.

Paul would have liked to have been able to observe his co-workers so that he could have given them better feedback, but both because of the worksite's gender segregation, which prevented males and females from much contact during the work day, and because the Fort was usually understaffed with often only one person at any given station, lead guides often felt frustrated with their ability to adequately contribute to their co-workers' evaluations.

Workers like Paul and Brynn wanted to succeed at their jobs and to receive recognition for their efforts. But because the site was not built to nurture workers in other ways, being a lead guide and passing tests stood in as objective markers of achievement. When I asked Paul if it was an easy transition going from guide to lead guide, he spoke with great pride about his achievements in his first year of working at the Fort that led to his being offered a lead guide position for the following year: "Well, I think it was natural, moving up because I had done so well my first year. As a first-year person I had taken and passed five tests and would have been studying for a sixth, which I had never gotten around to doing."[49] Paul took pride in having passed five tests and saw being promoted to the lead guide position as recognition for a job well done.

The pride Paul and other lead guides took in the role contrasted with the fact that others did not regard the positions "too seriously." When some lead guides acted as though they had managerial authority, it created dissension and fostered resentment among the staff.[50] Often when a lead guide would claim control, it was done so through the vehicle of claiming authenticity. Furthermore, attempts to control co-workers were often delivered and received in peculiarly gendered ways, as the examples above illustrate. Finally, although both males and females were hired as lead guides, interpreters with whom I interviewed and worked, did not complain of being micromanaged from the male lead guides, which strongly suggests lead guide dynamics did not function the same for both genders.

Skinning the Muskrat: *Performing Class and Masculinity*

Although the lead-guide dynamic did not function the same for both sexes, it does not mean that male staff members were free from co-worker surveillance. Male interpreters, no less than their female counterparts, were scrutinized in regard to how successfully they played games of authenticity. In particular male interpreters had their own surveillance rituals that were born out of the site's unique military culture, as some policed for signs that an interpreter was performing according to historical and contemporary conceptions of manliness.

Jay, who had worked several seasons as an interpreter when I had interviewed him, felt that whoever was assigned to play the sergeant on the drill squad "immediately became a lot more authoritarian" even after the change in Fort management in 2006.[51] In a particularly thoughtful appraisal of why this might be the case, Jay guessed that it could be attributed to "the way the leadership structure is set up at Fort Snelling."[52] Borrowing "shamelessly from [the Brazilian educator Paulo] Freire" (Jay's words), Jay noted that at the Fort "individuals don't really have a chance to participate authentically and bring themselves into the process to create, so that when they are put into these positions of *power*—even though it is just an artificial role-playing power—they abuse it in sort of an authoritarian way."[53] Complementing my analysis of why female lead guides micromanaged their co-workers, Jay believed that male interpreters who portrayed sergeants "immediately became a lot more authoritarian . . . not necessarily because it's their intent to; I mean, I think most probably don't realize that they're doing it. But it's just sort of the initial reaction that if you've never held power, if you've never held leadership, you tend to mimic those sort of authoritarian role models because that's all you know."[54] This exercise of power over others did not stop once military drill was over; when someone's musket failed to fire during drill, for example, some interpreters would call attention to this failure in the men's locker room at the end of the day.

Not everyone participated in this locker-room ritual, but to designate the group of male interpreters who regularly *did*, I will borrow a term from the world of reenacting and refer to them as the "hardcores." As opposed to "farbs" (a derogatory word meaning fakers, whose etymology is not entirely clear, possibly deriving from the phrase "far be it from real"), hardcore reenactors aim for "total authenticity," both in appearance and in mannerisms.[55] While scholars have frequently noted how hypermasculinity has shaped living history reenactment sub-cultures, my study shows that hypermasculinity similarly shaped the workplace culture of the Fort.[56]

Several of my male informants told me how the Fort's hardcores would sometimes yell at and other times make fun of those interpreters who either did not take the military aspects of interpretation as seri-ously or did not physically follow drill commands well. Henry recalled "there was a lot of strife [in the locker room] between the people who took the military program so serious to the point of thinking that we were in the real army opposed to those [for whom] it's just a job and a pretend army." Henry believed that the soldiers at Fort Snelling "would have been the worst trained in the Army" so that portraying less than perfect soldiers was the most authentic way to portray the past.[57] The hardcores disagreed, and felt it was most authentic to perform military maneuvers as they should have been performed. In either case, an attack on an interpreter's performance at military drill was often experienced as an attack on his modern-day self as a man and his "pride in [his] work."[58] Thus, the claims about how a guide portrayed a soldier of the past spilled over into a judgment about his manliness in the present.

Locker-room displays of manliness did not only manifest between men in arguments about the military drill. While female guides tended to col-lect hanks of yarns and checkered gingham cotton in their lockers, some male guides kept whiskey bottles and weapons in theirs. Although when I left the Fort in 2006, the new supervisors who were in place by then seemed to have nipped this practice in the bud, drinking in the men's locker room had long been a part of the culture at this worksite (possibly the previous management structure turned the blind eye because drink-ing was considered "authentic"). Henry recalled having seen a "whisky bottle cracked open at 9:20 in the morning and half of it consumed before we leave." He also was "amazed at the quantity of weapons that are actu-ally in the men's locker room." As he described, there were "lots of mus-kets and various firearms and edged weapons and swords in their lockers. They'll need it for interpretation once, so they'll have it for that, but they never seem to take it home and there almost seems to be [the question of] . . . who can collect the most weapons over the year." Then he joked, "I feel so unmanly; *I've* got a pocketknife and someone is pulling a ball and cap revolver out of his locker, [saying] 'yeah, I could put four holes in you in two seconds with this' and I'm like, 'don't hurt me!' "[59]

In terms of material culture, it was not just booze and muskets that were grounds for assessing a fellow interpreter's masculinity in the men's locker room—there was also a bell that a few of them would ring from time to time if a particularly attractive female visitor had been seen touring the Fort on any given day. As Jay recalled, "Men at the Fort were expected to ring a bell if they'd seen an attractive female visitor, and then they were expected to describe her and to describe sexual acts they would like to perform. Not necessarily like in a pornographic *Hustler*-type way, but in a 'Would you do her?/Yeah, I'd tap that!' stereotypical locker-room chatter."[60]

Many of the men were not entirely comfortable with locker-room conversation or antics—ranging from the blackface minstrel routines that purportedly had been performed a few times in the locker room by one of the male interpreters, to the ringing of the bell. However, it seems that most men either kept their objections silent or passively went along. One co-worker told me in conversation, "Well, I've never actually rung the bell myself," in order to distance himself from the ritual.[61] The bell ringing happened in the decisively masculine space of the locker room, and to object too passionately would have been to negate one's masculinity. Jay concluded that male interpreters who "were less socially popular would try and use the bell to relate to other co-workers" as a way to claim their space in the fraternity: "Like we've always had a number of kind of awkward folks and the bell and bell discussions were something of an equalizer of sorts because theoretically anyone could participate in the bell conversation."[62]

It should not be overlooked that male interpreters in the men's locker room were generally portraying soldiers, whom the site's training materials described as " 'the scum of the population of the older states,' 'the sweepings of the cities,' 'the dissipated, idle or improvident,' and 'the dregs of American society'. These expressions reflect the general truth that the dull, the lazy and the troublesome found the army an alternative to starvation or jail. Not all regulars deserved the reputation, but it had the effect of discouraging willing and able men from enlisting, thus reinforcing the stereotype."[63]

It would seem that the "bawdy" humor and masculine bravado that Oliver and others described as the prevailing culture in the men's locker room may have been related to how some workers interpreted and absorbed the roles they were asked to portray throughout the day. In a sense, acting in such a fashion may have been considered "authentic"— even though the lines were blurring between the past and the present.

Significantly, the Fort had two separate locker rooms for each gender—one for those playing working-class roles (the majority of the staff) and one for those playing middle- or upper-class roles (this is where the costumes and accouterments for those roles were kept). For females, these changing rooms were called "the women's locker room" (working-class roles) and "the ladies locker room" (middle- and upper-class roles), and for males the rooms were referred to as "the men's locker room" (for those portraying the roles of enlisted men) and "the civilian locker room" (for those portraying civilian men and officers). Over the course of a day, the one to three male interpreters who changed in the civilian locker room generally had few shared experiences with each other outside that locker room, or with co-workers who portrayed soldiers. Thus, it would be unlikely and awkward to razz each other about their work performance as part of locker-room conversation. Likewise, in the civilian locker room—where one changed clothes in the presence of just one or two male co-workers (to paraphrase one of my former co-workers) in *that* context, it would seem weird to ring a bell and get all worked up about that "hot Russian woman who had on the short skirt and the tank top."[64] Several men confessed that they preferred to be in the civilian locker room. Oliver, for instance eventually moved all of his gear to the civilian locker room because he preferred the atmosphere there: "I find that a lot of the men who portray officers or gentlemen at the Fort, at least attempt to elevate the level of their conversation above what I would willfully enjoy if I was the rest of the staff."[65] In the civilian locker room, some interpreters felt they could escape the pressures of the hardcores, and more easily perform class and gender identities with which they felt more at ease.

Jacob was another interpreter who mentioned a preference for changing into costume in the civilian locker room. He noted that he did not feel comfortable with the racist, sexist, and—in his words—"good old boys" views that a few co-workers felt free to express in the men's locker

room.[66] Though changing in the civilian locker room provided Jacob
with a certain distance from those "good old boys," he was still not
immune to the pressures of performing masculinity:

> There have been a few occasions where I had to do something I didn't
> want to do. Like the time they wanted me to skin the muskrat was
> not very fun. They already think I'm a wussy boy, the vegetarian;
> I'm just a little hippie kid. I didn't want to do it at the time, but look-
> ing at it from a historical standpoint, it was good that I had done it.
> I can say I've done it now and I know what it entails. It's not very
> much fun; it's smelly and bloody. [When they asked me to skin the
> muskrat] I was like, "You guys know I'm a vegetarian, right?" And
> they're like, "Yeah, that's why we want you to do it, Jacob."[67]

This incident occurred on a day when Jacob had been assigned to portray a fur trader. In dealing with the situation, he told me, he "couldn't
exactly say, 'It's not authentic for fur traders to skin muskrats.'" In
order to preserve his sense of manhood in the face of the hardcores, on
this occasion Jacob reluctantly went along with this game of authenticity and joined the fraternal "muskrat-skinning club." Even though he
was hazed into joining that club, in the interview Jacob took care to
differentiate himself from the men who pressured him to do it by calling them "weird" and comparing one to a "psycho."[68] In this particular
instance, one of the men who pressured Jacob to skin the muskrat was
also a member of the management team—so that the performance of a
certain kind of hypermasculinity was encouraged from multiple directions in the triadic labor model.

Committing, Engaging, Connecting, and Supporting

In his study of a "neo-bohemian" neighborhood in Chicago, sociologist Richard Lloyd found that workers in his study (namely artists who
earned their living as restaurant servers) experienced satisfying emotional work from jobs that encouraged them to explore their status as
hip "cultural creators."[69] Everyone in the triadic labor model benefited
from such an arrangement. Management benefited by employing these
artists because the restaurants gained a steady stream of creatively
skilled workers who were "easier to retain" because they bought "into

the employment culture" and were "not just passive servers catering to the whims of patrons, but active participants in the production of the overall ambiance, the creation of a 'really interesting place.' "[70] Tourists benefited by encountering a bit of the neighborhood's bohemian culture through servers who fused their creative identities as artists into their service jobs. And the artist/servers also benefited in having the freedom to express themselves at worksites that allowed them to forge a positive work identity, and distinguish themselves from "dabblers" (we might say "farbs") who were not committed to the production of the neighborhood's authentically edgy vibe.[71]

At the Fort, the distinctive environment that frontline workers produced for visitors, also rested on the production of an authentic ambience: local history that provided visitors the opportunity to "step back in time to the early 1800s."[72] In this manner, the Fort as a worksite benefited from hiring a certain kind of person who yearned to express his or her own creative identity in ways that produced the site's distinctive historic environment. One way that workers achieved this end was by actively acquiring knowledge and authentic craft skills, which produced the vibe of historical authenticity to visitors, and reinforced interpreters' sense of selves as unique and creative individuals. Not unlike the artist/servers in Lloyd's study, Fort interpreters who sought outward recognition of their efforts used claims of authenticity to pass judgment on which of their co-workers were just "dabblers" and which ones were worthy of being considered the real deal. This made for a divided workforce, whose focus was all too frequently turned from the shared enterprise of cultural creation, and turned toward battles over details. But Fort interpreters did not initiate this battle; they inherited it.

As had been the case since its first days as a living history museum in 1970, during the years of my study, management at Historic Fort Snelling seldom monitored the performance of workers on a day-to-day basis, which gave workers some relative freedom to play their games and execute interpretive decisions. But there was a false autonomy operating here. As I described in Chapter 1, early on in the site's history a culture of co-worker surveillance inspired by top-down military discipline was instituted at the Fort alongside fact-checking testing procedures designed to keep workers in line.

As one former manager explained it, these measures were put in place because of a lack of support for those who were hired to lead the site's early interpretive program: "I had a guide staff of forty three and I was the only supervisor . . . [and with a staff] working every day, seven days a week, with one supervisor, you obviously needed some sort of a hierarchy of supervisors on site. But the institution was not willing to authorize additional full-time or even part-time positions other than, simply, these seasonal, hourly positions."[73] Thus, the testing and internal hierarchical systems that were in place by the time I first took a job at the Fort in 1999 were symptomatic of wider, institutional issues of resources not being directed toward nurturing the interpretive programs, the frontline workers, or the supervisors at the Fort.

This lack of support had repercussions down the line. Though some interpreters I spoke to saw tests and lead guide opportunities as legitimate markers of achievement, most of those with whom I worked negatively experienced the culture of tests and co-worker surveillance, and reported feeling burdened by and excessively monitored by the Fort's measures of quality control. The games of authenticity that were so deeply entrenched in the workplace culture of the Fort served competing functions in the organization. Striving to be authentic could at times strengthen workers' positive work identities. Indeed, committed to their job for more than wages, interpreters' intrinsic emotional commitment breathed life into the production of the whole worksite when they played their games of authenticity. As part of the elaborate workplace games of authenticity, interpreters brought roosters to the worksite, hand-stitched dresses at home, studied military manuals on their own time, grew mutton-chop sideburns, read period novels to perfect dialect, and brought in road kill to skin for fur-trading demonstrations. Likewise, the skills and knowledge gained in playing these games of authenticity were often used to lure visitors into conversations about the past, and as such the games served the larger interests of the living history site, even as they were also tremendously rewarding for interpreters to play.

But at other times, these games were turned into tools of control: Some workers were accused of performing gender inaccurately, pressured to skin muskrats, or told that they were not qualified to play certain roles, or that they were getting their roles (or their stitches, or their marching, or their wood-stacking, or their facts) wrong altogether.

When used as control mechanisms, games of authenticity demoralized the interpretive staff, quelled creativity, and divided co-workers who had much to offer one another when they worked together as a team.

Although frontline workers at the Fort at times felt restricted by the organizational culture, strong desires to connect meaningfully with others in their workplace often weighed more heavily in their satisfaction with their work environment. Those who were dissatisfied, or disinvested in their jobs just left, but most interpreters stayed on for multiple seasons.[74] Why did they keep returning?

Once, when I was interviewing an interpreter who had worked at the site for nearly a decade, the tape ran out. I scribbled notes as she closed the interview by telling me about an email she had received a few days prior, one that moved her to tears because it made her think about the Fort, and the frustrations that she had with the limits of its institutional structure. My notes read: "I wish you enough tears to make you appreciate the happiness—enough hellos to balance the goodbyes." She tied this to the Fort by saying that as long as the job brings enough to balance the heartache, it's worth it, and that no job is perfect, but you just need enough rewards to keep you happy, to keep you coming back.[75]

Given the depth of investment from interpreters like the one here, it is clear that equally important to how committed workers are to their work, is how committed the overall organization is to engaging with, connecting to, and supporting its workers.

CHAPTER 5

INTERPRETING PAINFUL HISTORIES
Emotional Comfort and Connecting

J acob: *I think it's good that somebody talks about [slavery at the Fort], but I don't want it to be me. I feel somewhat uncomfortable talking about it.*

In Colonial Williamsburg—the country's most well-known living museum—we can see the genesis of living history's attempts to tackle the painful historical narrative of American slavery. With the stated aim of telling the story of eighteenth-century Williamsburg residents, Colonial Williamsburg was a tourist attraction for three decades before it attempted to interpret the lives of eighteenth-century free and enslaved African Americans, who made up roughly 50 percent of Williamsburg's population in the colonial era.[1]

. In the 1960s this living museum's first formal efforts to interpret African American history in one of the village's restored kitchens were instituted by means of a tape recording that described "the life of a slave cook."[2] Not everyone was comfortable with this interpretive addition to the site's programming. According to Anna Logan Lawson, whose research in the mid-1990s focused on the emergence of African American history at Colonial Williamsburg, "black members of the maintenance staff" were embarrassed by the tape recording, and their emotional discomfort led them to "hang their coats over the box containing the recording to keep visitors from hearing about slavery"—a gesture that both literally and figuratively worked to cover up historic interpretations of slavery's past; when management discovered what the workers were doing, management "abandoned" the tape recording.[3]

Lawson attributes the black maintenance workers' emotional discomfort to the historical climate of the 1960s—before the black power movements of the 1970s reclaimed slavery as "both the emblem of white oppression and the evidence of black strength."[4] Accordingly, in 1979—a few years after the television miniseries *Roots* brought the painful history of slavery into American living rooms—the Colonial Williamsburg Foundation began more earnest efforts to interpret a history of Williamsburg that included both African American social history and slavery by hiring six African American interpreters.[5] Soon thereafter, Colonial Williamsburg established the African American Interpretation Program (AAIP).[6] Before it was dissolved in 1997 (in favor of streamlining African American history with regular programming), the AAIP was charged with making the hard realities of American slavery, as well as slave culture, more visible to the public. For example, working with other departments at Colonial Williamsburg, the AAIP helped plan the controversial 1994 "Estate Sale" program, which drew a crowd of more than two thousand onlookers, and whose aim was to dramatize a historically based auction wherein four African American interpreters portrayed an enslaved family who were broken apart as they were sold among other forms of "property" to the "highest bidders," portrayed by white interpreters.[7]

It is clear from accounts in the popular press that this program stirred public emotion.[8] According to the *New York Times,* Baptist minister Dr. Milton A. Reid described the event this way: "This is 1994. As far as we have come, to go back to this for entertainment is despicable and disgusting. This is the kind of anguish we need not display."[9] This remark betrayed not so much Reid's desire to cover up the history of slavery, but his emotional and intellectual discomfort with the living historical medium in which the subject was to be treated. Could living history do justice to this painful subject?

Jack Gravely, the political director of the Virginia Branch of the National Association for the Advancement of Colored People (NAACP) thought that it could. Originally Gravely had organized protests against the performance, but after viewing the dramatization, he changed his position, seeing promise in living history's interpretive power: "Pain had a face. Indignity had a body. Suffering had tears."[10] While the press focused on the debate over whether tackling the topic of slavery was appropriate for living history interpretation—so often perceived as mere entertainment—little attention was paid to what the program meant for public history's proletariat who were lending their bodies and themselves to interpret the pain and indignity of the peculiar institution. How did interpreting painful histories affect those tasked with performing this emotionally charged history?

Drawing on interviews with Williamsburg interpreters, historian James Oliver Horton reported that African American interpreters who took part in the Estate Sale experienced "strong emotions—anger and extreme sadness, as well as pride at being part of this bold historical statement."[11] Horton also found that—even beyond the 1994 program— interpreters portraying enslaved persons at Colonial Williamsburg continued to experience conflicting emotional consequences, some finding "it uncomfortable to leave the colonial area in costume." Some reported feeling self-conscious being dressed as a slave, and having been victim to racist remarks while out in public, in costume.[12] For these interpreters, racism was not in the past, but a daily, lived experience.

Along similar lines, interpreters portraying slave-owners in the context of living history have also paid an emotional toll. For example, a January 1999 episode of WBEZ Chicago's *This American Life* (distributed by Public Radio International), focused on the consequences of role playing a cruel slave master in Conner Prairie's "Follow the North Star" program. This is an after-hours role-playing event wherein museum visitors pay to role-play as fugitive slaves on Indiana's underground railroad in 1836.[13] Conner Prairie's head of immersion programs, Dan Freas, has described the program as "so intense . . . that when it's over, we do a debriefing with psychological professionals, to make sure everyone's OK."[14]

The radio program focused specifically on the experience of Ron Copeland, whose role in the North Star program was to humiliate participants by yelling such phrases as, "Bucks step forward, breeders step back. Keep your eyes down. Don't you look at a white man. Don't you talk unless I talk to you." Not unlike Fort interpreter Henry (see Chapter 3), who had difficulty portraying a sergeant at the Fort, Copeland initially had difficulty getting into his character, but as the season progressed, he settled into the role. Copeland feared that portraying the cruel and dehumanizing slave master had changed him from someone who used to be soft-spoken and "laid back," to someone whose anger rose too quickly, and had caused him to scream and bark demands even out of character. "When you take off your costume," we hear Copeland say, "and you put on your civilian clothes to go outside and go home, you feel like 50 pounds have been [lifted] off each shoulder. All you want to do is get out of here, and get back to your life, to your home, to today, in 1998."[15] But while Copeland would go home and try to distance himself from his interpretive duties, often he found that at home he would replay the entire night of "Follow the North Star" over in his mind, and would try to justify his actions. He worried not only that he might have emotionally hurt a visitor, but also that the requirements of his job were taking a toll on his own emotional well-being.

In this final chapter I go back to my case study of the Fort to examine how interpreters at this living history site, often preoccupied by visitors' emotional comfort, chose to deal with Fort Snelling's more painful histories. My study shows that although interpreters theoretically had—to borrow from Stacy Roth's manual on interpretation—"the freedom to discuss just about any subject with a visitor," interpreters did not consistently exercise this freedom.[16] Rather, based on what I call "comfort cues"—such as signs from visitors (e.g., body language) or the group demographics according to race, gender, and/or age) that the interpreter would use to gauge whether to interpret some of the site's more painful histories (those relating to slavery, for instance, or American colonialism). Interpreters sometimes avoided painful histories not merely to protect what they perceived as visitors' emotional comfort, but rather to avoid agitating their own entrenched anxieties, especially relating to race and sexually exploitative power relations. While interpreters could bring their own interpretations and ideological investments to bear on their presentations of painful historical narratives, I argue that during my time as a guide, the site itself promoted programming that avoided eliciting painful emotion; instead the programming downplayed or attempted to ignore unequal power relationships in terms of race, class, and gender, and privileged the telling of a white, patriarchal history that erased controversial histories surrounding slavery, American colonialism, and American Indian/white relations.[17]

Interpreting Slavery at the Fort (1999–2006): *Symbolic Erasure*

From the moment Historic Fort Snelling became a living history museum in 1970—and until a year after the end of my seasonal employment there in 2006 (I discuss changes that began in 2007 later in this chapter)—the Fort's programming tended to erase the history of slavery at the site. An early planning document from 1969 suggests, however, that such erasures were not inevitable. As the restoration of Fort Snelling was progressing in the late 1960s, Governor Harold Levander chartered the Fort Snelling Sesquicentennial Committee to present the 1969 legislature with budgetary and programmatic recommendations regarding commemoration of the 150th anniversary of the laying of the Fort's cornerstone.[18] In the twelve-page "Fort Snelling Sesquicentennial Committee Report" issued to the governor, the committee not only recommended that military costumes and equipment be procured so that guides could represent "life at the fort as it was 150 years ago" but also "that appropriate recognition be given to the fact that Dred Scott, whose legal fight for status as a free man led to the historic Supreme Court decision of 1857, based his claim upon his residence at Fort Snelling as a servant of Dr. John Emerson. This could be done either in a special exhibit or through the interpretive center."[19]

When I began working at Historic Fort Snelling in 1999, within the Fort itself there was no "appropriate recognition" of the role that Fort Snelling played in the famous court case that Dred Scott and his legally wedded wife—Harriet Robinson Scott—launched in 1846.[20] A focus on military history, and the fixed nature of the 1827 programming, forestalled the need to formally train guides to interpret Dred and Harriet Scott's historic fight for freedom, beyond equipping them to provide cursory information. Enslaved persons did make up a small portion of the Fort's community in 1827, a fact that—while I worked there—few visitors would have known and few interpreters would have had the opportunity to discuss, given their interpretive charge to interpret the daily life of 1827 in the barracks, the sutler's store, the hospital, or the shops (carpenter's shop, blacksmith's shop, etc.). That said, interpreters stationed in the Commanding Officer's Quarters had the most logical opportunities to broach this difficult topic with visitors—and the decision to perform this emotional work would most often be shouldered by the female interpreters who were almost exclusively stationed to work there (both upstairs and down).

In their 1993 book about the Snelling family, former Fort interpreters and local historians Barbara and John Luecke compiled a list of "Servants of Colonel Josiah Snelling, 1820–1827" derived largely from journals and the "Accounts of Army Paymasters, 1819–1828."[21] From these documents the Lueckes found evidence that thirteen individuals worked as servants for the Snellings from 1820 to 1827. Of these thirteen, four worked for the Snelling family in 1827. Two were Swiss immigrants who had fled from a failed settlement in Rupert's Land (Canada).[22] The final two known servants in the household joined the workforce in the Snelling household in May 1827, when Colonel Snelling paid Mr. Bostwick of St. Louis, Missouri, $400 for a "Negro woman (Mary) and her child Louisa."[23] In the pay records, Mary is described as follows: "black complexion and eyes, wooly hair, 5' 4, Slave."[24] Although slave labor appears to account for half of the workforce in the Snelling household in 1827, the histories of Mary and Louisa mostly had been rendered invisible since the Commanding Officer's Quarters began being interpreted in the early 1980s.

This invisibility was encouraged by a number of factors. To begin, the Fort did not actively recruit African American interpreters to portray these roles, or others such as black fur traders, or free black domestic workers. In fact, in the collective memory of interpreters who had been at the site since the 1980s, prior to 2007 only two African American interpreters were recalled to have worked as paid interpreters at the Fort (both of them women); by contrast, hundreds of white interpreters had worked at the site since the 1970s. During my seven years working at the site, I worked with one African American interpreter. I met this interpreter (I'll call her "Kim") during the 1999 season (she had worked the season before, but did not return to work at the Fort after 1999).[25] As an interpreter, Kim portrayed the role of the enslaved woman Mary, and sometimes portrayed the role of a free black domestic.

The Fort also rendered slave labor (among other topics) invisible through interpretive labeling and exhibits that focused on military history and the daily lives of garrison soldiers. For example, in terms of prominent markers and exhibits at the Fort, the Fort Snelling History

Center (a modern interpretive center located outside of the historic
fort's walls) contained an exhibit on Fort Snelling's role in World War
II, while inside the historic fort interpretive exhibits focused on archae-
ology (in the Officer's Quarters), the history of medical practices (in the
reconstructed hospital barracks), and—in the longest stretch of exhibit
space—the "Wood Barracks house[d] an extensive exhibit on enlisted
men's life in the regular Army" that featured "room treatments" showing
the changes in the material conditions of soldiers' life in the nineteenth
century: "single or double squad rooms; fireplaces or stoves; plaster,
paneling or rough hewn logs."[26] The wood barracks exhibit also had a
small room dedicated to the interpretation of the Commanding Officer's
Quarters, which featured portraits of Colonel Josiah Snelling and his
wife Abigail Hunt Snelling (who lived at the post from 1820 to 1827) and
objects of material culture such as Abigail Snelling's mourning ring. The
preponderance of exhibits such as those described here produced an
"affective inequality" wherein visitors were guided to empathize with
the lives of soldiers and officers over other possible historical actors
(such as slaves, or American Indians, for example).[27]

This "affective inequality" was further reinforced by the management directive that interpreters treat all visitors who entered their station with deference, and to address them as if they were members of the
more privileged class of "officers or ladies," which encouraged visitors
to empathize with the perspectives of the fort's upper class in the same
ways that tourists at plantation museums are often invited to "empathize with the planter-class family who lived in the 'Big House.'"[28]
Meanwhile, the whiteness of interpreters who worked in the basement
of Commanding Officer's Quarters further worked to symbolically erase
the historically documented black slave labor. If white interpreters did
not mention that in 1827 the Commanding Officer's Quarters housed
slaves, few visitors would have suspected it. One visitor in the summer
of 2005, for example, explained her experience of not realizing that
the Snellings owned slaves, in this way: "We walked into the kitchen
and someone else, a woman—a visitor—was there talking to one of the
[white] cooks, who was sewing. And the woman asked the cook about
the room next to the kitchen. She asked her: 'So what's this room?' And
the cook answered: 'That's the servants' quarters.' And they started
talking about something else. I peeked in [to those quarters and saw]

there was a pantry, and a bed, and the cook was right there, so I assumed that must be where *she* slept—that she was the servant—so I walked on."[29] Until a future conversation with me, this visitor had no idea that in 1827 the room likely served as quarters for the Snellings' enslaved laborers.

While programming and the barracks and quarters exhibits presented interesting social histories in their own right, the combined messages of these mediums were that the most significant story to be told in this space was a military one.[30] And while a military history may not necessarily be a comfortable narrative, the Fort's packaging of the military story precluded the telling of other relevant histories, ones that might have gone further toward educating the public and interpreters alike on how to have conversations about some of the nation's more painful and emotionally uncomfortable historical narratives—like slavery—in one of the few public contexts where important conversations like these might take place.

Comfort Cues and Training

Although programming and visual cues erased the history of slavery at the Fort, whether or not to broach the topic was left to the discretion of interpreters or visitors. In interviews, interpreters stressed that *how* they chose to take up painful histories depended on who was standing in front of them. In her study of how college faculty in social work made decisions about how or whether to teach about oppression in their classes, sociologist Sharron M. Singleton found that faculty she interviewed followed three "distinct paths": "minimizing oppression content, rejecting all content on oppression, and explicitly including oppression content" in their courses.[31] As for historic interpreters, those I interviewed noted that the extent to which they would choose to minimize, reject, or explicitly engage in interpreting painful histories would be based on comfort cues that they perceived from visitors. Using those cues, interpreters would engage in what Singleton defined as "comfort work," which are "those steps taken . . . to achieve a tolerable level of personal ease"—which could vary considerably from interpreter to interpreter based on one's life experience.

For example, Maggie, a Fort interpreter, explained that she decided how to broach the topic of slavery at the Fort depending on "the look on people's faces, if nothing else."[32] When portraying a domestic working in the kitchen of the commanding officer's house, visitors often asked her if she slept in the room next to the kitchen (i.e., the "servants' quarters"). She said that she would respond to that question by saying, "No, I don't live there, that's [for] the servants that Colonel and Mrs. purchased in St. Louis." Then, Maggie waited to see if she had successfully dug her interpretive hole: if the visitors understood the implications of what she said—that the euphemism "servants" referred to enslaved persons—this could lead to further discussion. Maggie said she would go into the history of slavery at the Fort in the 1820s, or to break out of her 1820s character to talk about the Fort's subsequent role in the Dred Scott decision. But she was careful to note that this service was based on her gauging a comfort cue: "Again, it's body language and sometimes the kinds of questions they ask, or the quizzical look on their faces or whatever makes me think, 'Hmm, this is someone who wants to know more [about slavery] and I should tell them more and get out of character and do that.' I never hesitate to do that."[33] While Maggie noted that she tried to gauge the interest and comfort of visitors with regard to slavery in order to determine how she ought to address the subject, she also noted that she learned this strategy by "watching other people and developing [her] own style after a while" rather than being formally trained to engage with visitors on such matters.[34]

Commenting on the training received in this regard, Gavin remarked: "Well, there isn't much time from management and higher ups to study these things [like slavery or race] because they've got their own agendas and priorities, but they try to say, 'Don't make a big deal out of it,' and 'Try to make it palatable to the visitors' and, 'It's all in the training materials somewhere.' But I've never felt uncomfortable about it."[35] E. Arnold Modlin, Derek Alderman, and Glenn W. Gentry, in their study about tour guides, empathy, and affect in plantation house museums, found strong evidence to suggest that guides used "gendered and racialized assumptions" to determine what histories visitors might be interested in, "which perhaps reflect the proclivities of the guide as much as they do the visitor [and] represent a significant barrier to telling a more emotionally compelling story of the enslaved."[36] These assumptions were also operating at the Fort. Although Gavin claimed that he did not feel uncomfortable broaching difficult histories with visitors, he also noted that a visitor's race might influence the extent to which he might dwell on a subject such as slavery:

> I won't make a big deal about it if I have, you know, like, African American kids, I'm not going to go on and on about slavery. I'm going to talk about the things that were going on, what people were doing and building out here. And I may talk about the more happy role models. I might talk about George Bonga [a free black fur trader] or Dred Scott's wife. But we don't really have the resources and the training to really jump into race relations at all. We would just make people uncomfortable, so it's better to just mention, 'Yes, this really happened,' and 'This is what we know about it. What do you think about it? Do you think it's a good idea?' And then we just try to move on to something else.[37]

Here, race took the place of a body-language-informed comfort cue so that in the presence of African American children, Gavin would perform emotional work by adjusting his focus to dwell on "the more happy role models" in the spirit of not making anyone feel uncomfortable— probably, I would venture, even Gavin himself, whose own emotional comfort might have been compromised at the prospect of talking about slavery with African American children.

After acknowledging that Fort interpreters were not trained to deal with subjects like race or slavery or American Indian issues, Fort interpreter Karl responded to my question about how he broached these subjects in this way: "Succinctly, candidly, graciously, and with sensitivity. Don't expand on the subjects unless asked to. Do your research so you can expand if necessary."[38] In a related vein, Gavin felt that his options for interpreting racial issues with visitors were thwarted because he was not adequately trained to address historical race relations with visitors more substantively.

In light of the training materials offered to him, it is no wonder that Gavin chose to talk about the "more happy role models." Indeed, this decision conforms to directives in the only substantive manual available to interpreters about African American history at the Fort while I worked there—a thirty-one-page manual entitled, "African-Americans at Fort Snelling, 1820–1840: An Interpretive Guide" that was compiled in 1997 not by an MHS historian, but by an undergraduate intern. Although I began working at the site in 1999, the first I saw of this unrevised "Guide" was in 2004.[39]

The Guide has several components: It discusses race relations and slavery in the related contexts of St. Louis (Missouri), frontier Minnesota, and Fort Snelling; it gives an overview of notable and noted African Americans who lived in frontier Minnesota in the pre-territorial decades; and it offers suggestions for interpreting African American history in the context of its living history program. One of those suggestions is:

> Emphasize the variety of roles African-Americans played in the state's early history. Rather than focus on the negative aspects of black life, especially slavery, interpreters should emphasize African-American's positive contributions to Minnesota's history. While acknowledging that many of the region's blacks were slaves, costumed guides should highlight black fur traders, especially George Bonga, and free blacks, such as James Thompson and the Jacob Fallstrom family.[40]

To its author's credit, the Guide attempts to render a complex history of slavery and race relations in frontier Minnesota and Fort Snelling. Still, when offering interpretive suggestions for the Fort's costumed interpreters, it sometimes offers a decisively chipper spin on the primary sources. For example, the guide suggests that social relations between the garrison's enlisted soldiers and Fort Snelling slaves were not tense and that they would have "associated freely": "Because enlisted men and slaves occupied the lower-rungs of the Fort Snelling community they probably interacted with soldiers as relative equals. For example, the 'yellow woman' referred to in Colonel Bliss's reminiscences [Bliss lived at the Fort as a child] apparently had sexual relations with the garrison's enlisted men. As Bliss noted, 'she . . . became such an attractive belle among the soldiers that before leaving Fort Snelling we were obliged to make her a part of the cargo of the Steamer Warrior, and send her to St. Louis for sale.'"[41] Certainly there is more to extract from this particular "reminiscence"—namely Bliss's implication that the soldiers were using this woman sexually, possibly without her consent—but it is offered as proof that enlisted men and the enslaved fraternized "as

relative equals" without offering alternative readings about how the
enlisted men may have likewise considered this "yellow woman" a piece
of property, just as Bliss did when he notes that they were "obliged" to
sell her down-river.[42]

That management did not revise the Guide to reflect a more nuanced
historiographical treatment of the above account before distributing it
to interpreters as a training tool speaks to larger institutional issues
regarding how sexually charged power relations were not readily seen
as problematic—and in fact were seen by the male management as quite
natural. To take one example, in 1999 a male lead guide asked a new
female interpreter to portray a prostitute for an after-hours reenacting
event at the Fort. She would be the only woman on site, and the off-duty
male reenactors participating in the event would be "relaxing" with
alcohol around campfires at night.[43] Many of the men present would
not be Fort co-workers, but friends and guests of the male Fort workers.
The woman was to use suggestive play-acting to trick these "guests"
into giving her money, then go into an isolated building, telling them
to follow her in a few minutes. She was then to sneak out the back
window before they came in, so that the man entering would find only
a note on the table reading "You've been screwed for 25 cents."[44] This
was portrayed as a joke that the male Fort Snelling interpreters wanted
to play on their out-of-town visitors; the woman was simply the tool
they needed for the joke and she was being asked to do this as a "favor"
for a man who was senior to her (a lead guide) in her new job. The
female interpreter responded by writing a letter to the site manager,
expressing that she was declining this volunteer opportunity because it
was "objectifying [her] and putting [her] in danger."[45] In her letter, she
asked that no female interpreter be put in this position again. Although
in her interview she feared that she "might suffer later in terms of performance evaluations" she was glad when the "site manager came and
talked to [her] and said, 'Oh, I hadn't thought of it that way,' and they
didn't do anything [in retaliation]." The female interpreter felt that the
incident was related to worksite games of authenticity. As she phrased
it, "I guess they must have thought that every army camp historically
had whores, right? So we better have one."[46] It also speaks to the ways
that the military focus of the site may have naturalized unequal power
relations—and the ways in which the lines between present and past

could be blurred, causing distress to interpreters who expected to be treated as modern professional laborers, not as potential prostitutes or slaves simply because of their gender or race.

Clearly, there were consequences to the lack of adequate reflection on or training regarding these difficult issues. The Guide's reading of black/white relations on the frontier was echoed in the only mention of African Americans on the post that appeared in the standard interpreter training materials on a role-playing instructional sheet. Without offering primary or secondary sources, the role-playing instructional sheet contains five lines on white/black relations at the post in the 1820s (the same number of lines it offers for "saluting outside"—"saluting inside" takes an additional two lines): "During the 1820s slaves, free black servants, and fur traders were present on post. Enlisted men would have been very familiar on a social basis with these individuals, who—depending on their situation—may have actually led a more privileged and more comfortable life than many soldiers. Friendly social interchanges would likely be the normal mode between soldiers and civilian servants."[47] Not only is this context brief, it disproportionately focuses on the relative comfort of some slaves, free black servants, or black fur traders—albeit without offering any evidence to support the suggestion that many of the soldiers may have been worse off than these black individuals, or to support the supposition that the soldiers were on friendly terms with the black individuals who they may have encountered at the Fort.

Both pieces of training literature offer optimistic views of the past. To be fair, the Guide does mention that there may have been a "negative aspect to black life" at Fort Snelling in the 1820s—but nevertheless encourages interpreters not to focus on it. In accentuating the positive, such an approach to historical interpretation is consistent with a dominant strain in contemporary conservative ideology, which holds that only harm can come of dwelling on the negative aspects of the past. Neoconservatives like David Horowitz have frequently argued that bringing up the traumas of history invites racial conflict in the present.[48] But even without adhering to neoconservative ideology, interpreters feared igniting conflict in the present if they became the conduit for talking about painful histories with visitors. As Jacob noted in his interview: "I think it's good that somebody talks about [slavery at the fort], but I don't want it to be me. I feel somewhat uncomfortable talking about it."[49] The dearth of formal training on the history of slavery and race relations in the 1820s, as well as the lack of training on how to have conversations with visitors about these histories, is in part why interviewees like Jacob reported feeling awkward about interpreting painful histories with visitors.

By the same token, the lack of training may also help explain why some interpreters conveyed painful histories so *ineffectively*. Some interpreters, for example, used racist language in character, without providing visitors with a framework for understanding larger historical contexts for nineteenth-century race relations. In contrast to the Conner Prairie interpreter mentioned at the start of this chapter, Fort interpreter Oliver noted that some of his co-workers did not seem to feel at all uncomfortable espousing racist sentiments in front of the public when cloaked in the first-person viewpoints of their "characters."

> This summer I had a couple of interesting experiences with some of the male staff members who, very pointedly, were using these [racist] words in front of the public at various times throughout the summer. And I would find myself sort of nervously laughing or trying to modify or moderate that view in some fashion right in front of the public, just to make sure that they got the point, that they understood the difference [between past and present]. . . . [It] made me uncomfortable [to hear co-workers] utter these words, and express these opinions about the "dirty savages" and "we want to kill us some Indians," and so on and so forth. It made me very uncomfortable.[50]

For his part, Oliver chose not to express racist views or use outdated (and potentially offensive), or racist language in front of visitors. He further noted that he would "never attempt to get into those situations [of interpreting historic race relations] with children" or with "senior citizens, simply because they grew up in a different time" when "many of those same phrases or expressions [used in the early nineteenth century were] being offered up." For Oliver, age served as a comfort cue that could potentially safeguard his own uneasiness; when he did interpret historical viewpoints that concerned race, he said he "tend[ed] to shoot for people more my own age, between the 25 to 55 range" with the hope that they'd possess a mindset "close enough" to his. Ultimately, however, Oliver felt that using expressions such as "the red man" or "niggers"—even if historically appropriate—would make him feel uneasy: "I'm always afraid that I'm going to open a door for a bigot to walk right into and it's going to make *me* mighty uncomfortable, so I just avoid that."[51] Such an avoidance strategy may have had more to do with racial anxieties in the present than about the past—a theory that anthropologist Eric Gable also found to be true for Colonial Williamsburg's white interpreters who tended to avoid the topic of miscegenation at that living history museum.[52]

Not all interviewees, however, betrayed such entrenched anxieties. Elijah, who had more than ten years of experience working as an interpreter at the site when I interviewed him, self-consciously addressed the limits of interpreting painful histories in the context of a service-oriented historic site that was preoccupied with visitor comfort. He had the following to say about interpreting emotionally uncomfortable histories at the Fort:

> We try and make it real P.C. out there [and say things like] "Oh no, the Indians are our friends, la de da." Nuh-uh. [Actually,] the soldiers were attacking the Indians, and doing all sorts of horrible stuff to the Indians. There were some shootings down by the river in the winter: The Indians were constantly coming to [a U.S. Indian agent named Lawrence] Taliaferro and complaining about the soldiers, on just how awful they were; there were some rapes of the Indian women in one of the local villages and Taliaferro and Snelling were trying to figure out what to do about it. [Fort Snelling] was not a fun place to be. It was not a cheery site.[53]

Elijah acknowledged that the history of Fort Snelling was more complicated and vexed with conflict and turmoil than contemporary promotional brochures suggested, but he also acknowledged that he was not simply free to talk about any subject because of his position as an employee for the Minnesota Historical Society:

> I'm on the payroll for the [Minnesota Historical Society] and if I'm in costume and I'm spouting all kinds of terrible things and that visitor is upset and goes away, [saying] "I'm never going back there again, those schmucks," you know, that's not what we're trying to do. But I

think if I meet some visitors who are willing to get involved in some
controversial things, the most I can hope to do is to pique their interest enough and say, "Hey, yeah, there were some ugly things that
went on here, and I'll talk about them a little bit, but you can read
more at the library, or you can talk to some other people about that
more." You know? I don't try and give them the whole story. I try
and say, "Well, yeah, slavery was alive and well. In fact, Taliaferro
and Snelling had some [slaves], and when you go over to the [Com-
manding Officer's] house you might want to ask them about that."[54]

Elijah captured the difficulty of interpreting emotionally charged issues
in the context of a service-economy job. While performing the past and
delivering historical narratives, these workers were expected to serve
museum visitors by smiling, greeting them, and being attentive to comfort cues. Meanwhile, like other workers in the new economy whose job
it is, largely, to produce feelings, interpreters I interviewed performed
comfort work in order to protect their own emotions and feeling states,
often by resisting exposure to situations that might have caused distress
for either themselves, their employers, or the visitors. As Elijah reminds
us, he was "on the payroll" for the Minnesota Historical Society. In
this light, an interpreter's shying away from painful histories should
be understood as a condition of their labor as workers in the service
economy.

The Evolution of Interpretative Programming at the Fort (post-2006)

At a certain point, as freelance writer and volunteer Fort interpreter
Rick Magee noted in a 2009 *Legacy Magazine* article, the interpretive
program at Historic Fort Snelling "was perceived to be stagnant . . .
stuck in 1827."[55] There was "declining attendance over time." Finally,
"reviewers from the American Association of Museums strongly urged
that first-person methods be replaced by third-person interpretation."[56]

By May 2008, when I returned to the Fort for a research trip to conduct
follow-up interviews with supervisors and staff and to examine the new
program changes first-hand, the MHS had brought in a new manager,
a new program manager, three new site supervisors (each drawn from
the interpretive staff), and created a new position: a program developer.

After a year of working on site, in 2007 the Fort's new program manager instituted major programmatic changes, which included transitioning to what some staff at the site began calling a "modified third-person" method of costumed interpretation.[57] As one site supervisor described it: "You're not pretending to be somebody else, and you're not pretending to be in another time, but you maintain conventions of the period, and you maintain as neutral [a] language and vocabulary as you can. The main premise is that you've created an aesthetic of the period for the public and you don't want to ruin it by using modern slang."[58] First-person interpretation remained at the Fort only with specified interpreters called "History Players" who portrayed Colonel or Mrs. Snelling at specified times during the day.

Several individuals who worked at the Fort in 2008 believed that the move away from first-person methods also stemmed from the new management's desire to avoid any further incidents of "bad behavior" from a small handful of interpreters who used derogatory language or expressed potentially offensive opinions with the defense that it would have been historically appropriate for their first-person character. Late in the 2006 season, for example, one of the Fort's three site supervisors overheard a female interpreter who was working in the Commanding Officer's Quarters kitchen refer to the enslaved persons who worked there—Mary, and her daughter, Louisa—as either "niggers, or negros, or negroids; we're not exactly sure which variation of that word she used to describe them, but essentially she was discussing the Snelling's slaves [with visitors], and the way that she presented it to them ended the conversation and they left. . . . This was this employee's third incident of that nature."[59] The move to modified third-person provided the site's new management with a quick way to rid the Fort of these kinds of issues, because in third-person it would be easier for management and supervisors to enforce a culturally sensitive (and contemporary) lexicon at the work site.

When I worked at the HFS, the Fort's *Staff Administrative Handbook* instructed staff on the importance of being "Culturally Sensitive and Aware." A February 2007 revision of the handbook contained an entirely new section called "Language & Ethnicity," which included a list of "Appropriate Terms, From the Minnesota Historical Society Glossary & Style Guide" that defined terms such as "African American,"

"American Indian," "Dakota," "Ojibwe," "U.S.-Dakota War," and "gay." "Inappropriate Terms" were also listed, along with explanations on why such terms would be unsuitable to use in front of the public.[60] Such a glossary augmented the training for interpreters to engage in potentially charged topics while minimizing the risk that interpreters would (intentionally or unintentionally) offend visitors.

On a related note, moving to third-person interpretation was also a way to curb some of the other "weird stuff" that was going on "in a first person environment," including interpreters who were portraying non-commissioned officers "who had [co-workers] stand in the corner when they wouldn't shut up" and "Catholic bashing."[61] As one supervisor told me in 2008, "now if you Catholic bash, it's you who's Catholic bashing; it's not your character."[62]

According to another supervisor, the move to third-person also "opened a lot of great opportunities at the Fort."[63] One of these opportunities was the expansion of gender-neutral interpretation in the blacksmith and carpenter shops: "[We have] female blacksmiths now. It's not even a question anymore. One of the arguments against it was there never would have been a woman blacksmith at an army post, but when first person went away, it was no problem."[64] Another opportunity was for interpreters to widen the scope of historical narratives that they needed to be prepared to engage with the public. The lion's share of the Fort's interpretive programming would now focus on the first twenty years of the Fort's history (1820–1840), though, as Rick Magee has noted, because of the third-person format, "the staff has been freed" to more naturally move beyond the early frontier history of the Fort to interpret not only slavery, but also "the U.S.-Dakota War, the World Wars, and many other stories."[65]

By 2008, notable expansions to the Fort's interpretive programming were signs in the Commanding Officer's Kitchen that addressed sensitive issues (two signs were labeled "Slavery in Minnesota" and "The Commandant's Servants," for instance), as well as the addition of the Dred and Harriet Scott Quarters—located beneath the Fort's stone hospital building and staffed by a noncostumed interpreter. In addition to being open to the public as an interpretive station during the summer season, the quarters were also added to the core curriculum of the Fort's school tour programs. These developments came about in 2007, as part of the new management's goal that season, "to try to deal more directly with the presence of African-Americans and slavery as it relates to the Fort and surrounding community from the period of 1820–1862."[66] To that end, in May 2007, interpreters received a new eight-paged (single-spaced) training manual titled "Interpreting African-Americans and Slavery at Fort Snelling."[67] Also that season, two African Americans were hired as interpreters—one who chose to work expressly in the Dred and Harriet Scott Quarters.[68]

Initially, some interpreters found it difficult to engage with the public on the issue of slavery in Minnesota. Speaking again to the emotional discomfort that surrounds reckoning with the history of slavery, one supervisor noted that when managers and supervisors began the task of getting interpreters "to start to talk about slavery, we had staff that wouldn't say the word 'slave.' We really had to work hard to get people to say 'slave.' . . . We actually sat down with some of them, and had them say 'slave' [and told them that] African Americans are not going to appear from nowhere and start attacking you because you've said the word *slave*. And people are not going to personally attack you because you've violated one of their concepts of the universe by saying there were slaves in Minnesota."[69] Still other interpreters were emotionally distressed about how to address how slaves were treated at the Fort. Site supervisors issued a memo that explained: "As nice as it may be to console the whole idea of slavery [in Minnesota] as 'not so bad,' the truth is we simply don't know enough to make such an assertion."[70]

My own observations at the Fort in October 2008—as well as conversations with interpreters who had worked in the Dred and Harriet Scott Quarters—suggest that the issue of slave treatment was a key concern for some Fort visitors, as well. While many visitors to this station were willing to engage with interpreters about the history of the Scotts and the role of the Fort in their court case, other visitors just popped their heads in to look at the space without wanting to talk with interpreters. Still others merely observed the material culture objects in the room, verbally remarking that the room looked not unlike other working people's quarters at the Fort; several offered comments to the effect of, "This doesn't look so bad."[71]

National Park Service curator Patricia West has noted that the kitchen at President Martin Van Buren's Lindenwald presented a similar interpretive dilemma. Because modern visitors to Lindenwald's kitchen experience it as a clean, pleasant, and cool space, interpreters have had to "offset this powerful information" by discussing the "misrepresentation" and conveying how—for Van Buren's servants—the kitchen would have been "defined by heat, dirt, and heavy work."[72] Interpreters stationed in the Dred and Harriet Scott Quarters were likewise charged with the task of conveying to Fort visitors that regardless of one's opinion of the relative comfort or quality of the Scott's quarters, Dred, Harriet, their two daughters, and the some other twenty-five to thirty-five individuals who were enslaved at Fort Snelling between 1820 and 1840, "did not have the pretense of self-determination, [and] they were at the 'mercy' of a master."[73]

The move to third-person interpretation and to self-consciously address African American history and slavery at the Fort has been the most important change in the Fort's programming since the 1980s when the Fort shifted to modified first-person interpretation and expanded interpretation of civilian and women's roles. Notably, promotional ad copy for the Fort's opening weekend in May 2010 explicitly highlighted the Fort as a place where one could come to learn about the history of slavery: "At Historic Fort Snelling, try out the History Hunt program for kids and get a special Fort Kid's button. Take a Dred Scott Freedom Tour, which follows the history of slavery at the fort, culminating with the story of Dred and Harriet Scott and their bid for freedom."[74]

Making the Dred Scott Freedom Tour a key component of the Fort's opening weekend activities is in the spirit of the Minnesota Historical Society's (MHS) larger goal of gradually rebranding the Fort as a place where complex stories about the past can be told that go beyond a heroic view, and of engaging more deeply with the stories of African Americans, women, families, and American Indians—the latter being key to the MHS's goal of interpreting the "complex story" of the Fort's role in "American colonialism in the Northwest Territory."[75]

Indeed, a far cry from previous ad copy that tended to promote a nostalgic view of the Fort as an outpost in the wilderness, ad copy to promote Fort visitation in 2010 cast much broader strokes: "Explore the lives of the soldiers and civilians who called the fort home, learn about the transformation of the fort throughout its history, hear the silent voices of slaves kept in bondage in a free state, delve into the checkered

Figure 8. "Captured Sioux Indians in Fenced Enclosure on Minnesota River below Fort
Snelling," circa 1862–1863. Photograph by Benjamin Franklin Upton (1818–).
Courtesy Minnesota Historical Society.

history of the fort and American Indians, and much much more."[76]
Along these lines, the MHS's Indian Advisory Committee had long been
advocating for interpretive changes at the Fort, and a 2007 MHS internal
report about the efficacy of a new visitor center at the Fort, notes that
the "Native American and African American stories will be particularly
significant" in future interpretive planning at said location.[77]

American Indians at the Fort: *Imprisonment and Activism*

In 2007, while African American history took on increased prominence in
the Fort's interpretive programming, interpreting American Indian history at the Fort proved to be an even more vexing endeavor. The Fort—a
clear symbol of American colonialism—was built on the Dakota sacred
site of Bdote, which, according to the Dakota's creation story, was the
site of Dakota genesis. But the land just outside of the Fort's stone walls
is also a site of historical trauma for the Dakota; in response to the U.S.-
Dakota War of 1862, over the winter of 1862–63, the U.S. Army imprisoned approximately 1,700 Dakota Indians—mostly women, children, and
elders—in a concentration camp outside of the Fort's walls (fig. 8).

The imprisonment, and the 150-mile forced march to Fort Snelling that preceded it, were the first steps toward the eventual expulsion of Dakota from Minnesota in the wake of the war that eastern bands of Dakota had declared on the United States in 1862 due to multiple and long-standing grievances. At the onset of the war, Dakota were facing starvation, and settlers were illegally squatting on their reservation land. The U.S. government—which was not providing food promised to the Dakota—had no incentive to stop the squatters because the government stood to profit more from the (largely German) immigrants on the land than they did from the American Indians.

As a result of inadequate shelter and poor conditions while imprisoned at Fort Snelling, some 300 Dakota lost their lives, and 38 warriors were put to death by hanging in Mankato—the largest mass execution in U.S. history.[78] Furthermore, in 1865, two prominent Dakota leaders—Medicine Bottle and Sakpe—were executed at the Fort after the United States found them guilty of war crimes for their part in the U.S.-Dakota War.

Viewing the Fort as "an icon of American colonialism," Dakota activists and allies launched the Take Down the Fort Campaign in June 2006, and requested "that Historic Fort Snelling be demolished, the land returned to a pristine condition, and finally returned to the care and jurisdiction of Dakota people."[79] As the Take Down The Fort website correctly points out, there was precedent for the Minnesota Historical Society turning the management of at least one state historic site over to a Minnesotan indigenous population, and in the summer of 2009 the Lower Sioux Indian Community began to manage the Lower Sioux Interpretive Center. However, given the MHS's renewed investment in lobbying for funds to renovate the Fort, at the time of this writing there are no signs to suggest that the MHS intends to turn over management of the Fort to the Dakota, much less to demolish the state's flagship historic site.

In February 2010, twenty Take Down the Fort activists protested MHS's request for state funding that would go, in part, toward renovating the Historic Fort Snelling campus. Staged at the state capitol in the midst of MHS's own Rally for History, the Take Down the Fort representatives unfurled banners to announce the goal of their campaign and named the fort as a shameful symbol of American colonialism.[80] In addition to the Take Down the Fort Campaign, Dakota activists chose the Fort as a staging ground more generally to protest their past and present colonization. For example, in May 2008, activists objected to a wagon train of celebrants dressed in pioneer garb who were passing through the Fort as part of a 100-mile commemorative trek to honor Minnesota's statehood sesquicentennial.[81] As Dakota scholar Waziyatawin Angela Wilson has observed, the celebrants' portrayal of the sesquicentennial wagon train was inaccurate (since most migrants to Minnesota arrived by water) and the symbols of pioneers in their wagons neatly packaged the historical narrative of Minnesota settlement into a nostalgic framework that naturalized westward expansion and perpetuated the myth of white settlers moving into an empty and virgin landscape.[82] While the sesquicentennial wagon train was not a sanctioned activity of the Minnesota Historical Society, that the Dakota activists chose the Fort as the site to protest the commemorative activity speaks volumes to how the Fort is a contested site for competing historical narratives about the past.[83] Not unlike John Barnes's observations about the site of the Bear River Massacre—which took place in Southern Idaho in 1863, and ended in the slaughter of 300 Shoshone Indians—the Fort is just one of many spaces in the history of the United States wherein the "historical landscape . . . is anything but settled."[84]

No doubt that as the Minnesota Historical Society begins to rebrand the Fort as a place where one can learn about the "checkered history of the fort and American Indians," they will have a difficult road ahead of them.[85] Though the Fort's living history program had benefited from the fairly consistent presence of two Dakota interpreters since the 1990s, as is the case at other North American living history sites, the power of mere representation of minority groups among the interpretive ranks is limited. As Peers has noted, "few sites have appointed Native staff at the managerial level; the vast majority are seasonal workers, with little input into decisions about content for interpretation, or budgets."[86] Likewise, because the Fort has not (yet) prioritized Native perspectives as central to its operations, the MHS will need to do more than simply recruit additional Native interpreters. Indeed, Peers's study of historic reconstructions that employ Native interpreters concluded that merely "adding to the messages that historic reconstructions communicate without changing key aspects of their representations of the past, or structures of power in the present" does not do much "for changing the status quo" and can even work toward perpetuating "aspects of colonial control."[87]

Living History's Limits

Since the late 1990s a number of scholars have focused on the intellectual, emotional, and therapeutic benefits for visitors to museums and historic sites, and have argued that visitors seek out these places not only for entertainment, or to merely learn about the past, but because they wish to have an "affective or emotional experience."[88] Additionally, my research shows that interpreters, too, sought meaningful intellectual and emotional interactions with others by engaging with site visitors about history. But at times, as this chapter shows, this desire to experience a positive emotional connection with visitors was precisely what prevented some interpreters from engaging with painful site histories, even while other interpreters saw opportunities for emotional connection by navigating such difficult terrains. For those interpreters who did engage with histories that were very painful for some—uncomfortable for others—the stakes were raised, and interpreters ran the risk of suffering emotional costs.

In concluding this chapter it is important to reiterate that living history interpreters should not shy away from interpreting painful histories, but management (and critics) must take into account that interpreting these histories with the public in a nonscripted environment is hard work and can be emotionally taxing. Between demonstrating tasks like blacksmithing or laundry, drawing meaningful connections across time, and monitoring their own and the visitors' emotional states, interpreters engaged in presenting painful histories might find themselves working—to borrow a metaphor from a different mode of labor production—on an ever-accelerating assembly line of emotional production. Interpreters willing to risk emotional discomfort and broach these stories may well engage the public with meaningful counternarratives—and they should be supported in doing so through proper training that would include regular access to relevant primary sources, work-sponsored study groups, up-to-date manuals that incorporate the newest historical scholarship, and instruction on how to engage in emotionally charged conversations with visitors.

That said, it may well be that the transformative power of living history to interpret painful past events at the Fort is limited, not only because of the constraints of the interpreter-visitor service interaction but also because the Fort itself may carry too much symbolic weight as a site of American military might. In 2009 Minnesota historian Bruce White argued as much in his provocative blog entry on why he believes the Fort should be gradually deconstructed:

> Inevitably the story of Historic Fort Snelling, that diamond-shaped monolith, is a military story. The fundamental fact about the fort—as reconstructed and as interpreted—is that it is a fortress and that for many years since its reopening, when you walked into the fort you went through a gate, and often there was an interpreter there, dressed as a soldier, guarding that gate. The reconstructed fort created a logic of its own. One could try to give a different message inside the fort, but what did the fort itself say when no one was speaking? What did the mere presence of the fort say? The message was a military message and it told the story of the colonial conquest of the 19th century.[89]

As Scott Magelssen has argued with regard to Plimoth Plantation, efforts to subvert "the mythical nostalgic ideal" are quickly undermined when dominant myths and symbols are reproduced "to reaffirm" those myths.[90] Inside its stone walls, a flag waves, and soldiers march; they fire muskets, and ignite cannon charges at regularly scheduled times—reproducing familiar symbols of American military pageantry. In the wake of such powerful symbols, stories of slavery that do not end in freedom and stories of war that end in a dishonorable conquest may disrupt the dominant message produced by the Fort's diamond-shaped wall, but they are too often quieted in the wake of the patriotic messages that reaffirm what so many visitors—in my experience—came to expect.

As I explained in Chapter 1, the Fort's military and state-centered messages were foregrounded early on in the site's history as a reconstructed living history museum.[91] Indeed, as White also notes, the idea of reconstructing the fort was generated out of Minnesota's state centennial in 1958; likewise, the target date for completion of the Fort was in order to rally the public in a celebration of the Fort's 1970 sesquicentennial, and the Fort's peak attendance was during the nation's bicentennial. As nation-building exercises, commemorations such as these

Figure 9. "Memory wreaths are brought to the Round Tower under the auspices of the Daughters of the American Revolution. The Old Trails Chapter presented a tablet to Fort Snelling commemorating the sixty men who died at Camp New Hope during the winter of 1819–1820," September 11, 1915. Courtesy Minnesota Historical Society.

privilege dominant memories over others, and are designed so that celebrants might affirm the ideals of festival organizers, imagining themselves as connected to each other, as Benedict Anderson might argue in his important work *Imagined Communities,* as part of a horizontal fraternity, bound through national identity (fig. 9).[92] These are powerful myths—and ones that many people set great store by. Indeed, Historic Fort Snelling's heaviest days of attendance remain patriotic holidays (the Fourth of July and Memorial Day weekend) where a mythic narrative of American egalitarianism is promoted, and painful histories of race, class, and gendered oppressions are silenced by the cumulative symbolic weight of military uniforms and patriotic tableaux (fig.10).

In managing this particular historic site, the Minnesota Historical Society, as a state-run organization, finds itself pulled in multiple directions: ethical (and scholarly) responsibilities to tell the full and "checkered" story of the Fort on the one hand—civic obligations to make the site available for those patriotic pilgrims looking for a national sacred

Figure 10. "Soldiers at Restored Fort Snelling," September, 1973. Photograph by Monroe P. Killy (1910–2010). Courtesy Minnesota Historical Society.

space to confirm their own place in the American story on the other. Sites that carry such powerful symbolic weight, aided by interpreters who work in these spaces, might do well do to take up the challenge of historicizing their own creation as museums and touristic spaces. As Cathy Stanton has suggested for Lowell, if sites could start to "interpret themselves" the public might be better equipped to recognize the roles these places have played in reproducing mythic narratives, and in silencing painful histories.[93] With new understanding of how living history museums and living history interpreters have historically shaped public meaning, new conversations can begin.

EPILOGUE

Taking a historical perspective shows us that the mushrooming of first-person living history museums across the landscape in the early 1970s was coterminous with the expansion of the service and knowledge economies. Largely charged with the tasks of performing preindustrial skills for postindustrial tourists, interpreters at these sites became the linchpins of living museums' ability to produce meaningful experiences for visitors. The growing body of scholarship on these types of public historical spaces has shown that while frontline interpreters have been valued for their interpersonal and affective potential as "customer service superstars," they have also tended to be devalued within the hierarchy of knowledge production and management overall.[1]

This book seeks to illuminate the experience of the frontline interpreters at one such worksite, with the aim of informing future practice through a better understanding of past practice. In a time when funding pressures for museums and other cultural institutions are mounting, leaders invested in strengthening the vitality of their cultural organizations must address the individual and collective interests among those working for wages in the creative cultural economy. Nuts-and-bolts issues such as fair pay, job security, career counseling, and benefits are essential but not sufficient to creating institutions that sustain and develop workers who love history, seek connections with the public, experience great pleasure in the games of enacting the past, and strongly believe in the importance of the cultural role they perform. The challenges of connecting the goals and priorities of knowledge workers in offices, to those of contingent workers on the front lines is not unique to public history, and lessons may be learned from other cultural institutions.

I can draw one such example from one of my own work experiences—this time, outside of Fort walls. In fall 2004, as a graduate student at the University of Minnesota, I began volunteering for a union-organizing campaign at the University of Minnesota called Graduate Teaching and Research Assistants Coalition (GradTRAC), whose aim was to organize roughly 4,500 graduate student employees. GradTRAC was affiliated with the United Electrical and Machine Workers (UE), who had successfully organized the graduate teaching and research assistants at the University of Iowa in 1996. Finding myself in the perpetual cycle of job insecurity that is graduate student employment, in January 2005 I applied for and was offered a six-month contract with UE to work as an organizer on the campaign.

In my job as an organizer, I served on the front lines of the union campaign, speaking one-on-one with graduate student employees from across the university. I brought to the job interpersonal skills I had learned on other frontline jobs in the knowledge and service economies—skills I had picked up waitressing, teaching, and interpreting. I also brought a lot of commitment; though I knew I would not be employed as a union organizer for the long haul, I was willing to invest far more time than was compensated by my hourly wage. I needed those financial wages but also gained emotional compensation and personal fulfillment from working with colleagues toward an end greater than myself.

This should sound familiar. It certainly felt familiar to me at the time. The lived experience of working this job while writing up my research about interpreters at Historic Fort Snelling demonstrated a compelling connection between these seemingly disparate jobs in the cultural economy. Despite sharing similar concerns about issues such as job security and fair pay, those we spoke to who opposed unionization tended to see the lean and insecure years of graduate student employment as the price to be paid for their own future success in the job market. In addition, many anti-union science and engineering research assistants saw themselves as a fundamentally different class of worker from the English-composition teaching assistants with fewer lucrative job prospects.

By contrast, those in favor of unionization tended to see themselves as a class of knowledge workers who saw the benefit of securing a contract with their employer not only for themselves, but also for future contingent workers within this institution. In essence, two competing worldviews emerged among the graduate student employees we spoke to: one individualist, the other collectivist. We lost the election 1,292 to 1,779. In our postelection analysis, we agreed that given these competing worldviews, achieving solidarity in a 4,500-person bargaining unit seemed insurmountable.

Aligning such competing worldviews about how people perceive their labor is a tall order, and this is no less true at cultural institutions like the University of Minnesota than at cultural institutions like Fort Snelling. Worksites in the knowledge economy and culture industries—with increasingly individualized needs across workforces, and entrenched institutional management methods and historical systems in place—do not offer particularly fertile ground for collective-bargaining efforts. Therefore, efforts to change organizational cultures often sputter out. Causes of this failure are myriad: the complex mix of personalities, historical ways of running operations, fear of causing conflict, burnout, self-interest, worksite politics, stretched resources, or because those at different positions in the organization may not feel their ideas for improvement matter to management, and thus they see themselves as less connected to others laboring within their shared enterprise.

Over twenty years ago Richard Handler and Eric Gable noted an organizational divide at Colonial Williamsburg during a 1990–91 contract dispute between the unionized hotel and restaurant workers and management, wherein both management *and* "low-level" interpreters in the historic areas were opposed to the hotel and restaurant workers' demands for pay increases and improved health benefits. Both groups worked for hourly wages, and their collective labor was vital to the overall success of Williamsburg's living historical endeavor. And while they shared similar workplace goals as well as concerns of job security, low wages, and devaluation, the anthropologists found that the interpreters did not see themselves in common cause with the hospitality workers because in order "to preserve what they [the interpreters] imagined were positions of tenuous privilege, they could not condone a labor disturbance, much less participate in one."[2]

At the Fort, the major exception to the hesitancy to confront work-place and organizational issues was the Minnesota Historical Society Interpreters Caucus (see Chapter 2), wherein interpreters throughout the state joined to articulate the value of their labor and to improve the conditions of their individual working lives. Had the Caucus members persisted in those efforts instead of disbanding in 1996, who knows whether they might have achieved some of the changes they sought, at least within the interpretive workforce. Perhaps, had common cause amongst interpreters been fostered, the culture of co-worker surveil-lance that was ubiquitous during my years working at HFS would have been transformed. Perhaps workers' energies might have been channeled away from conflict over "authenticity" and more fruitfully directed toward ensuring they were receiving proper training on how to engage in emotionally charged topics with visitors, regular access to relevant primary sources, work-sponsored study groups, and up-to-date manuals that incorporated the newest historical scholarship—in addi-tion to basic issues of pay, benefits, and job security.[3]

Even though many felt the sting of being devoted to work not gen-erally regarded as a "real job," interpreters I met invested themselves passionately in their skilled interpretive work far beyond their meager financial wages. And yet, like the graduate student workers at the uni-versity and the interpreters at Colonial Williamsburg, they tended to see themselves as individual laborers—not as a class of workers with common concerns—and tended to view their cultural work as a privi-lege. Should seasonal or contingent cultural employees expect jobs that offer development, organizational support, benefits, or the possibility of earning a living wage without holding a second job? Seen another way, what would employers and organizations have to gain by provid-ing frontline cultural workers opportunities to share ideas and voice concerns without fear of retaliation—or to work in a place that is struc-tured to nurture workers at all levels—whose labor contributes to the shared enterprise of cultural creation and sharing knowledge about our society, our past?

Climbing the hill of organization change is daunting. So what does this study offer to those seeking organizational change, particularly with regard to frontline workers in the knowledge economy? Hiring and retaining workers who are committed and intrinsically motivated to perform cultural work that matters to them is one step toward building a strong team of leaders within an organization. It can be difficult, as we have seen, to create success across an entire organization, but the aim is to support rather than manage those who are doing things on their own to better the organization. Management can encourage individual development through training and find out what individuals like to do, what they are good at, and what they need to do their best.

Organizations responsive to users can support and assist workers by finding out what workers want to do or improve or change on behalf of their role within the organization. In other words, change comes at the grassroots level by treating frontline workers like they truly are an organization's most valuable assets. Rather than revert to top-down management that monitors what workers are doing or judges them, or instead of fighting against each other within the organization, a culture focused on coaching and development could give frontline workers a voice in the work they care about, fostering opportunities and the support they need, while encouraging creative approaches to workplace issues, and recognizing successes along the way.

Given the increasingly user-centered environments of this economy, there is no better time for top-down cultural organizations to begin the tough work of embracing the principles of participatory democracy where the perspectives and experiences of those at the front line are taken seriously, where they are given a seat at the table, where their emotional and intellectual labor is valued and nurtured. Constantly drawing on feedback from the front lines (as well as from the public) is an iterative process that allows institutions to constantly improve and adjust as new information comes available. Oddly, this practice of refining our views based on new information is central to the historical profession, but is less often practiced in large top-down public history institutions, where there is a widening gulf between those in the offices and those working on the front lines. As the front line is the clearest route to working directly with the public that our cultural institutions aim to serve, those at all levels of an organization have a stake in hearing their voices, and ensuring the dignity of that labor.

On the front lines of public history, change "on the shop floor" begins with bringing frontline work into view as labor. I have done that with this book, contributing to the growing literature on knowledge- and service-sector work since the late 1990s. Critics from within the academy have long lamented the dangers of Disneyfying history at sites that rely on the labor of the public history proletariat without advocating for ways our society might nurture these workers to become better historians, better communicators, and better bridge builders between past and present for a public that craves connection.[4] We have much to lose if these frontline workers are treated as disposable commodities, but we have much to gain if we begin to value and strengthen the important cultural work that they perform.

Beginning the conversation about how to bring dignity to the labor of cultural workers—including those whose labor supports the culture industry—may be more important than ever as government purse strings grow tighter, public institutions increasingly privatize, and institutions of culture rely more heavily on the labor of part-time, temporary, and contingent workers. It is a worthwhile endeavor to cross-fertilize conversations about how to bring dignity to our collective labor by integrating a range of perspectives, by ensuring that everyone has a voice, and that everyone has a seat at the table. In so doing, we might better collaborate with each other as we collectively learn to be critical agents of, and advocates for, our shared passion.

NOTES

Introduction

1. Because the worksite described in this these pages is undergoing constant change, I refer to the culture that is the focus of this study in the past tense. This is important to note because programmatic and managerial shifts (which I address toward the end of the book) have been implemented since I last worked as a costumed interpreter at the Fort.

2. Rosalind Gill offers a preliminary study of growing workloads for academics who experience emotional and mental stress, in part, because of expectations surrounding email proliferation in "Breaking the Silence: The Hidden Injuries of Neo-liberal Academia," in *Secrecy and Silence in the Research Process: Feminist Reflections,* ed. Roisin Ryan-Flood and Rosalind Gill (London: Routledge, 2009).

3. For a study of how feminized, emotional labor is often devalued in the workplace, see Kenneth J. Meier, Sharon H. Mastracci, and Kristin Wilson, "Gender and Emotional Labor in Public Organizations: An Empirical Examination of the Link to Performance," *Public Administration Review* 66, no. 6 (November–December 2006): 899–909.

4. For an examination of how devaluation and exploitation has taken hold in the arts and the academy, see Andrew Ross, "The Mental Labor Problem," *Social Text* 63 (Summer 2000): 1–31. Drawing a careful connection to the academy, Ross notes that those who "accept a discounted wage out of 'love for their subject' has helped not only to sustain the cheap labor supply [in the knowledge economy] but also to magnify its strength and volume" (23).

5. For studies using the extended case method, see Michael Burawoy, *Manufacturing Consent: Changes in the Labor Process Under Monopoly Capitalism* (Chicago: University of Chicago Press, 1979); see also Michael Burawoy et al., *Global Ethnography: Forces, Connections, and Imaginations in a Postmodern World* (Berkeley: University of California Press, 2000); and Michael Burawoy et al., "Critical Sociology: A Dialogue between Two Sciences," *Contemporary Sociology* 27, no. 1 (January 1998): 12–20, 15.

6. Richard Handler and Eric Gable, *The New History in an Old Museum: Creating the Past at Colonial Williamsburg* (Durham, NC: Duke University Press, 1997); Cathy Stanton,

The Lowell Experiment: Public History in a Postindustrial City (Amherst: University of Massachusetts Press, 2006).

7. Laura Peers, *Playing Ourselves: Interpreting Native Histories at Historic Reconstructions* (Lanham, MD: AltaMira Press, 2007).

8. Stephen Eddy Snow, *Performing the Pilgrims: A Study of Ethnohistorical Role-Playing at Plimoth Plantation* (Jackson: University Press of Mississippi, 1993).

9. I assigned pseudonyms to all informants and chose quotations not to single out individuals, but because the words they represented revealed larger trends about the living museum as a worksite. To those who are familiar with the Fort, some individuals might be recognizable, particularly in cases where the individual held a unique position (as with management, or supervisors, lead guides, etc.), but even in those cases I have taken pains not to single out individuals who are named within the context of interviews or through my participant-observation fieldwork. When I use real names, it is because those individuals were public figures (as with the director of the Minnesota Historical Society), or because the individual was credited as an author or actor in an archival document, published or unpublished. Since other researchers would be able to identify these individuals in the archives, it is appropriate to refer to them by the names used within those documents.

10. Nine of the thirty-two interviews were collected in 2008 and 2009. These interviews focused either on the early years of the Fort as a living history museum (1970s and 1980s) or on the changes at the Fort since I had left it in 2006. In the course of their careers, five of these nine interviewees had served as managers or supervisors at the Fort; two had served only as interpreters, and one had served only as a volunteer. Seven of these interviews were with men, and two were with women. Two interviews were follow-up interviews with individuals whom I had formally interviewed before. The remaining twenty-three interviews took place between 2001 and 2003, and thus the programming, management, work conditions, and other issues about which the informants spoke referred to their experiences at or before that time. The interviewee group comprised sixteen males and seven females, which roughly represented the ratio of male to female interpreters at this military history site. All but five interviewees from this group had earned a bachelor's degree or higher at the time of the interview, and all but one racially identified as white.

11. The Minnesota Historical Society Archives (MHSA) contains a wealth of materials on the history of Fort Snelling. For this study, I focused especially on MHSA materials that spoke to the military fort's transition to a historic site, and that shed light on the emerging interpretive workforce—especially from the 1960s through the 1980s.

12. These photocopies are in my possession. I was also given photocopies of another employee-produced document from the mid-1990s called "The Hospital Journal"—a journal placed in the Fort's hospital, where interpreters stationed there recorded their thoughts (in prose, doodles, and cartoons) during times when visitation was slow.

13. The records at Historic Fort Snelling proved invaluable. There, I was fortunate to have been given access to nonsensitive documents (i.e., no personnel files) that lent insight into changes over time in the Fort's work culture, especially in terms of programming and employee training.

14. In terms of both context and disclosure, it is important to note that during my fieldwork from 2001 to 2006, I also held jobs as a teaching assistant, a research assistant, and a graduate student instructor at the University of Minnesota. Furthermore, in 2004

I began volunteer work for a union-organizing campaign called GradTRAC (Graduate Teaching and Research Assistants Coalition), whose aim was to organize the graduate employees at the university. To that end, for six months in 2005, I was a paid employee of the United Electrical and Machine Workers (UE), with whom GradTRAC was affiliated. I discuss this further in the epilogue.

15. The title is a self-conscious nod to two other studies. The first is Charles Phillips and Patricia R. Hogan's 1984 study of history professionals titled *The Wages of History: The AASLH Employment Trends and Salary Survey* (Nashville, TN: American Association for State and Local History, 1984). For aspiring and practicing historians the conclusions of this study are bleak. In a nutshell, the historians who participated in the survey were generally found to be underpaid and underemployed; and the prospects for employment, or higher earnings tended to be even less promising for women in the profession. The second is David Roediger's landmark study, *The Wages of Whiteness: Race and the Making of the American Working Class* (New York: Verso, 1991, 2000). In *Wages,* Roediger (one of my first professors at the University of Minnesota) traces the intersections between race and class in the nineteenth century, noting especially how one's "whiteness" was traded in as a kind of "wage" that was used to assert power over those who could not claim said identity. While this book examines twentieth- and twenty-first-century service workers, and not nineteenth-century working-class laborers, I do examine issues of race, particularly in Chapter 5.

16. Denise Meringolo, *Museums, Monuments, and National Parks: Toward a New Genealogy of Public History* (Amherst: University of Massachusetts Press, 2012).

17. See Constance Schulz, "Becoming a Public Historian," in *Public History: Essays from the Field,* ed. James B. Gardner and Peter S. LaPaglia (Malibar, FL: Krieger Publishing, 2004), 23–43.

18. Merrill J. Mattes, "Richard H. Maeder, Superintendent, 1973–1977," chap. 9 of *Fort Laramie Park History, 1834–1977* (Denver, CO: Rocky Mountain Regional Office, National Park Service, September 1980), www.nps.gov/fola/historyculture/upload/FOLA_history.pdf; J. Faith Meader, *Fort Pulaski National Monument, An Administrative History* (Atlanta, GA: Cultural Resources, Southeast Region, National Park Service, December 2003), www.nps.gov/history/history/online_books/fopu/fopu_ah.pdf; Michael Welsh, "Fort Davis and The Living History Initiative, 1966–1980," chap. 6 of *A Special Place, A Sacred Trust: Preserving the Fort Davis Story,* Intermountain Cultural Resources Center, Professional Paper no. 58 (Santa Fe, NM: Division of History, National Park Service, 1996), www.nps.gov/history/history/online_books/foda/adhi/adhi6.htm; Liping Zhu, "Interpretation and Visitation," chap. 4 of *Fort Union National Monument: An Administrative History,* Southwest Cultural Resources Center, Professional Papers no. 42, (Santa Fe, NM: Division of History, National Park Service, 1992), www.nps.gov/history/history/online_books/foun/adhi/adhi4b.htm; Jane T. Merritt, "Park Staff and Administration," chap. 9 of *Fort Vancouver National Historic Site, Administrative History* (Seattle, WA: Pacific Northwest Region, National Park Service, 1993), www.nps.gov/history/history/online_books/fova/adhi/chap9.htm. Also of significance, the Association for Living History, Farm and Agricultural Museums was founded in 1970 to promote the "growth and professionalization" of living history in museum settings. ALHFAM home page, www.alhfam.org/index.php.

19. Jay Anderson, "Living History," *A Living History Reader, Volume 1, Museums,* ed. Jay Anderson (Nashville, TN: American Association for State and Local History, 1991), 6.

20. For example, Colonial Williamsburg, which was financially backed by J. D. Rockefeller II, initially focused its interpretation on the town's historic elite when it was founded in 1927. The interpretive focus began to shift in the late 1960s, and a focus on the "'the other half' and the dispossessed, and less on the silk-pants patriots" became a focus of the new historians working at the living history museums during the 1970s and 1980s. See Handler and Gable, *The New History,* 79. For a critique of Handler and Gable's conclusions see Cary Carson, "Lost in the Fun House: A Commentary on Anthropologists' First Contact with History Museums," *Journal of American History* 81, no., 1 (June 1994): 137–45; and Cary Carson, "Colonial Williamsburg and the Practice of Interpretive Planning in American History Museums," *Public Historian* 20, vol. 3 (Summer 1998): 11–51.

21. From within the ivory tower, the concern about living history's failures to satisfactorily interpret the past is typified in a *Museum News* article from 1978 whose title announced its central argument—"It Wasn't That Simple"—wherein historian Thomas Schlereth chastised living history museums for being "lodged in the 'consensus' historiography of the 1950s." Thomas J. Schlereth, "It Wasn't That Simple," *Museum News* 56, no.1 (January–February 1978): 39–40. Schlereth's criticisms of living history museums were echoed three years later by fellow historian Michael Wallace in "Visiting the Past: History Museums in the United States," *Radical History Review* 25 (1981): 63–96. In 1984 the first book-length account of the living history movement—*Time Machines: The World of Living History,* written by folklorist Jay Anderson—was decisively more optimistic than Schlereth. Anderson answered historians' critiques by providing examples of living history interpretation at its finest and most pedagogically promising. But while he praised living history museums for being "memory machines" that transported visitor and interpreter alike into feeling as though they had journeyed through time, he did not probe the significance of his industrial-era metaphor. Certainly, if the living history museum was a time machine, the frontline interpreters were its interchangeable parts. Jay Anderson, *Time Machines: The World of Living History* (Nashville, TN: American Association for State and Local History, 1984). In 1989, Kate Stover echoed Anderson's optimism in Kate F. Stover, "Is it REAL History Yet?: An Update on Living History Museums," *Journal of American Culture* 12, no. 2 (Summer 1989): 13–17.

22. Dean MacCannell, *The Tourist: A New Theory of the Leisure Class* (Berkeley: University of California Press), 36.

23. By 1815, the rebuilding of Fort Dearborn (Chicago) was underway, and the construction of several military defense outposts in the region began in 1816: Fort Crawford (Prairie du Chien), Fort Armstrong (Rock Island), and Fort Howard (Green Bay). Fort St. Anthony—renamed Fort Snelling in 1825—was established in 1819 under the direction of Colonel Henry Leavenworth. Under Colonel Josiah Snelling's direction, however, the Fort's first location was abandoned and moved to its current location on the bluffs overlooking the place where the Minnesota and Mississippi rivers converge. See Theodore Christian Blegen, *Minnesota: A History of the State* (Minneapolis: University of Minnesota, 1967, 1975), 99–100.

24. American Indians at the Fort have been portrayed in the first person only by interpreters who identified as either Ojibwe or Dakota. For an analysis of how First Nations and Native American interpreters have experienced the work of living historical interpretation at living history museums in Canada and the United States, see Peers, *Playing Ourselves.*

25. Minnesota Historical Society, "New Fort Snelling Visitor Center," www.nps.gov/miss /parkmgmt/upload/November%209%20History%20Report.pdf, 5.

26. Cary Carson, "The End of History Museums: What's Plan B?" *Public Historian* 30, no. 4 (Fall 2008): 16.

27. Ibid., 19.

28. John H. Falk and Beverly K. Sheppard, *Thriving in the Knowledge Age: New Business Models for Museums and Other Cultural Institutions* (Walnut Creek, CA: AltaMira Press, 2006), 110.

29. "Old Sturbridge Village 2009 Visitors Up 32%," press release, Old Sturbridge Village, March 10, 2009, www.osv.org (no longer available).

30. "Conner Prairie achieves increased attendance and revenue for 2009 season," press release, Conner-Prairie, November 18, 2009, www.connerprairie.org/Newsroom /News-Releases/2009/Conner-Prairie-achieves-increased-attendance-a-(1).aspx.

31. On free choice learning, see John H. Falk, *Lessons without Limit: How Free-Choice Learning is Transforming Education* (Walnut Creek, CA: AltaMira Press, 2002).

32. Ken Bubp and Dave Allison, "Opening Doors to Great Guest Experiences," *AASLH History News* 62, no. 2 (Spring 2007): 20–23.

33. "ALHFAM Annual Meeting & Conference 2012—Call for Papers," http://alhfam.org (no longer available).

34. The term "interactive service worker" was coined by sociologist Robin Leidner. See Robin Leidner, *Fast Food, Fast Talk: Service Work and the Routinization of Everyday Life* (Berkeley: University of California Press, 1993), 1. Alternatively, noninteractive service workers would include those workers who have no or limited face-time with the public. For example, at a fast-food restaurant, the line cook making French fries is a noninteractive service worker, whereas the checker at the register is an interactive service worker.

35. Cameron Lynne Macdonald and Carmen Sirianni, "The Service Society and the Changing Experience of Work," in *Working in the Service Society,* ed. Macdonald and Sirianni (Philadelphia: Temple University Press, 1996), 3.

36. Arlie Russell Hochschild, *The Managed Heart: Commercialization of Human Feeling* (Berkeley: University of California Press, 1983); Macdonald and Sirianni, "The Service Society and the Changing Experience of Work," 3.

37. *Student Employee Training Guide,* Job Services, Rev 2/03/2009 pk, p. 6: www.scc.los-rios.edu/Documents/pio/StudentEmployeeTraining.pdf; Junior Fowler Restaurants, LLC & Cooper Fowler Restaurants, LLC, *Restaurant Employee Manual,* Revision Date: March 31, 2007, p. 16, http://jrfowler.com/Employee%20Manual.pdf.

38. *Staff Administrative Handbook,* Historic Fort Snelling, Staff Training Materials (2004) [hereafter HFS], 9.

39. Falk and Sheppard, *Thriving in the Knowledge Age,* 45. In terms of monetary wages, the Bureau of Labor Statistics states that in 2008 the national mean hourly wage for those working as tour guides was $10.40. The state government is listed as the "top paying industr[y] for this occupation." See Bureau of Labor Statistics, "Occupational Employment and Wages, 39-6021, Tour Guides and Escorts," May 2008, www.bls.gov/ oes/2008/may/oes396021.htm.

40. Falk and Sheppard, *Thriving in the Knowledge Age,* 205, 206.

41. Ibid., 206.

42. William T. Alderson and Shirley Payne Low, *Interpretation of Historic Sites,* rev. 2nd

ed., originally published in 1976 by the American Association for State and Local History (Walnut Creek, CA: AltaMira Press, 1996), 69–70. Other notable guides for live interpretation include Barbara Levy Abramoff, Sandra Mackenzie Lloyd, and Susan Porter Schreiber, *Great Tours! Thematic Tours and Guide Training for Historic Sites* (Walnut Creek, CA: AltaMira Press, in cooperation with the National Trust for Historic Preservation, 2001); Alison L. Grinder and E. Sue McCoy, *The Good Guide: A Source Book for Interpreters, Docents and Tour Guides* (Scottsdale, AZ: Ironwood Press, 1985); Jennifer Pustz, *Voices from the Back Stairs: Interpreting Servant's Lives at Historic House Museums* (Dekalb: Northern Illinois University Press, 2010). Andrew Robertshaw, "From Houses into Homes: One Approach to Live Interpretation," *Journal of Social History Curator's Group* 19 (1992): 14–20; Stacy F. Roth, *Past Into Present: Effective Techniques for First Person Interpretation* (Chapel Hill: University of North Carolina Press, 1998); and Freeman Tilden, *Interpreting Our Heritage,* 3rd ed. (Chapel Hill: University of North Carolina Press [1977] 2007).

43. *Staff Administrative Handbook,* HFS, 1. Historians Daniel J. Walkowitz and Lisa Maya Knauer have noted that by the mid-twentieth century "state-legitimizing agendas . . . often determined whether or not the funding spigot flowed" for many public historical ventures—a claim that is born out in this excerpt from the Fort's *Staff Administrative Handbook.* Daniel J. Walkowitz and Lisa Maya Knauer, "Introduction: Memory, Race, and the Nation in Public Spaces," in *Contested Histories in Public Space: Memory, Race, and Nation,* ed. Knauer and Walkowitz (Durham, NC: Duke University Press, 2009), 9.

44. Tammy S. Gordon, *Private History in Public: Exhibition and the Settings of Everyday Life* (Lanham, MD: AltaMira Press, 2010), 97.

45. Cary Carson, "The End of History Museums," 19. Similarly, in her 2010 presidential address to the National Council on Public History (NCPH), Marianne Babal implored NCPH members to remember that "people's engagement with history is innately emotional." Marianne Babal, "Sticky History: Connecting Historians with the Public," in *Public Historian* 32, no. 4 (Fall 2010), 76–84; 81.

46. MacCannell, *The Tourist,* 13.

47. Ibid., 83.

48. Tilden, *Interpreting Our Heritage,* 18.

49. Stanton, *The Lowell Experiment,* 179.

50. Ibid.

51. Gordon, *Private History in Public,* 109.

52. Peers, *Playing Ourselves,* and Peers, "'Playing Ourselves': First Nations and Native American Interpreters at Living History Sites," *Public Historian* 21, no. 4 (Fall 1999): 39–59.

53. Author's field notes, St. Paul, MN: April 30, 2001.

54. Matthias Benz, "Not for the Profit, but for the Satisfaction?—Evidence on Worker Well-Being in Non-Profit Firms," *Kyklos* 58, no. 2, 155–76; 157.

55. Ryan [pseud.], interview by author, Minneapolis, May 2002.

56. Leidner, *Fast Food, Fast Talk.*

57. Ryan [pseud.], interview by author.

58. Paula R. Dempsey, "Interactive Service and Professional Culture: Academic Reference Librarians in an Emerging Context," in *Advances in Library Administration and Organization,* vol. 24, ed. Edward D. Garten, Delmus E. Williams, James M. Nyce (Bingley, UK: Emerald Group Publishing Limited, 2006), 91–116.

59. Bureau of Labor Statistics, see "Personal Care and Service Occupations: Tour Guides and Escorts," www.bls.gov/oco/oco20055.htm; see also O-Net Online, "Summary Report for: 39-6021.00—Tour Guides and Escorts," www.onetonline.org/link/summary/39-6021.00, which includes an overview of the requirements for the following job titles "Docent, Tour Guide, Museum Guide, Discovery Guide, Historical Interpreter, Guide, Interpreter, Science Interpreter, Museum Docent, Museum Educator," and lists an average hourly wage of $11.42. In Stephen Eddy Snow's ethnography of Plimoth Plantation, Snow observes that starting pay in 1983 was "four dollars per hour and in 1985, five dollars"—an "economic reality [that] reflects the questionable, if not downright lowly, professional status of the interpreter." Snow, *Performing the Pilgrims*, 122.

60. Sociologist Jennifer Pierce has identified a similar performance of care among paralegals. Pierce's ethnographic research shows that female paralegals frequently practiced caretaking behavior for attorneys with the aim of being singled out and praised through nods of approval and complements. While Fort workers were not necessarily caretaking for their superiors, like Pierce's overworked paralegals interpreters were emotionally, not financially compensated for their caretaking work. Jennifer L. Pierce, *Gender Trials: Emotional Lives in Contemporary Law Firms* (Berkeley: University of California Press, 1995).

61 Snow, *Performing the Pilgrims*, 132.

62. Gavin [pseud.], interview by author, Minneapolis, September 5, 2002.

1. Performing a Public Service

1. Richard J. Weiss to Division of State Parks, Minnesota Department of Conservation, letter dated May 12, 1965. File folder: "Fort Snelling: Correspondence, Resolutions etc. Leading up to preservation of Old Fort Snelling," Minnesota Historical Society Archives, St. Paul, Minnesota (hereafter cited as MHSA).

2. In 1858 the War Department sold the military reservation of Fort Snelling to Franklin Steele, a businessman and land speculator. Sheep grazed at the Fort from 1858 until 1861, at which time Steele leased the land back to the U.S. government to use as an induction station during the Civil War. See Russell W. Fridely, "Fort Snelling, from Military Post to Historic Site," *Minnesota History* 35, no. 4 (December 1956): 178–92, 183. Fridley notes that Steele held legal title to the land until 1871 (184). For a brief biography of Steele (albeit one that portrays Steele as emblematic of the rugged and courageous businessmen who helped to "tame the frontier"), see Rodney C. Loehr, "Franklin Steele, Frontier Businessman," *Minnesota History* 27 (December 1946): 309–18.

3. Legal scholars Lea VanderVelde and Sandhya Subramanian argue that Harriet Robinson Scott (who was twenty-three years younger than her husband, Dred) was likely the initiator of the Scott's lawsuit initiated in 1846. However, because of laws of coverture, the lawsuit needed to be filed under Harriet's husband's name. See Lea VanderVelde and Sandhya Subramanian, "Mrs. Dred Scott," *Yale Law Journal* 106, no. 4 (January 1997): 1033–1122. For more on Fort Snelling's relation to the Dred Scott Decision of 1857, see David Vassar Taylor, *African Americans in Minnesota* (St. Paul: Minnesota Historical Society Press, 2002).

4. The imprisonment, and the 150-mile forced march to Fort Snelling that preceded it, were the first steps toward the eventual expulsion of Dakota from Minnesota that was initiated in response to the U.S.-Dakota War of 1862. For a history of the U.S.-Dakota War, see especially Waziyatawin Angela Wilson, "Decolonizing the 1862 Death Marches," *American Indian Quarterly* 28. nos. 1/2, Special Issue: Empowerment Through Literature (Winter–Spring 2004): 185–215; and also Kurt D. Bergemann, *Brackett's Battalion: Minnesota Cavalry in the Civil War and Dakota War* (St. Paul: Minnesota Historical Society Press, 2004); Kenneth Carley, *The Dakota War of 1862*, 2nd ed. (St. Paul: Minnesota Historical Society Press, 2001); *Through Dakota Eyes: Narrative Accounts of the Minnesota Indian War of 1862*, ed. Gary Clayton Anderson and Alan R. Woolworth (St. Paul: Minnesota Historical Society Press, 1988); Elden Lawrence, *The Peace Seekers: The Indian Christians and the Dakota Conflict* (Sioux Falls, SD: Pine Hill Press, 2005); and Duane Schultz, *Over the Earth I Come: The Great Sioux Uprising of 1862* (New York: St. Martin's Press, 1992). For a local historical account of the Dakota internment at the Fort, see Corinne L. Monjeau-Marz, *Dakota Indian Internment at Fort Snelling, 1862–1864* (St. Paul, MN: Prairie Smoke Press, 2006).

5. At this time, the Fort was popular with locals because it was home to a trick horse named Whiskey. Marilyn L. Slovak, "'Smartest Horse in the U.S. Army': Whiskey of Fort Snelling" *Minnesota History* 61, no. 8 (Winter 2009/10): 336–45.

6. Depicting scenes from Minnesota history on the interior walls of this original 1820s building, the murals were painted by Iowa artist Richard Haines. The Minnesota Historical Society helped to staff this museum with a steward, prior to the Fort's decommissioning in 1946, and again in the late 1950s.

7. For a general history of the Fort through the mid-1950s, see Russell W. Fridley's "Fort Snelling, from Military Post to Historic Site."

8. This shift in custodial responsibilities initially left the post's Round Tower Museum and its Work Progress Administration murals without a steward, until the Minnesota Historical Society resumed staffing the site in the late 1950s (as it had done prior to the Fort's decommissioning). Minnesota Department of Conservation, Minnesota Historical Society, "Agreement Relating to Fort Snelling State Historical Park," File folder: "Fort Snelling: Correspondence, Resolutions etc. Leading up to preservation of Old Fort Snelling," box 147.D.9.1, MHSA.

9. G. Hubert Smith to Russell Fridley, letter dated May 21, 1956, in folder "Fort Snelling 1956–1962 (correspondences maps, memos, etc.)" box 147.D.9.1, MHSA. See also Jay Edgerton, "Old Fort Snelling is Endangered," *Minneapolis Star,* May 16, 1956, 11A.

10. Russell Fridley, "Fort Snelling: From Military Post to Historic Site," 178–92, 191.

11. "Progress at Old Fort Snelling as Reported by Samuel H. Morgan," *Hennepin County History* (Winter 1967): 16–23, 18.

12. William J. O'Brien, "Notes for Presentation to Minnesota Planning Association," February 5, 1965: "Folder: Fort Snelling Restoration Committee, 1964, 1965," box 147.D.9.1, MHSA.

13. The FSRC included William J. O'Brien, state representative, St. Paul; Fred C. Andersen, chairman of the board, Andersen Corporation, Bayport; Philip C. Bettenburg, architect, St. Paul; Brooks Cavin, architect, St. Paul; F. Robert Edman, coordinator, Minnesota Outdoor Recreation Resources Commission; Russell W. Fridley, director, Minnesota Historical Society; Ronald M. Hubbs, president, St. Paul Insurance Companies, St. Paul; Karl Humphrey, architect, Wayzata; Clinton Johnson, manager, Fort Snelling

State Park; Rodney C. Loehr, professor of history, University of Minnesota; Chester J. Moeglein, adjutant general of Minnesota; Samuel H. Morgan, president, Fort Snelling State Park Association; Leslie W. Myers, chairman, Hennepin County Historical Society; Wayne H. Olson, commissioner, Minnesota Department of Conservation; and Walter N. Trenerry, president, Minnesota Historical Society. *Fort Snelling*, prepared by Minnesota Outdoor Recreation Resources Committee with the Minnesota Historical Society, MORRC Report 15 (St. Paul: The Commission, May 1965), 80.

14. Ibid., 110. For an essential history on the roots of historical pageantry see David Glassberg, *American Historical Pageantry: The Uses of Tradition in the Early Twentieth Century* (Chapel Hill: University of North Carolina Press, 1990).

15. An annual event since 1962, in 2010, the Fort Michilimackinac Reenactment pageant boasted that it was "the longest running FREE attraction in the State of Michigan." www.fmpcfestival.org/.

16. John Grossman, "In Theatre of Life . . . You Get Into the Act/Scene: Fort Snelling," undated document, Unprocessed Papers and Archives at Historic Fort Snelling, St. Paul, MN (hereafter cited as HFS).

17. William J. O'Brien, "Notes for Presentation to Minnesota Planning Association," MHSA.

18. Mike Wallace, *Mickey Mouse History* (Philadelphia: Temple University Press, 1996), 199. For provocative case studies of historic preservation efforts in a U.S. context see Max Page and Randall Mason, ed., *Giving Preservation a History: Histories of Historic Preservation in the United States* (New York: Routledge, 2003).

19. See Cathy Stanton, *The Lowell Experiment: Public History In a Postindustrial City* (Amherst: University of Massachusetts Press, 2007), 3. In addition to Stanton, for a discussion of postindustrial heritage sites, see Michael Frisch, "De-, Re-, and Post-Industrialization: Industrial Heritage as Contested Memorial Terrain," *Journal of Folklore Research* 35, no. 3 (September–December 1998); and Mike Wallace, "Industrial Museums and the History of Deindustrialization," in *Mickey Mouse History,* 87–100.

20. Draft of press release dated Tuesday, October 11, 1966. File folder: "Fort Snelling 1965–1966," MHSA.

21. Ibid.

22. "Minnesota's Oldest and Newest School House," dedication ceremony remarks [draft] by Russell W. Fridley, p. 3. File folder: "Fort Snelling, 1965–1966," box 188, 147.D.2.5 (B), MHSA.

23. Architectural historian Alison K. Hoagland examines the history of interpretation at Forts Laramie and Bridger, but focuses solely on their built environments: "Although there are other viable means of interpretation, including signs, brochures, exhibits, films, and living history performances, these remain more ephemeral than the buildings, which constitute the most permanent attribute of a site." See Alison K. Hoagland, "Architecture and Interpretation at Forts Laramie and Bridger," *Public Historian* 23, no. 1 (Winter 2001): 27–54; 28.

24. *Fort Snelling*, prepared by MORRC with the MHS, 49.

25. Ibid., 105.

26. Merrill J. Mattes, "Richard H. Maeder, Superintendent, 1973–1977," chap. 9 in *Fort Laramie Park History, 1834–1977* (September 1980), www.nps.gov/fola/historyculture/upload/FOLA_history.pdf.

27. Loren Johnson, "At Alan Woolworth's Request I Have Written This Critique of the

1967 Fort Snelling Interpretive Program," folder, Fort Snelling, box 198, 147.D.3.35 (B), MHSA.

28. Ibid.

29. Ibid.

30. Ibid.

31. Fort Snelling Sesquicentennial Committee, "Fort Snelling Sesquicentennial Committee Report" (St. Paul: The Committee, 1969).

32. In 1969, the sesquicentennial committee consisted of its chairman, Mr. Thomas H. Swain (of St. Paul Insurance Companies), Mr. Arnulf Ueland (vice chairman of the committee), Mr. Russell Fridley (secretary of the committee, and director of the MHS), Mr. Jarle Leirfallom (commissioner of conservation), Mr. J. Kimball Whitney (commissioner of economic development), Mr. U. W. Hella (director, parks and recreation services), Mr. Samuel H. Morgan (attorney at law), Mr. Raymond D. Black (president, Fort Snelling State Park Association), Mr. Alcuin G. Loehr (commissioner of veterans affairs), Mr. Peter Popovich (attorney at law), Senator Gordon Rosenmeier, Representative Richard W. Fitzsimons, Dr. Theodore Blegen, Mrs. Stephen R. Brodwolf, Mrs. Adolph Johnson, Mr. Dan Gustafson (Minneapolis Building and Construction Trades Council). "Fort Snelling Sesquicentennial Committee Report" (1969).

33. Ibid.

34. While Mattes's language is unclear here, I am inclined to think that the latter woman was portraying an officer's maid as part of the living history demonstration, not that she actually was a maid. Mattes, "Richard H. Maeder, Superintendent, 1973–1977."

35. J. Faith Meader, *Fort Pulaski National Monument, An Administrative History* (Atlanta, GA: Cultural Resources, Southeast Region, National Park Service, December 2003), www.nps.gov/history/history/online_books/fopu/fopu_ah.pdf, 41.

36. Frances Davey and Thomas A. Chambers, " 'A Woman? At the Fort!' A Shock Tactic for Integrating Women's History in Historical Interpretation," *Gender and History* 6, no. 3 (November 1994): 468–73.

37. "An Interpretive Program for Fort Snelling Restoration," HFS.

38. Jane T. Merritt, "Park Staff and Administration," chap. 9 of *Fort Vancouver National Historic Site, Administrative History* (Seattle, WA: Pacific Northwest Region, National Park Service, 1993), www.nps.gov/history/history/online_books/fova/adhi/chap9.htm.

39. "An Interpretive Program for Fort Snelling Restoration," HFS.

40. According to the NPS 1978 Master Plan for Fort Larned, in Kansas, the post's "Commanding Officer's Quarters, [was] in adaptive use as quarters for the park historian." In the Plan, however, "Management . . . determined that onsite employee quarters will be eliminated." See National Park Service, "The Plan," chap. 6 of *Master Plan, Fort Larned National Historic Site, Kansas* (November 1978), www.nps.gov/history/history/online_books/fols/master_plan/sec6.htm.

41. Freeman Tilden, *Interpreting Our Heritage,* 3rd ed. (Chapel Hill: University of North Carolina Press, 1977), 9.

42. "An Interpretive Program for Fort Snelling Restoration," HFS, 1.

43. Ibid.

44. Ibid.

45. "Tour Guiding," folder: FHA Historic Sites, Misc. items, 1970s, MHSA.

46. "Tourist Guide Performance Evaluation," Ramsey House, September 21, 1970, MHSA.

47. "An Interpretive Program for Fort Snelling Restoration," HFS. (See section titled "Post Dependents," 2).

48. Patricia West, " 'The New Social History' and Historic House Museums: The Lindenwald Example," *Museum Studies Journal* 2 (Fall 1986): 22. On the interpretation of domestics at historic house museums, see Margaret Lynch-Brennan, "The Servant Slant: Irish Women Domestic Servants and Historic House Museums," in *Her Past Around US: Interpreting Sites for Women's History,* ed. Polly Welts Kaufman and Katharine T. Corbett (Malabar, FL: Krieger Publishing, 2003), 121–43; Bonnie Hurd Smith, "Women's Voices: Reinterpreting Historic House Museums," in Polly Welts Kaufman and Katharine T. Corbett, *Her Past Around US,* 87–101; Jennifer Pustz, *Voices from the Back Stairs: Interpreting Servant's Lives at Historic House Museums* (Dekalb: Northern Illinois University Press, 2010); and Patricia West, "Uncovering and Interpreting History at Historic House Museums," in *Restoring Women's History through Historic Preservation,* ed. Gail Lee Dubrow and Jennifer B. Goodman (Baltimore: Johns Hopkins University Press, 2003), 83–95.

49. When the buildings called the "shops" were reconstructed, the men stationed there to interpret crafts such as blacksmithing and carpentry would also be more isolated from the majority of the staff.

50. At the living history museum, visitors could purchase souvenirs (often replicas or period-appropriate items) at this reconstructed building.

51. Susan Porter Benson, *Counter Cultures: Saleswomen, Managers, and Customers in American Department Stores 1890–1940* (Champaign: University of Illinois Press, 1988), 177.

52. Historic Fort Snelling, Training Session Schedules, 1979 Season, HFS. Incidentally, supplementary training sessions for female interpreters were not instituted until the bicentennial season.

53. "Symposium: The Representation of Women's Roles at the Oliver Kelley Farm," (with Amy Sheldon, Thomas A. Woods, Joan M. Jensen, and Jo Blatti—contributing editor) *Oral History Review* 17, no. 2 (Fall 1989): 91–105.

54. Amy Sheldon, "Gender, Language, and Historical Interpretation," in "Symposium: The Representation of Women's Roles at the Oliver Kelley Farm," *Oral History Review* 17, no. 2 (Fall 1989): 91–105.

55. Candyce [pseud.], interview by author, Minneapolis suburb, February 5, 2003.

56. William T. Alderson and Shirley Payne Low, *Interpretation of Historic Sites,* rev. 2nd ed. (Walnut Creek, CA: AltaMira Press, 1996), 122.

57. Steve Osman, "Living History Evolution and Change at a Historic Site, or From Dogma to Side Show," panel/debate with Plimoth Plantation, Association for Living History, Farm and Agricultural Museums (ALHFAM) conference, June 1989, 2–3.

58. Richard W. Dienst, "At Fort Snelling on April 11–13, 1975," HFS.

59. Also, vis-à-vis the presence of the media (e.g., the local news)—interpreters became accustomed to being viewed as objects of modern-day curiosity as they performed their work displays. In the introduction I discuss "work displays," a term coined by Dean MacCannell.

60. Percy to HFS Management, undated, circa 1973, HFS. By contrast, others were attracted to the idea of an overnight immersion training, at least some of those like Todd, who worked at the Fort in the late 1990s had read about the Fort's immersion training when he was a teenager in the 1980s. He felt "let down" when he found out during his job interview that the Fort "did away with that." Todd [pseud.], interview by author, Minneapolis, September 2002.

61. Percy to HFS Management, undated, circa 1973, HFS.

62. Jay Anderson, *Time Machines: The World of Living History* (Nashville, TN: American Association for State and Local History, 1984).

63. As Jenny Thompson notes in her ethnographic study of twentieth-century war reenactors, distinguishing between a "reenactor" and an "interpreter" can be a bit slippery. For example, at public events some "reenactors present themselves as historical interpreters" and greatly value the pedagogical possibilities of living history. Jenny Thompson, *War Games: Inside the World of Twentieth-Century War Reenactors* (Washington DC: Smithsonian Books, 2004), 108.

64. Cathy Stanton, "Being the Elephant: The American Civil War Reenacted" (master's thesis, Vermont College of Norwich University, 1997), 44.

65. *The First Minnesota Volunteer Infantry,* www.firstminnesota.org (no longer available).

66. Charles [pseud.], e-mail to author, August 4, 2009. Other fort interpreters from the 1970s have placed this legal action as having occurred during the 1976 season (Mike [pseud.] e-mail to author, September 6, 2011).

67. John J. Wood (deputy director) to All Minnesota Historical Society Personnel, memo. Subject: "Job Openings" January 21, 1980, HFS. According to the memo, although this was a supervisory position, it was also seasonal, and the hourly wage was low. For example, the position was advertised in 1980 to offer $4.93 per hour, whereas Historic Site Guides started at $3.89/hour that same year.

68. See "The Landing," *Three Rivers Park District,* www.threeriversparks.org/parks/the-landing.aspx.

69. John J. Wood (deputy director), to John Hackett (historic site operations manager), memo. "Subject: Hiring of Historic Fort Snelling Summer Interpretive Staff," March 5, 1982, HFS.

70. Program notes, no author, dated 1982/1983, HFS. Warren Leon and Margaret Piatt's assessment of living history museums in the late 1980s lamented a similar staff turnover at Old World Wisconsin—a popular midwestern living history museum. Because of low wages, and the lack of job security afforded by seasonal employment, the authors noted that "many [interpreters] stay for just a single season." Warren Leon and Margaret Piatt, "Living-History Museums," in *History Museums in the United States: A Critical Assessment,* ed. Warren Leon and Roy Rosenzweig (Champaign: University of Illinois Press, 1989), 80. Because of turnover, the authors assert that Old World interpreters were unlikely to develop "a complete range of teaching techniques" with the "unfortunate result . . . that even serious visitors to Old World Wisconsin [were] not likely to detect the subtle differences between cultures presented at various farms" (80). The focus of Leon and Piatt's critique is directed at the negative effects that this turnover had for Old World Wisconsin visitors, not for the workers. Low wages and seasonal employment are not the only reasons an otherwise talented interpreter might decide not to pursue working as an interpreter. Often, there are emotional considerations as well. To take one example, Stephen Eddy Snow notes that one of Plimoth's most talented interpreters quit her job after just two seasons there "because of the low pay, the lack of job security, and mainly, because of the negative experience of her colleagues' competitiveness and hostility. Stephen Eddy Snow, *Performing the Pilgrims: A Study of Ethnohistorical Role-Playing at Plimoth Plantation* (Jackson: University Press of Mississippi, 1993), 137.

71. Christina Maslach, *Burnout: The Cost of Caring* (Hillsdale, NJ: Prentice-Hall, 1982). Stephen Eddy Snow notes that burnout was especially common among Plimoth's

interpreters when tourist visitation was in high gear, and interpreters were encountering "two or three thousand visitors a day." At those time, notes Snow, lunch breaks
away from interpretive stations—which interpreters did not always take—were "desperately needed." Snow, *Performing the Pilgrims,* 72.

72. Although it is not clear what prompted the MHS to raise guide wages, one document
from 1982 suggests that upper management wanted to curb the turnover rate and
retain workers from season to season, as a cost-saving measure. Wood to Hackett, "Hiring of Historic Fort Snelling Summer Interpretive Staff," memo. March 5, 1982, HFS.

73. Osman, "Living History Evolution," 4.

74. Gavin [pseud.], interview by author, Minneapolis, September 5, 2002.

75. Ibid.

76. During the rebuilding and reconstruction of the Fort, its stone barracks were rebuilt.
Interpreters explained to the public that the barracks originally housed two full companies of roughly eighty men of the Fifth Infantry, referring to them to as Company A
and Company H. Since paid HFS interpreters portrayed only Company A, occupying
only one section of the barracks, it is likely that the group of former employees who
were now volunteering at the Fort decided to call themselves Company H so that they
could believably hang out in their own separate section of the barracks, one that the
historical "Company H" might have inhabited. My thanks go to Edward Louis Reidell
for suggesting this scenario as the reason for the "Company H" moniker.

77. Gavin [pseud.], interview by author.

78. Snow, *Performing the Pilgrims,* 132.

79. The reference to the site's initial focus on strict-first person interpretation as "dogma"
is drawn from Osman, "Living History Evolution and Change at a Historic Site," 4.

80. I discuss "games" and "consent" Chapter 4.

81. Gavin [pseud.], interview by author.

82. Ibid.

83. Charles [pseud.] interview by author, Minneapolis, July 2009. Incidentally, Charles
did meet his future wife at HFS. Similarly, at Fort Union in New Mexico, two of the
initial three interpreters hired to do living history interpretation "kick[ed] off the
living history program for the summer of 1975" by getting married to each other, in
a real wedding ceremony in which all attendees (including the minister) were "clad
in period clothing." Liping Zhu, "Interpretation and Visitation," chap. 4 of *Fort Union
National Monument, an Administrative History,* Southwest Cultural Resources Center,
Professional Papers no. 42, (Santa Fe, NM: Division of History, National Park Service,
1992), www.nps.gov/history/history/online_books/foun/adhi/adhi4b.htm.

84. Osman, "Living History Evolution," 4.

85. A fire in 1981 forced the newly restored Commanding Officer's House to close. This
original building was reopened in 1983. An early interpretive plan (1982) for the Commanding Officer's House suggested staffing the house with a trained actress who would
portray Mrs. Abigail Snelling, the colonel's wife. See Maureen McKasy-Donlin, "Commandant's House Interpretation and Furnishings Plans" (master's thesis, State University of New York, College at Oneonta, 1982).

86. Osman, "Living History Evolution," 4.

87. Ibid., 7.

88. Ibid., 6.

89. Susan Collins Lehmann, Cabrillo Historical Association, "The Development of Planning

Within the Park Service," chap. 9 of *The Administrative History of Cabrillo National Monument* (1987), www.nps.gov/history/history/online_books/cabr2/adhi9.htm.

2. "Our Seat at the Table"

1. Gavin [pseud.], interview by author, Minneapolis, September 5, 2002.
2. Ibid.
3. Ibid.
4. Erik J. Olsrud, from the song "I'm a Troopie Named Stroopsiuskey," 1989. When Olsrud worked for the MHS at Historic Fort Snelling, he wrote this song about the politics of working as an employee for the MHS. It includes a critique of the budgetary appropriations for the Minnesota History Center in light of the cuts for sites.
5. Nina M. Archabal, "The New Minnesota History Center: Looking Back at the Journey," *Minnesota History* 53, no. 3 (Fall 1992): 117–23; 121.
6. The Minnesota Historical Society was founded the year that Minnesota became a U.S. Territory, in 1849. See Valerie Hauch, "150 years ago: The Founding of the Minnesota Historical Society," *Minnesota History* 56, no. 1 (Winter 1999–2000): 444–51. On the formation of state historical societies, see H. G. Jones. ed., *Historical Consciousness in the Early Republic: The Origins of State Historical Societies, Museums, and Collections, 1791–1861* (Chapel Hill: North Caroliniana Society and North Carolina Collection, 1995); and Leslie W. Dunlap, *American Historical Societies, 1790–1860* (Madison, WI: Cantwell Printing Co., 1944).
7. Archabal, "New Minnesota History Center," 122.
8. Ibid. As Archabal recalled, "The Society's executive council concluded that $14 million would be needed from the private sector to complete the building, to purchase special equipment for storage and care of collections, and to develop the first museum exhibitions."
9. Nick Coleman, "Budget Threatens Some Historic Sites," *St. Paul [MN] Pioneer Press,* December 3, 1992.
10. Gavin [pseud.], interview by author. The MHS raised the funds, and by 1992 the building was completed, positioning the state's oldest institution—the Minnesota Historical Society—to continue "its historic mission to collect, preserve, and tell the Minnesota story into the next century." Nina M. Archabal, "New Minnesota History Center," 122.
11. In terms of using archival traces to examine the history of the interpretive work force during the 1990s, material related to the Caucus is the most significant source material that I found, and to which I was provided access.
12. Harriet Zuckerman and Ronald G. Ehrenberg, "Recent trends in funding for the academic humanities & their implications," *Daedalus* 138, no. 1 (Winter 2009): 124–46; "Museums in the United States at the Turn of the Millennium: An Industry Note," presented at Museum Governance in a New Age, conference of the U.S. Museum Trustee Association, October 4–7, 2001; Stephen E. Weil, "A Success/Failure Matrix for Museums," *Museum News* (January/February 2005): 36–40; Harold Skramstad, "An Agenda for American Museums in the Twenty-First Century," *Daedalus* 128 (1999): 109–28.
13. In 2004, for example, while the Minnesota Historical Society drew 50.6 percent of its revenue from state funds and 7.5 percent from federal, county and state grants, 11.9 percent came from individuals and corporations, and 30 percent from earned income.

Minnesota Historical Socicty, "2004 Annual Report," Minn. Publication 05-0312, 8.

14. Minnesota Council for Nonprofits, "Nonprofit Workforce Hurt by Government Cuts, Slow Economic Recovery" (March 2004), www.mncn.org (no longer available).

15. Jan Masaoka, Jeanne Peters (with Stephen Richardson), "A House Divided: How Nonprofits Experience Union Drives," *Nonprofit Management & Leadership* 10, no. 3 (Spring 2000): 305–17.

16. In 1985, for example, the Service Employees International Union (SEIU), enjoyed considerable success in its militant "Justice for Janitors" campaign, a movement that began in Colorado to improve the working conditions and terms of employment for janitors, and was largely driven by its rank-and-file constituency of women, minority, and immigrant workers. Justice for Janitors, with more than 200,000 members, has employed strategies ranging from strikes, militant protests, civil disobedience, and hunger strikes with the goal of winning "better wages, basic benefits, and job security for janitors who clean buildings in major cities and suburbs," www.seiu.org (no longer available). Another high profile example of the turn to organizing service workers is the Starbucks Workers Union (SWU), which organized in 2004 as part of the Industrial Workers of the World (IWW), with a platform that emphasizes fair compensation, job security and health coverage, www.starbucksunion.org/about-starbucks-union /how-iww-starbucks-workers-union-making-work-better.

17. This move to organize the nonprofit sector was in part, responding to the market trend toward privatizing in which "governments began turning jobs once done by union- ized employees over to nonprofit workers, causing unionized companies and nonprofit groups to compete routinely for government contracts." See Jennifer C. Berkshire, "Nonprofit Groups Turn to Unions to Organize Workers and Collaborate on Common Causes," *The Chronicle of Philanthropy* (November 21, 2002), http://philanthropy.com/ article/Nonprofit-Groups-Turn-to/52443/.

18. On this new trend in union organizing campaigns, see: Dan Clawson and Mary Ann Clawson, "What Has Happened to the US Labor Movement? Union Decline and Renewal," *Annual Review of Sociology* 25 (August 1999): 95–119; Richard W. Hurd, Lowell Turner, Harry C. Katz, eds., *Rekindling the Movement: Labor's Quest for Rel- evance in the Twenty-First Century* (New York: Cornell University Press, 2001); and Ruth Milkman and Kim Voss, eds., *Rebuilding Labor: Organizing and Organizers in the New Union Movement* (New York: ILR, Cornell University Press, 2004).

19. On labor activism at university campuses, see Marc Dixon, Daniel Tope, and Nella Van Dyke, " 'The University Works Because We Do': On the Determinants of Campus Labor Organizing in the 1990s," *Sociological Perspectives* 51, no. 2 (June 2008): 375–96; Toni Gilpin et al., *On Strike for Respect: The Clerical and Technical Workers' Strike at Yale University, 1984–1985* (Chicago: C. H. Kerr, 1988); and D. M. Herman and J. M. Schmid, eds., *Cogs in the Classroom Factory: The Changing Identity of Academic Labor* (Westport, CT: Praeger, 2003). The key accounts of Minnesota's labor activism at the end of the twentieth century focus on the Hormel Strike in Austin, Minnesota. See Peter Rachleff, *Hard-Pressed in the Heartland: The Hormel Strike and the Future of the Labor Movement* (Boston: South End Press, 1993); Hardy Green, *On Strike at Hor- mel* (Philadelphia: Temple University Press, 1990). For accounts of earlier Minnesota labor activism, see Jennifer Delton, "Labor, Politics, and African American Identity in Minneapolis, 1930–1950," *Minnesota History* 57 (Winter 2001–2002): 418–34; Tasslyn Frame, "The Workers of St. Anthony Falls as Pictured in the Manuscript Censuses of

1895, 1900, and 1910," *Hennepin History* 22–35; William Millikan, "Defenders of Business: The Minneapolis Civic and Commerce Association Versus Labor During W.W. I," *Minnesota History* 50 (Spring 1986): 2–17; William Millikan, *A Union against Unions: The Minneapolis Citizens Alliance and Its Fight against Organized Labor, 1903–1947* (St. Paul: Minnesota Historical Society Press, 2001); and David Riehle, "Labor Found a Friend: W. W. Erwin for the Defense," *Ramsey County History* (Winter 2008): 18–26.

20. For a history of AFSCME Local 3800, see Tom O'Connell and Don J. Dinndorf, "Pioneers of the Past, A Brief History of AFSCME Council 6," www.afscme3800.org/history. Likewise, the Harvard Union of Clerical and Technical Workers (HUCTW)—currently affiliated with AFSCME—negotiated their first union contract in 1989. Rejecting the hard-lined militancy often associated with union campaigns, HUCTW organizers chose a gendered approach heavily influenced by feminism that stressed " 'mutual listening' rather than 'demanding' as a negotiation strategy" and privileged " 'kindness and respect' as its motto in the treatment of everyone." See Susan C. Eaton, " 'The Customer Is Always Interesting': Unionized Harvard Clericals Renegotiate Work Relationships," *Working in the Service Society*, ed. Cameron Lynne Macdonald and Carmen Sirianni (Philadelphia: Temple University Press, 1996), 291–33; 302.

21. The Federal Minimum wage in 1993 was $4.25. In 1989, Colonial Williamsburg interpreters were earning around $8.00 an hour. See Jean McNair, "Discontent Among the Colonists; Williamsburg Employees Irked by Pay, Conditions," *Washington Post*, February 13, 1989, capital edition.

22. Gavin [pseud.], interview by author.

23. Eric Ferguson, interview by author, March 27. 2006. Figure taken from Marco Good, "Report from Forest History Center," *MHS Interpreters Caucus*, April 1994. Apparently the figure was not "disproportionate to its percentage of the total budget" although it is unclear to what extent the cuts made elsewhere in the MHS budget would have an effect on employees' wages (or on management's salaries). Nonetheless, it was clear to Marco Good, an interpreter at the Forest History Center, that site management did not want his workers to feel like the sites were unfairly cut. As Good writes about a management/employee meeting: "We began by crunching the old numbers from the cuts, where some adjustments have been made. Our site manager, Skip Drake, made the point that the Sites Division was not cut disproportionate to its percentage of the total budget: of $1.2 million in cuts, $815,000 came from other divisions of the MHS, and $345,000 came from Historic Sites. The concern there is to reduce the public perception that the St. Paul History Center is being funded at the expense of the sites."

24. Coleman, "Budget Threatens Some Historic Sites."

25. Eric Ferguson, interview by author.

26. "What Goes On at a Meeting?" *MHS Interpreters Caucus*, May 1994. Certainly, other workplace grievances preceded the classification changes in 1993, grievances that no doubt spurred on the (failed) efforts to have AFSCME union representation. As I explained in Chapter 1, some interpreters had long been upset, for example, that MHS did not compensate employees for hours spent on work-related activities outside of work, including the time spent studying for exams employees were required to take and pass before working with the public.

27. See National Association for Interpretation, "What is NAI," www.interpnet.com /about_nai/index.shtml.

28. *MHS Interpreters Caucus*, May 1994.

29. Notes from the 1993 "Hospital Journal" (an employee journal in which employees stationed in the Fort's hospital mused, drew, and wrote) suggests that initial meetings were held at the Fort. A journal entry from September 8, 1993, states that they were set to have a meeting at the new Minnesota History Center: "Meeting at another site is a step forward. Next step is getting participants from outstate and metro sites that have normally been quiet."

30. "Priorities for the Coming Year," *MHS Interpreters Caucus,* February 1994.

31. Good, "Report from Forest History Center."

32. Ibid.

33. "Meeting Report," *MHS Interpreters Caucus,* August 1994.

34. Ibid.

35. Ibid.

36. Jean Hewlett Moline, "Survey Results," *MHS Interpreters Caucus,* November 1994.

37. Respondents' genders were not noted in the survey. I have elected to refer to respondents in the masculine (he/his) because most interpreters were male at the two largest sites: Historic Fort Snelling, and Forest History Center.

38. Anonymous respondent, "Survey Results," *MHS Interpreters Caucus,* November 1994.

39. Various anonymous respondents, "Survey Results."

40. Anonymous respondent, "Survey Results."

41. Anonymous respondent, "Survey Results."

42. Ibid.

43. Wendy Brown, *Edgework: Critical Essays on Knowledge and Politics* (Princeton, NJ: Princeton University Press, 2005), 42–43.

44. Ibid.

45. Anonymous respondent, "Survey Results."

46. Eric Ferguson, interview by author, March 27, 2006. Ferguson pointed out to me that some of those who opposed permanent status did so because they feared they would be expected to work year-round, which would legitimately interfere in their other work. This helps explain why some would object to "permanent" status. But it also brings up other questions, such as, what decisions might this employee make about his work life if he could have a full-time position within the Minnesota Historical Society that provided a comfortable living wage and benefits? What if his "first income" job provided the same so that he would not have to find a second income job "valuable to maintain lifestyles"?

47. Anonymous respondent, "Survey Results."

48. Thanks to Kevin P. Murphy, who suggested the "mistress" metaphor to me.

49. Jackie Krasas Rogers, *Temps: The Many Faces of the Changing Workforce* (Ithaca, NY: Cornell University Press, 2000), 116. On the subject of temporary workers in the new economy, see also Richard S. Belous, "How Human Resource Systems Adjust to the Shift toward Contingent Workers," *Monthly Labor Review* 112 (1989); Robert E. Parker, *Flesh Peddlers and Warm Bodies* (New Brunswick, NJ: Rutgers University Press, 1993); Vicki Smith, "The Fractured World of the Temporary Worker: Power, Participation, and Fragmentation in the Contemporary Workplace," *Social Problems* 45, no. 4 (November 1998): 411–30.

50. Rogers, *Temps,* 113.

51. Ibid., 89.

52. Various anonymous respondents, "Survey Results."

53. Michael Kinsman, "For Many Employees, Temporary Is Permanent: Some Like It, But Most Are Stuck without Benefits," *Star Tribune,* Minneapolis, November 13, 1994, Metro edition.

54. Eric Ferguson, "Rehire," *MHS Interpreters Caucus,* November 1994.

55. Kinsman, "For Many Employees, Temporary is Permanent."

56. Ferguson, "Rehire."

57. Eric Ferguson, "The Temping of America," *The Historic Interpreter,* September 1995. Note that the newsletter was renamed.

58. Ibid.

59. Ibid.

60. Chris Tilly, *Half a Job: Bad and Good Part-Time Jobs in a Changing Labor Market* (Philadelphia: Temple University Press, 1996), 1.

61. Tilly drew these figures from the U.S. Bureau of Labor Statistics, "Employment and Earnings," January 1994. See Tilly, *Half a Job,* 3.

62. "Minutes Strategic Planning Human Resources Subcommittee," February 1, 1994, HFS.

63. "Our 1994–95–96 Key Goals," Minnesota Historical Society, Historic Sites Department, January 3, 1995, HFS.

64. "Our 1994–95–96 Key Goals," 15.

65. Ibid.

66. Rachel Tooker, draft of "Welcome Letter," 1994, HFS.

67. Tooker, "Welcome Letter," 1994, HFS.

68. It should be noted that among the (nonsensitive) human resources documents to which I was given access at HFS, I only saw copies of the drafts for these pages, and for the welcome letter. As such, my analysis is focused on the cleanest copies of these drafts, but not necessarily on the final copies.

69. "An Introduction to your Employment at MHS Historic Sites," 1994, HFS. The identification card, incidentally, was made of a lightweight cardstock paper (like a business card). It was not laminated, and was not made to last.

70. Ibid.

71. "Minutes for the Strategic Planning Human Resources Subcommittee," February 1, 1994, HFS.

72. "Our 1994–95–96 Key Goals," 16.

73. "Text of the Sick Leave Proposal," *MHS Interpreters Caucus,* January 1995.

74. Kudos were given with caution, however, as a prior MHS study of departmental structures and pay scales compared MHS seasonal interpreters wages and benefits with that of other national interpretive programs, rather than taking into consideration the discrepancies between interpreters in various MHS divisions. Noted Ferguson: "The only comparison that is relevant to Historic Sites interpreters is to interpreters in our own Education Dept. An Education Dept. interpreter who had formerly worked in Historic Sites once remarked to me that it was almost like working for a different employer. Perhaps that comparison should be made, since it seems incongruous for the departments to be so different." Eric Ferguson, "Interpreter Focus Group Meets for New Guide Study," *MHS Interpreters Caucus,* July 1995.

75. Eric Ferguson, "A Seasonal Gets on an Employee Committee," *MHS Interpreters Caucus,* July 1995.

76. Ibid.

77. A hand-written, interpreter-produced "Hospital Journal" entry dated September 9,

1993, for example, describes that making calls into the school programs coordinator resulted in a job reposting for an interpretive position, presumably at the History Center, so that seasonal applicants could be considered for the position.

78. Eric Ferguson, "MHS Should Reinstate Policy of Interviews for Qualified Internal Job Applicants," *The Historic Interpreter,* June 1996.

79. Olsrud, "I'm a Troopie Named Stroopsiuskey," song, 1989.

80. As elsewhere throughout the book, I have not provided pseudonyms for names that appear in archival documents, but nor have I draw from archival documents that might be considered sensitive (i.e., personnel files, etc.). I would like to affirm that while the lyrics of this parodic song by Erik Olsrud express ire for the MHS's then director Nina Archabal (a public figure), in quoting from the song it is not my intention to out upper management of the MHS or Olsrud, but to highlight how a seasonal worker at the Fort creatively expressed both frustration with and investment in his interpretive job. It is possible, even likely, that Olsrud never met Archabal, but used her as a straw-man figure to symbolize the top of the hierarchy within the MHS, whereas interpreters such as himself were toward the bottom.

81. Tilly, *Half a Job,* 1.

82. As noted in Olsrud, "I'm a Troopie Named Stroopsiuskey."

83. AASLH's Historic House Affinity Group Committee, *How Sustainable Is Your Historic House Museum?* (Fall 2008), 10.

84. A look at the Lower East Side Tenement Museum website suggests that the museum offers around eleven tours per day on weekdays, and twenty tours per day on weekends. One online source claims that in the nearly four weeks from September 8 to October 3, 2008, 625 tours were offered. See "Fight at the Museum," *NY Press,* October 22, 2008, http://nypress.com/fight-at-the-museum/.

85. UAW Local 2110 represents the collective bargaining efforts of other New York museum workers from the Museum of Modern Art, the New York Historical Society, and the Bronx Museum of the Arts. See www.2110uaw.org.

86. Public Service Alliance of Canada, News Release, "Museum workers vote to strike," August 28, 2009, www.psac.com/news/2009/releases/34-0809-e.shtml; and Media Advisory, "Striking Canadian War Museum employees to organize Remembrance Day activities," November 9, 2009, www.psac.com/news/2009/releases/71-1109-e.shtml.

87. "Determination of appropriate units for labor organization representation," 5 USC § 7112, www.law.cornell.edu/uscode/5/7112.shtml.

88. The ongoing battle between per-diem workers and the museum drew headlines in May 2008 when New York State Senator Tom Duane resigned from the museum's board and stated in a letter to the museum that he was, "most disturbed by the museum's continued obstruction of the union organizing drive being mounted by its part-time tour guides." See "Worked up over museum dispute, Duane quits board," *The Villager* 77, no. 49 (May 7–13, 2008).

89. Andy Urban, e-mail correspondence with author, May 2, 2010. Urban had worked as both a full-time and part-time employee at the Lower East Side Tenement Museum.

90. Kat Hinkel, "Solutions Series 1: The Robin Hood Rule," *Museos Unite!* March 17, 2010 (http://museosunite.blogspot.com/2010/03/solutions-series-1-robin-hood-rule.html).

91. *Museos Unite!* http://museosunite.blogspot.com/.

92. On France's 2009 museum worker strikes, see *Museos Unite!* and *New York Times* online blog postings (respectively) by Kirsten Teasdale, "Museos on Strike at 1/5th of

France's Museums," December 5, 2009, http://museosunite.blogspot.com/2009/12
/museos-on-strike-at-15th-of-frances.html; and by Maîa De La Baume, "Strike
Spreads in France Over Museum Staff Cuts," December 4, 2009, www.nytimes.
com/2009/12/04/arts/design/04strike.html. On England, see Kirsten Teasdale's
Museos Unite! posting, "In Which I Make Awkward Transitions between Topics:
Salary Survey Update + Museos On Strike," February 16, 2010, http://museosunite.
blogspot.com/2010/02/in-which-i-make-awkward-transitions.html; and "London's
National Gallery staff strike over £7 pay rate," *BBC News,* http://news.bbc.co.uk/2/
hi/uk_news/england/london/8518310.stm.

93. Teasdale, "In Which I Make Awkward Transitions between Topics."

94. Eric Ferguson, "We're Disbanding," *The Historic Interpreter,* May 1996.

95. Dan Clawson, *The Next Upsurge: Labor and the New Social Movements* (Ithaca, NY: ILR
Press, 2003), 26.

96. Ibid.

97. Author's field notes, Historic Fort Snelling, April 2, 2001.

98. Al Gini, *My Job, My Self: Work and the Creation of the Modern Individual* (New York:
Routledge, 2001), 2. At the same time, there is no evidence to suggest that any interpreters were staunchly opposed to the Caucus, even while some did not support its
efforts universally.

99. Richard Handler and Eric Gable, *The New History in an Old Museum: Creating the Past
at Colonial Williamsburg* (Durham, NC: Duke University Press, 1997), 218–19.

3. The Wages of Living History

1. Oliver [pseud.], interview by author, Minneapolis, October 2002.

2. Author's field notes, conversation with Becky [pseud.] April 23, 2004. Becky, a costumed
interpreter whom I met at Conner Prairie, articulated similar frustrations to me when she
said: "Today something hit me when I was out on the grounds, that visitors don't realize
the effort we put into it, the dedication." Describing how visitors seemed not to appreciate their efforts, she said that sometimes while interpreting to visitors, she found herself
upset, and thinking how the public did not seem to get that she was, in her words,
"facilitating educational experiences!" But then, in a move that Arlie Hochschild would
recognize as an exercise in the worker being empathic with the public's needs over her
own, Becky added: "But, I suppose they shouldn't see any of that, and they should
only remember the experience, and not worry about [the effort we put into] doing the
training." Hochschild would call this an uneven emotional exchange between customer
and client: "Where the customer is king, unequal exchanges are normal, and from the
beginning customer and client assume different rights to feeling and display. The led-
ger is supposedly evened by a wage." Arlie Russell Hochschild, *The Managed Heart:
Commercialization of Human Feeling* (Berkeley: University of California Press, 1983), 86.

3. Five years was the chosen benchmark because it was the length of service for the
enlisted men in the army of the early republic. For example, my name on the role call
read "A. Tyson 1999, 2001–2006."

4. Erving Goffman, *Stigma: Notes on the Management of a Spoiled Identity* (New York:
Simon and Schuster, 1963, 1986), 4.

5. Ibid.

6. Karla Erickson, *The Hungry Cowboy: Service and Community in a Neighborhood Restaurant* (Jackson: University Press of Mississippi, 2009), 31.

7. Elijah [pseud.], interview by author, Minneapolis, February 11, 2003.

8. Ibid.

9. Oliver [pseud.], interview by author.

10. In order to see how working as a costumed historical interpreter is stigmatized, one can look to popular culture. In Comedy Central's *South Park* episode "Super Fun Time" (no. 1207, April 23, 2008) for example, workers at the town's local living history museum Pioneer Village are repeatedly ridiculed for not breaking character and for taking their jobs far too seriously.

11. Jean McNair, "Discontent Among the Colonists; Williamsburg Employees Irked by Pay, Conditions," *Washington Post*, February 13, 1989, capital edition.

12. "Apply for a Job," Colonial Williamsburg Foundation, Museum Interpreter A—Bassett Hall, www.hrapply.com/cwf/AppJobList.jsp. In 2005, starting positions for interpreters were advertised at $8.35/hour. I obtained the information about the rate of pay for Colonial Williamsburg from their human resources webpage, www.history.org/Foundation/human_resources/#. In 2005, in order to link to the page that would tell me what positions were offered and what their rate of pay was, I had to first click on a button saying that I would agree to comply with standards of customer service at Colonial Williamsburg. As such I was affirming a positive answer to the following questions: "Are you friendly? Will you do everything possible to make our guests feel welcome? Will you smile and be helpful to guests, coworkers, and supervisors?" This is consistent with Handler and Gable's 1997 study of corporate culture at Colonial Williamsburg wherein one of the workers at the museum stated, "You're being paid to be hospitable. . . . You cannot be sharp or short [with visitors] because it's a hospitality and courtesy violation for which you can be fired." Richard Handler and Eric Gable, *The New History in an Old Museum: Creating the Past at Colonial Williamsburg* (Durham, NC: Duke University Press, 1997), 170.

13. Author's field notes, conversation with Becky [pseud.] April 23, 2004.

14. According to the Bureau of Labor Statistics (BLS), in 2005, historical interpreters could expect to earn an average of $9.10/hour as workers in the "leisure and hospitality industry." The BLS projected hourly wage for this class of workers in April 2005 in Table B-4. "Average hourly earnings of production or nonsupervisory workers on private nonfarm payrolls by industry sector and selected industry detail, seasonally adjusted," www.bls.gov/news.release/empsit.t17.htm (no longer available). By 2008, the BLS estimated the national mean hourly wage for those working as "Tour Guides" to be $10.40. "Occupational Employment and Wages, 39-6021, Tour Guides and Escorts," May 2008, www.bls.gov/oes/2008/may/oes396021.htm.

15. Paul [pseud.], interview by author, Minneapolis, April 2001.

16. Ibid.

17. Julie Elmore, "National Park Service Employee Satisfaction and Employee Retention" (master's thesis, Nicholas School for the Environment and Earth Sciences, Duke University, May 1, 2006).

18. Handler and Gable, *New History*, 190.

19. Ibid.

20. Ibid., 189.

21. See especially Erickson, *Hungry Cowboy*.

22. Gideon Kunda, *Engineering Culture: Control and Commitment in a High-Tech Corporation* (Philadelphia: Temple University Press, 1992), 215–16.
23. I define emotional labor in the introduction. See especially Hochschild, *Managed Heart*.
24. Elijah [pseud.], interview by author, Minneapolis, February 11, 2003.
25. Alyssa [pseud.], interview by author, Minneapolis, April 2001.
26. Author's field notes, quoting Donald [pseud.] in a training session, Historic Fort Snelling, April 2, 2001.
27. Paul [pseud.] interview by author.
28. Ibid.
29. Ibid.
30. See Freeman Tilden, *Interpreting Our Heritage*, 3rd ed. chap. 1 (Chapel Hill: University of North Carolina Press, 1977); "An Interpretive Program for Fort Snelling Restoration," unidentified author (John Grossman files), c. 1970, Unprocessed Papers and Archives at Historic Fort Snelling, St. Paul, MN (hereafter cited as HFS).
31. Tilden, *Interpreting Our Heritage*, 4.
32. Ibid., 38.
33. Karl [pseud.], interview by author, Minneapolis, February 10, 2003.
34. Ibid.
35. Ibid.
36. Hochschild, *Managed Heart*.
37. Ibid., 33.
38. Maggie [pseud.], interview by author, Minneapolis, October 2002.
39. Lois H. Silverman, "The Therapeutic Potential of Museums as Pathways to Inclusion," in *Museums, Society, Inequality,* ed. Richard Sandell (London: Routledge, 2002), 69–83, 75.
40. Maggie [pseud.], interview by author.
41. Ibid.
42. Erickson, *Hungry Cowboy;* Hyun Jeong Kim, "Hotel Service Providers' Emotional Labour: The Antecedents and Effects on Burnout," *International Journal of Hospitality Management* 27 (2008): 151–61; Genevieve Lovell, "Can I Trust You? Meaning, Definition and the Application of Trust in Hospitality Service Settings," *Tourism and Hospitality: Planning and Development,* 6, no. 2, 145–57.
43. Maggie [pseud.], interview by author.
44. Oliver [pseud.], interview by author.
45. Henry [pseud.] interview by author, Minneapolis, September 25, 2002.
46. Ibid.
47. Ibid.
48. Kunda, *Engineering Culture,* 215. There is an emerging literature on self-monitoring in the workplace, which examines the differing levels of stress experienced by "high self monitors" (i.e., those who find it easy to shift their perspectives to those around them) and "low self monitors" (those who have a strong sense of their "true selves"). See Catherine D. Rawn, "Self-Monitoring," in *Encyclopedia of Social Psychology,* Roy F. Baumeister and Kathleen D. Vohs, eds. (Thousand Oaks, CA: Sage Publications, 2007); and Ajay Mehra and Mark T. Schenkel, "The Price Chameleons Pay: Self-Monitoring, Boundary Spanning and Role Conflict in the Workplace," *British Journal of Management* 19, no. 2 (2008): 138–44.
49. Brynn [pseud.] interview by author, Minneapolis suburb, February 13, 2003.

50. Ibid.
51. Ibid. For an account of Abigail Snelling's life, see Janis Obst, "Abigail Snelling: Military Wife, Military Widow," *Minnesota History* 54, no. 3: 98–111.
52. Brynn [pseud.] interview by author.
53. Ibid.
54. Oliver [pseud.], interview by author.
55. Ibid.
56. Martin [pseud.], interview by author, Minneapolis suburb, January 29, 2003.
57. Silverman, "Therapeutic Potential of Museums," 69–83.
58. Alyssa [pseud.], interview by author.
59. Ibid.
60. Ibid.
61. Ibid.
62. Ibid.
63. Henry [pseud.] interview by author.
64. Ibid.
65. Likewise, Alyssa's task would be to digest a performance wherein she would easily exhibit stereotypically feminized labor, as a deferent domestic.
66. Author's field notes, Ennis [pseud.] in conversation with author, Minneapolis, January 2005.
67. Author's field notes, Sean [pseud.] in conversation with author, Minneapolis, September 2005.
68. Todd [pseud.], interview by author, Minneapolis, September 2002.
69. Ibid.
70. Jon Keljik, "Fort Snelling Follies," *The Rake* (July 2006): 14–15.
71. Ibid.
72. Ibid.
73. This kind of public crafting is distinct from the "Stitch and Bitch" phenomena of middle-class women gathering together to knit in community that some have identified as proliferating in the early twenty-first century, possibly as a comfort-seeking response to the social unrest caused by 9/11. See, for example, an article published in January 2003 in *The Phoenix* from by Nina Willdorf, "Hello, 1950s: Cold War culture makes a comeback," www.bostonphoenix.com/boston/news_features/top/features/documents/ 02090163.htm. Others have characterized this return to the yarn as less a yearning for the comforts of the 1950s, but as a desire for an edgy, woman-centered solidarity, wherein women began to "meet at bars" for stitch and bitch sessions "complete with martinis and attitude." Annin Barrett, "A Stitch in Time: New Embroidery, Old Fabric, Changing Values," *Textile Society of America Symposium Proceedings,* January 1, 2008, http://digitalcommons.unl.edu/cgi/viewcontent.cgi?article=1079&context=t saconf. Notably, scholars such as Elizabeth Groeneveld have traced this twenty-first-century boom of knitting, crocheting, and other crafting to having been promoted in third-wave feminist periodicals in the mid 1990s, "Join the Knitting Revolution: Third-Wave Feminist Magazines and the Politics of Domesticity," *Canadian Review of American Studies* 40, no. 2 (June 2010): 259–77. In contrast to such recent trends, I am arguing that the female living history interpreter's urge to knit or hand sew after-hours resulted from such tasks having been mapped on one's body during the work day.
74. Henry [pseud.], interview by author.

75. Stephen Eddy Snow, *Performing the Pilgrims: A Study of Ethnohistorical Role-Playing at Plimoth Plantation* (Jackson: University Press of Mississippi, 1993), 132.
76. "Robert" is a pseudonym.
77. Author's field notes, Minneapolis, October 18, 2008.
78. Goffman, *Stigma*, 14.
79. Cathy Stanton, *The Lowell Experiment: Public History in a Postindustrial City* (Amherst: University of Massachusetts Press, 2006), 177.
80. Stanton, *Lowell Experiment*, 178.
81. Brynn [pseud.], interview by author.

4. Pursuing Authenticity

1. Michael Burawoy, *Manufacturing Consent: Changes in the Labor Process Under Monopoly Capitalism* (Chicago: University of Chicago Press, 1979); Rachel Sherman *Class Acts: Service and Inequality in Luxury Hotels* (Berkeley: University of California Press, 2006), 112.
2. Even interpreters very skilled at digging interpretive holes would sometimes withhold engaging with the public depending on their own physical and emotional needs. For example, an animated half hour long conversation about early nineteenth-century medical treatments might be emotionally rewarding, but it might also exhaust an interpreter so much that he or she might decide *not* to expend so much energy with the next group of visitors.
3. Burawoy, *Manufacturing Consent*.
4. I discuss "work displays" in the introduction to this book.
5. Goffman has called this "negative deference"—showing contempt toward those whom one would otherwise be expected to defer. Erving Goffman, *Interaction Ritual* (New York: Pantheon Books, 1967), 88.
6. For an examination on the roots of American's fascination with authenticity, see Miles Orvell, *The Real Thing: Imitation and Authenticity in American Culture, 1880–1940* (Chapel Hill: University of North Carolina Press, 1989).
7. See Stephen Eddy Snow, *Performing the Pilgrims: A Study of Ethnohistorical Role-Playing at Plimoth Plantation* (Jackson: University Press of Mississippi, 1993) and Richard Handler and Eric Gable, *The New History in an Old Museum: Creating the Past at Colonial Williamsburg* (Durham, NC: Duke University Press, 1997).
8. Sherman *Class Acts*, 112. In addition to equipping me to more effectively engage in the game of digging interpretive holes, my skills also enabled me to engage in the worksite game of trading skills with co-workers. This bartering game worked when an interpreter entered into an agreement with a co-worker whereby a product born of one's acquired period skills would be traded for something produced by a co-worker—often (though not always) for a product that someone had made using skills that oneself did not possess, which led to a lot of cross-gender trading. Over the years I had traded knitted and sewn handiwork with co-workers in exchange for two hand-carved wooden spoons, a lovely flint and a hand-forged steel striker, a plaid hand-sewn pocket to tie around my waist, a hand-carved ball and cup game, and a hand-forged steel knife in a leather holster. While those who had acquired considerable skills cooking and baking were not able to trade in on those particular skills for durable goods, they often

received recompense in the form of compliments, and a reputation among co-workers for being a good cook. And, of course, the success of one's meal, or of one's handcrafted product, ultimately hinged on whether others approved of it as "authentic."

9. E. Doyle McCarthy, "Emotional Performances as Dramas of Authenticity," in *Authenticity in Culture, Self and Society,* ed. Philip Vannini and J. Patrick Williams (Surrey, England: Ashgate, 2009), 241–57; 242.

10. Elijah [pseud.], interview by author, Minneapolis, February 11, 2003.

11. Judith Rollins describes a feeling of "ressentiment" (from the French verb *ressentir*) as "more than hostility; it is a long-term, seething, deep-rooted negative feeling toward those whom one feels unjustly has power or an advantage over one's life. Judith Rollins, *Between Women: Domestics and Their Employers* (Philadelphia: Temple University Press, 1985), 227.

12. Linda Fuller and Vicki Smith, "Consumers' Reports: Management by Customers in a Changing Economy," in *Working in the Service Society,* ed. Cameron Lynne Macdonald and Carmen Sirianni (Philadelphia: Temple University Press, 1996), 76.

13. Ibid.

14. Alyssa [pseud.], interview by author, Minneapolis, April 2001.

15. Aili McGill, "Defining Museum Theater at Conner Prairie," in *Enacting History,* ed. Scott Magelssen and Rhona Justice-Malloy (Tuscaloosa: University of Alabama Press, 2011), 99. McGill reports that because "autonomy is the standard at Conner Prairie—most interpreters rarely have any supervision as they interact with guests, meaning that they are not accustomed to regular constructive feedback. Often, the presence of a supervisor made them feel threatened or scrutinized, rather than helping them feel someone was taking on the role of director and coordinating 'the big picture.' "

16. Leidner, *Fast Food, Fast Talk.*

17. John Grossman, "Army Life in the Early 19th Century," Historic Fort Snelling Training Materials (1977, updated and revised by Thomas G. Shaw, 2004).

18. "Army Life" is itself organized into five sections (the Military System of the U.S., the Regulars, Barracks Life, Garrison Routine, and the Northwest Frontier). As its title suggests, this part of the HFS training materials focused on the lives of the regular enlisted soldiers, and provided only scant information on women and American Indians. Thus, because it did not contain footnotes or provide sources to be consulted, there is no way to tell from the text itself where the author drew conclusions and descriptions, such as when he uses quoted phrases to characterize (and single out) the post's laundresses as "usually middle-aged immigrant women: 'a little old Irish campwoman, who had much true Irish wit and her small withered face was full of fun.' By reputation," asserts the author without citing his source, "they were 'good, honest, industrious wives,' although fond of drink, martially inclined, minutely familiar with their rights, and rough in manner; still, they were kind at heart and always ready to help." Grossman, "Army Life," 48.

19. Handler and Gable, *New History,* 78–101.

20. Grossman, "Army Life," 78. Calhoun served as the U.S. Secretary of War from 1817 to 1824, and more or less gave the marching orders for the establishment of the frontier posts along the Mississippi.

21. Similarly, Stephen Eddy Snow reported that early on in the development of Plimoth Plantation's living history program in the early 1970s "difficult examinations were given to interpreters on a regular basis . . . [and interpreters were expected] to be able to elucidated specific themes for the visitors." Snow, *Performing the Pilgrims,* 37.

22. Tara [pseud.], interview by author, St. Paul, April 18, 2001.
23. Ibid.
24. Ibid.
25. This changed when the Fort shifted to third-person modified interpretation in 2007.
26. Jacob [pseud.], interview by author, Minneapolis, September 25, 2002.
27. Performance reviews did not open the doors to internal advancement, but if interpreters failed their performance reviews they risked not being hired back the next season—or being fired.
28. Fuller and Smith, "Consumers' Reports," 76.
29. Craig [pseud.], interview by author, St. Paul, February 21, 2001.
30. Notably, two of the three tests developed by interpreters themselves were designed to be taken open-book.
31. Alyssa [pseud.] interview by author. Alyssa attributed management's decision to cast these new interpreters as a case of image management: "There was also some kind of, what would you call it? Not sexism, but looks-ism—when they pick the pretty girls to be in the play."
32. Reserving Colonel Snelling's role for one or two interpreters had been the custom at the Fort at least since the 1980s, but with the overturn in management in 2006, ceased to be the case.
33. Paul [pseud.] interview by author, St. Paul, April 2001.
34. Craig [pseud.], interview by author.
35. Ibid.
36. Kathleen [pseud.], interview by author, St. Paul, September 10, 2002.
37. Snow, *Performing the Pilgrims*, 75.
38. Author's field notes, Historic Fort Snelling, August 2002.
39. Author's field notes, Historic Fort Snelling, July 2002.
40. Elizabeth is a pseudonym.
41. Author's field notes, Historic Fort Snelling, July 2002.
42. Writes Smith-Rosenberg: "Nineteenth-century American society did not taboo close female relationships but rather recognized them as a socially viable form of human contact—and, as such, acceptable throughout a woman's life. Indeed it was not these homosocial ties that were inhibited but rather heterosexual feelings." Carroll Smith-Rosenberg, "The Female World of Love and Ritual: Relations Between Women in Nineteenth-Century America," *Signs* 1 (1975): 1–29; 27.
43. Carol Hymowitz, "In the Lead: The Confident Boss Doesn't Micromanage or Delegate Too Much," *Wall Street Journal*, March 11, 2003, Eastern edition.
44. Jared Sandberg, "Bosses Who Fiddle With Employees' Work Risk Ire, Low Morale," *Wall Street Journal*, April 25, 2006, Eastern edition.
45. Ibid.
46. Brynn [pseud.] interview by author, Minneapolis suburb, February 13, 2003. This lack of supervisory authority, according to one long-time staff member, Gavin, occurred in the late 1980s to early 1990s when the lead guide position was formed out of what had previously been called "Level 3s." During this shift, the "Level 3s" became "lead guides" and in the process, they, as Gavin said, "avoid[ed] any language in the job descriptions of these lead guides that would indicate that they were supervisors." Nonetheless, as Gavin noted, "they were still performing all kinds of work performed in other situations like supervisors. They were writing out schedules for people. They

were scheduling events. They were planning events like they still do. They were going around checking on people, helping them with breaks. They could *not* hire and fire. Let's face it, you and I know that [lead guides] work closely with [management] . . . they plan special events and organize things and go shopping and lots of things: they're really on the management team." Gavin [pseud.], interview by author, Minneapolis, September 5, 2002.

47. Brynn [pseud.] interview by author.
48. Vicki Smith, "The Fractured World of the Temporary Worker: Power, Participation, and Fragmentation in the Contemporary Workplace," *Social Problems* 45, no. 4 (November 1998): 411–30; 418. As Smith notes, this behavior is "consistent with Kanter's structural opportunity hypothesis." See Rosabeth Moss Kanter, *Men and Women of the Corporation* (New York: Basic Books, 1993).
49. First year employees were only required to take one such of these tests, so that Paul's passing into five specialty areas in his first year can be viewed as exceptionally ambitious. That he named the passing of five tests as a marker of his achievement is testament to the seriousness with which he regarded that test taking.
50. Craig [pseud.], interview by author.
51. Jay [pseud.], interview by author, Chicago, November 20, 2008.
52. Ibid.
53. Ibid. See Paulo Freire, *Pedagogy of the Oppressed*, translated by Myra Bergman Ramos (New York: Continuum, 2000). There are also some interesting parallels here to the controversial experimental psychology study, known as the "Stanford Prison Experiment." In this 1971 study, the volunteer subjects who were assigned to play the roles of prison guards became abusive and autocratic. See C. Haney, W. C. Banks, and P. G. Zimbardo, "Interpersonal dynamics in a simulated prison," *International Journal of Criminology and Penology* 1 (1973), 69–97.
54. Jay [pseud.], interview by author.
55. See (especially Chapter 2) Tony Horwitz, *Confederates in the Attic: Dispatches from the Unfinished Civil War* (New York: Pantheon Books, 1998). See also *Men of Reenaction*, VHS, directed by Jessica Yu, Carousel Films, 1997.
56. For a list of scholarly sources that examine reenactment culture, see Chapter 1.
57. Henry [pseud.], interview by author, Minneapolis, September 25, 2002. In Chapter 1, I examined how this military chain of command developed among the male interpretive staff in the 1970s. In the wake of a limited supervisory presence, management encouraged this military culture at the worksite as a way to keep the Fort's crew of male interpreters in line, literally and figuratively. While the intensity of this military chain of command gradually waned throughout the 1990s and 2000s, it did not entirely disappear.
58. Henry [pseud.], interview by author.
59. Ibid.
60. Jay [pseud.], interview by author.
61. Author's field notes, male interpreter in conversation with the author, Historic Fort Snelling, June 2006.
62. Jay [pseud.], interview by author.
63. Grossman, "Army Life," 10.
64. Author's field notes, male interpreter in conversation with the author, Historic Fort Snelling, July 2, 2006.

65. Oliver, [pseud.], interview by author, Minneapolis, October 2002.

66. Jacob [pseud.], interview by author.

67. Ibid.

68. Ibid.

69. Richard Lloyd, *Neo-Bohemia: Art and Commerce in the Postindustrial City,* 2nd ed. (New York: Routledge, 2006, 2010), 135.

70. Ibid.

71. Ibid., 98, 130.

72. Historic Fort Snelling, "Media Room," http://events.mnhs.org/media/kits/sites/hfs/index.cfm.

73. Former manager, interview by author, Minneapolis, July 23, 2009.

74. According to a Fort supervisor employed at the site as of 2011 (but who wished to remain anonymous), "seasonal turnover is usually between 10 to 20 percent or 5 to 10 people from a staff of 50 to 60 individuals." Anonymous, email correspondence with the author, December 26, 2011.

75. Author's field notes, February 13, 2003.

5. Interpreting Painful Histories

1. In 1978, material culture scholar Thomas Schlereth critiqued living museums in the United States for being "lodged in the 'consensus' historiography of the 1950s," where they functioned as "historical shrines" that encouraged "a worship" of the nation's myths, symbols and heroes. Thomas J. Schlereth, "It Wasn't That Simple," *Museum News* 56, no. 1 (January–February 1978): 36–41.

2. Anna Logan Lawson, "The Other Half": Making African American History at Colonial Williamsburg" (PhD dissertation, University of Virginia, 1995), 119.

3. Ibid.

4. Ibid.

5. Lawson notes that a handful of African Americans had interpreted Williamsburg history before the 1970s, including two African American housekeepers who worked in the 1930s for Dr. W. A. R. Goodwin, the man credited for encouraging Rockefeller to provide the capital needed to begin the Colonial Williamsburg founding and subsequent restoration. Ibid., 110, n. 25.

6. In 1989, museum studies scholar Kate F. Stover praised both Colonial Williamsburg and Plimoth Plantation for producing complicated visions of the past, particularly noting the former's establishment of the AAIP. Kate F. Stover, "Is It REAL History Yet?: An Update on Living History Museums," *Journal of American Culture* 12, no. 2 (Summer 1989): 3–17. The AAIP spearheaded such programs as "The Other Half Tour" and interpretation of the Carter's Grove Slave Quarter. In part because Carter's Grove was competing with the downtown living history museum for visitors, in 2007 Colonial Williamsburg sold Carter's Grove (eight miles southeast of the colonial capital) to Halsey Minor, founder of CNET (an Internet publishing company). See Michelle Washington, "Carter's Grove mansion sells for $15.3 million," *PilotOnline.com,* http://hamptonroads.com/2007/12/carter%2526%2523039%3Bs-grove-mansion-sells-$15.3-million. On the larger significance of this sale, see Cary Carson, "The End of History Museums: What's Plan B?" *Public Historian* 30, no. 4 (Fall 2008): 9–27.

7. This "Estate Sale" was part of a trend in interpretation at the time, launching the year after Thomas Jefferson's Monticello introduced plantation tours that focused on slave culture at the mansion and the same year that the National Park Service began its own ambitious interpretive assessment program, which sought to redesign programs at Civil War battlefields, and sites such as Arlington House (the Robert E. Lee memorial) and George Washington's Birthplace National Monument, to include the history of enslavement. See Lois E. Horton, "Avoiding History: Thomas Jefferson, Sally Hemings, and the Uncomfortable Public Conversation on Slavery," in *Slavery and Public History: The Tough Stuff of American Memory*, ed. James Oliver Horton and Lois E. Horton (New York: The New Press, 2008), 135–50; Dwight T. Pitcaithley, " 'A Cosmic Threat': The National Park Service Addresses the Causes of the American Civil War," in *Slavery and Public History*, ed. James Oliver Horton and Lois E. Horton, 169–86. The "Estate Sale" was scheduled in conjunction with one of the museum's regular programs, "Publick Times"—a three-day event that included a recreation of an auction whose purpose was to demonstrate how colonials handled debt and estate settlements. See "Slave Quarter at Carter's Grove," Colonial Williamsburg Foundation, www.history.org/Almanack/places/hb/hbslave.cfm.

8. For an examination of how battles over memory are connected to the impulse to memorialize with public expressions of emotion, see Erica Doss, *Memorial Mania: Public Feeling in America* (Chicago: University of Chicago Press, 2010).

9. Associated Press, "Tears and Protest at Mock Slave Sale," *New York Times*, October 11, 1994.

10. Ibid. But while Gravely saw value in the event after viewing it, the NAACP maintained that he "spoke only for himself" while the organization "remained concerned about slave auction portrayals and would discuss it further with officials of Colonial Williamsburg." See Associated Press, "NAACP Disavows Official's Views of Re-enactment," *The Virginian-Pilot*, October 12, 1994. Five years later, in 1999, the Virginia NAACP upheld its critique of the 1994 auction, not because they thought that dramatizing slavery was wrong, but because they believed the event "treated the subject [of slavery] as a trifling aside." Dan Eggen, "In Williamsburg, the Painful Reality of Slavery," *Washington Post*, July 7, 1999. In March 1999, Colonial Williamsburg put forth efforts to make African American interpretive programming more central to the programming at large, namely by launching the "Enslaving Virginia" program, which consisted of ongoing dramatizations and living history reenactments designed to flesh out various aspects of life for the enslaved in colonial Virginia, to demonstrate the heterogeneity of the colony's black population, and to "show [how] slavery in Williamsburg affected everyone, regardless of color, wealth, or social status." The Associated Press, "CW Focusing on Issue of Slavery Employees Excited—And Worried, *Richmond [Virginia] Times-Dispatch*, March 14 1999, city edition. Speaking to the mission of "Enslaving Virginia," Harvey Bakari, Williamsburg's development manager of the program explained it as "about the contradiction between freedom and slavery in Colonial America, but . . . also about the contradictions of race in America today. . . . One minute, [the public will] be standing and cheering when Patrick Henry talks about liberty, but the next minute they have to confront the reality of racial discrimination. . . . When they react the way they do, people almost seem to be attempting to right the wrongs of the past, to step into history and say, 'Don't do this!' " Quoted in Dan Eggen, "In Williamsburg, the Painful Reality of Slavery," *Washington Post*, July 7, 1999.

11. James Oliver Horton, "Slavery in American History: An Uncomfortable National Dialogue," in *Slavery and Public History,* ed. James Oliver Horton and Lois E. Horton, 53. See also Karen Grigsby Bates, *Toll, Rewards of Playing a Slave at Brattonsville,* www.npr.org/templates/story/story.php?storyId=4992408.

12. Horton, "Slavery in American History," 35–55.

13. See Scott Magelssen, "This Is a Drama. You Are Characters": The Tourist as Fugitive Slave in Conner Prairie's "Follow the North Star," *Theatre Topics* 16, no. 1 (March 2006): 19–34; and Amy M. Tyson, "Crafting Emotional Comfort: Interpreting the Painful Past at Living Museums in the New Economy," *Museum and Society* 6, no. 3 (November 2008): 246–62. In my 2008 article for *Museum and Society* I compare this service encounter to an elaborate sadomasochistic ritual. As with sadomasochism, for example, the event was largely scripted, we visitors took on a role that we understood was designed to make us experience some kind of pain, we entered into the theatrical display understanding what is expected of us in our role, and in terms of the role-playing, we were only pushed as far as we would concede. While not explicitly addressing Conner Prairie, Alison Landsberg's work confronts the challenges posed by a range of projects using "experiential memory." See Alison Landsberg, *Prosthetic Memory: The Transformation of American Remembrance in the Age of Mass Culture* (New York: Columbia University Press, 2004).

14. See Donovan Webster, "Back to the Frontier," *Smithsonian Magazine,* May 2008, www.smithsonianmag.com/travel/da-frontier.html?c=y&page=2.

15. Alix Spiegel, "Act One: Doing Good By Doing Bad," *This American Life,* episode 120, "Be Careful Who You Pretend to Be," January 22, 1999, www.thisamericanlife.org/radio-archives/episode/120/Be-Careful-Who-You-Pretend-to-Be. There are parallels here to the controversial experimental psychology study, known as the "Stanford Prison Experiment." In this 1971 study, the volunteer subjects who were assigned to play the roles of prison guards became abusive and autocratic. See C. Haney, W. C. Banks, and P. G. Zimbardo, "Interpersonal dynamics in a simulated prison," *International Journal of Criminology and Penology* 1 (1973): 69–97.

16. "First and foremost," Roth urges, museums considering integration of "sensitive material" should ensure that it "be meaningful within the purpose of a program and complement sponsors' larger missions." Secondly, she advises, "museums . . . should analyze their image and their audience before acting. They must assess the value of shaking complacent audiences who are more accustomed to idyllic pasts. Institutions that would rather avoid public backlash may want to leave well enough alone." Stacy F. Roth, *Past Into Present: Effective Techniques for First Person Interpretation* (Chapel Hill: University of North Carolina Press, 1998), 161–62.

17. Jennifer L. Eichstedt and Stephen Small, *Representations of Slavery: Race and Ideology in Southern Plantation Museums* (Washington DC: Smithsonian Institution Press, 2002). The authors apply the term "symbolic annihilation" to sites that erase slavery through euphemisms such as "servant" (260). Jennifer Pustz also draws on Eichstedt and Small's work in her book, *Voices from the Back Stairs: Interpreting Servant's Lives at Historic House Museums* (Dekalb: Northern Illinois University Press, 2010).

18. Fort Snelling Sesquicentennial Committee, "Fort Snelling Sesquicentennial Committee Report" (St. Paul. MN: The Committee, 1969).

19. Ibid.

20. Dred Scott and Harriet Robinson Scott were enslaved when they were brought to live

at the Fort in the 1830s. They met at Fort Snelling and were pronounced legally wed by Major Lawrence Taliaferro, the post's Indian Agent, and the once-owner of Harriet Robinson. Legal scholars Lea VanderVelde and Sandhya Subramanian argue that with regard to the Scotts, it was likely that Taliaferro (who was Harriet Robinson's "master") intended to free both individuals from bondage when he pronounced them legally married. The Scott's court case, *Dred Scott v. Sanford* (initiated in 1846), resulted in the landmark 1857 Dred Scott Decision in which the U.S. Supreme Court both prohibited the enslaved, or those descended from Africans brought into the country as slaves and now living in free states, from becoming citizens (thus barring their legal right to sue); the decision also declared that the federal government had no constitutional basis to prohibit slavery in the territories. Indeed, as the 1969 committee noted, it was the Scott's time spent living at Fort Snelling (in free territory, per the Northwest Ordinance of 1787, and the Missouri Compromise of 1820) that helped them prepare the ground-work for their court case. Notably, in 1837—a few years before the Scotts launched their case—another enslaved woman who had lived at Fort Snelling ("Rachael") had used a similar argument of having lived on free soil as grounds in her ultimately successful Missouri court case, *Rachael v. Walker,* in which she won her freedom. The Fort Sesquicentennial Committee does not mention Rachael, nor do they mention the major role that Harriet played in the Scotts' court case. Indeed, Harriet's leading role was not fully recognized in the historiography of the Dred Scott Decision until Lea VanderVelde and Sandhya Subramanian, "Mrs. Dred Scott," *Yale Law Journal* 106, no. 4 (January 1997): 1033–1122; 1041. For more information about the Scotts' case and their family, see also Paul Finkelman, "The Dred Scott Case, Slavery and the Politics of Law," *Hamline Law Review* 20 (Fall 1996): 1–42; and Barbara Bennett Woodhouse, "Dred Scott's Daughters: Nineteenth Century Urban Girls at the Intersection of Race and Patriarchy," *Buffalo Law Review* 48 (Fall 2000): 669–701.

21. Barbara and John Luecke, *Snelling: Minnesota's* First *First Family* (Eagan, MN: Grenadier Publications, 1993): Appendix L, 261.

22. Ibid.

23. Colonel Josiah Snelling, *Journal of 1827,* Minnesota Historical Society Manuscript Collection, 130.

24. Colonel Snelling's monthly salary was $75 a month; he also received a monthly allotment of $10 a month to pay for the clothing and food rations of two servants. For colonels the army allotted $2.50 per month for clothing allowance and 20 cents per day for food rations, for up to two servants. Luecke, *Snelling,* Appendix L, 261.

25. "Kim" is a pseudonym.

26. See Minnesota Historical Society, "Historic Fort Snelling: Wood Barracks," www.mnhs.org/places/sites/hfs/tour/woodbarr.html.

27. See E. Arnold Modlin Jr., Derek H. Alderman, and Glenn W. Gentry, "Tour Guides as Creators of Empathy: Marginalizing the Enslaved at Plantation House Museums," *Tourist Studies,* 11, no. 1 (April 2011): 3–19.

28. Ibid., 15.

29. Author's field notes, conversation with author, Minneapolis, September 2005. On the use of terminology such as "domestics," "servants," and "slaves," at historic house museums, see Eichstedt and Small, *Representations of Slavery,* 260; and Pustz, *Voices from the Back Stairs,* 40–41.

30. Rendering painful histories invisible such as slavery was also encouraged because the

site's scheduled programming focused on day-to-day life within a military garrison in ways that did not necessarily invite questions about some of the Fort's messier histori- cal terrains. For example, infantry drills were featured at 11 a.m. and 2 p.m. each day during the regular season; cannon drills were featured at 1 p.m. and 4 p.m. If a visitor made it to the Commanding Officer's Quarters after the cannon drill, they would have the opportunity to see dinner served, which in my experience tended to prompt ques- tions about how meals were prepared or about the Snelling's eating utensils, rather than, for example, on working conditions for domestic workers or enslaved persons in the early republic.

31. Singleton also found that decisions about the extent to which they would engage with the uncomfortable subject matter depended on "overlapping influences from personal and professional values as well as life experiences, work settings and characteristics of the student population." Sharron M. Singleton, "Faculty Personal Comfort and the Teaching of Content on Racial Oppression," in *School Social Workers in the Multicul- tural Environment: New Roles, Responsibilities, and Educational Enrichment*, ed. Paul Keys (New York: The Haworth Press, Inc. 1994), 16.

32. Maggie [pseud.], interview by author, Minneapolis, October 7, 2002.

33. Maggie [pseud.], interview by author.

34. Ibid.

35. Gavin [pseud.], interview by author, Minneapolis, September 5, 2002.

36. Modlin, Alderman, and Gentry, "Tour Guides as Creators of Empathy," 16. See also Eichstedt and Small, *Representations of Slavery*, 20.

37. Gavin [pseud.], interview by author.

38. Karl [pseud.], interview by author, Minneapolis, February 10, 2003.

39. Max L. Grivno, "African-Americans at Fort Snelling, 1820–1840: An Interpretive Guide," (unedited photocopy), Historic Fort Snelling Training Materials, 1997. This Guide later served as the foundation for Grivno's article, "'Black Frenchmen' and 'White Settlers': Race, Slavery, and the Creation of African-American Identities along the Northwest Frontier, 1790–1840," *Slavery and Abolition* 21, no. 3 (December 2000): 75–93. Inter- preters were provided with the unrevised "Interpretive Guide" once during my seven years working at the Fort. It is important to note that the Guide is not representative of Grivno's views, which have, inevitably, been revised and refined in the years since he was an intern in the late 1990s (Grivno, personal email communication, March 2, 2009). Moreover, I want to draw a clear distinction between the Guide and Grivno's views as a researcher who works on the subject of slavery and emancipation, and whose PhD dissertation on slavery—"'There Slavery Cannot Dwell': Agriculture and Labor in Northern Maryland, 1790–1860 (PhD dissertation, University of Maryland), 2007 (http://drum.lib.umd.edu/handle/1903/7259) has received the highest honors awarded by the Southern Historical Association. My real concern is to draw attention to the Fort's erasures, not to take issue with the unrevised work of an intern in the 1990s.

40. Grivno, "Interpretive Guide," 27.

41. Ibid. Colonel John H. Bliss was the son of Major Bliss, who commanded Fort Snelling from 1833 to 1837. The reminiscences that the Guide quotes are derived from: Colonel John H. Bliss, "Reminiscences of Fort Snelling," *Collections of the Minnesota Historical Society* 6 (St. Paul. MN: The Pioneer Press Company, State Printers, 1894), 335–53. The paragraph from which the Guide quoted reads: "At St. Louis the last of our necessary

purchases was made, to wit: a nice-looking yellow girl and an uncommonly black man. On arriving at our final destination, she proved to be a very good servant, but became such an attractive belle among the soldiers that before leaving Fort Snelling we were obliged to make her a part of the cargo of the Steamer 'Warrior,' and send her to St. Louis for sale. The man, Hannibal by name, was a most excellent and faithful fellow." Bliss is recollecting a memory from when he was nine years old.

42. Speaking to training inadequacies with regard to interpreting issues relating to sex, interpreter Martin remarked: "It seems like from an interpretive perspective it's left up to the interpreter [if they want to raise uncomfortable historical instances of miscegenation and rape]. If you want to bring that up with a visitor, that's okay; I think it is appropriate. . . . But the support tools should be there if people want to talk about it. But there isn't anything." Martin [pseud.], interview by author, Minneapolis suburb, January 29, 2003.

43. Alyssa [pseud.], interview by author, Minneapolis, April 2001.

44. Ibid.

45. Ibid.

46. Ibid.

47. Role-playing hand out, un-dated photocopy, Fort Snelling Training Materials.

48. See, for example, David Horowitz, *Uncivil Wars: The Controversy over Reparations for Slavery* (San Francisco: Encounter Books, 2002). This mode of thinking is evident in his sensationalist argument against slavery reparations, wherein Horowitz claims that "the renewed sense of grievance—which is what the claim for reparations will inevitably create—is neither a constructive nor a helpful message for black leaders to be sending to their communities and to others." David Horowitz, "Ten Reasons Why Reparations for Blacks is a Bad Idea—and Racist, Too" reprinted in *Reparations for Slavery: A Reader,* ed. Ronald P. Salzberger and Mary C. Turck (Lanham, MD: Rowman and Littlefield, 2004), 127–39; 129. Similarly, President Ronald Reagan, in his 1983 "Evil Empire" speech to the Annual Convention of the National Association of Evangelicals, argued for an objective yet optimistic view of history: "Whatever sad episodes exist in our past," he said, "any objective observer must hold a positive view of American history, a history that has been the story of hopes fulfilled and dreams made into reality." Ronald Reagan, "Remarks at the Annual Convention of the National Association of Evangelicals," Orlando, Florida, March 8, 1983.

49. Jacob [pseud.], interview by author, Minneapolis, September 25, 2002.

50. Oliver [pseud.], interview by author, Minneapolis, October 2002.

51. Ibid.

52. Eric Gable, "Maintaining Boundaries, or 'Mainstreaming' Black History in a White Museum," in *Theorizing Museums: Representing Identity and Diversity in a Changing World,* ed. Sharon Macdonald and Gordon Fyfe (Oxford, UK: Blackwell, 1998).

53. Elijah [pseud.], interview by author, Minneapolis, February 11, 2003. Speaking to this issue, it's useful to take just one excerpt from Major Taliaferro's journal, dating from December 6, 1827: "Three Deg. Colder this morning than yesterday. Snowing at 9 o'clock with a freezing wind—The Soldiers were troublesome to the Indian Women who are encamped near the Agency—their husbands & friends being out hunting. I was called up at 2 o'clock last night to drive them out of the Sioux Lodges. Several of the Sioux women have (by Some means not easily accounted for) contracted the

Vanerial [sic] disease—some of them badly." Transcript of *Lawrence Taliaferro Papers,* Minnesota Historical Society Microfilm Collection, roll 3. Vols. 6–14 Journals, 1821–36, December 6, 1827.

54. Elijah [pseud.], interview by author.

55. Rick Magee, "A Fork in the River: Experiencing the Change from First- to Third-Person Interpretation at Historic Fort Snelling," *Legacy Magazine* (November 19, 2009), http://onlinelegacy.org/2009/11/a-fork-in-the-river-experiencing-the-change-from-first-to-third-person-interpretation-at-historic-fort-snelling/.

56. Ibid.

57. While in the 1980s, the formal move from strict first-person interpretation to modified first-person interpretation was the result of a bottom-up movement wherein interpreters found it necessary to break out of period character to better meet visitors' needs and to better address their questions, in 2007 the move to modified third-person was a top-down decision that the Fort's new program manager introduced, with the support of the Minnesota Historical Society's upper management.

58. Site Supervisor A, interview by author, Minneapolis, October 17, 2008.

59. Site Supervisor B, interview by author, Minneapolis, October 18, 2008.

60. Historic Fort Snelling, "Interpretive & Museum Shop Staff, Administrative Handbook," revised February 2007, 8–9. One former interpreter recalled that during a morning meeting in 2007, when one of the site supervisors "read through a list of racial slurs that were not allowed, instead of this being an instance where people were like 'I can't believe that this [kind of language] is actually happening here,' [some interpreters] challenged [the supervisor] on certain words, like 'there's the United Negro College Fund, so why can't I say "negro?'—that sort of thing." Jay [pseud.], interview by author, Chicago, November 20, 2008.

61. Site Supervisor A, interview by author.

62. Ibid.

63. Site Supervisor B, interview by author.

64. Ibid.

65. Magee, "A Fork in the River."

66. [No author attributed in document] "Interpreting African-Americans and Slavery at Fort Snelling," May 2007.

67. On May 1, 2007, interpreters also received an email memo from one of the new site supervisors entitled "American Indian & Soldier relations at Ft Snelling 1827," which was an effort to set the historical record straight on racialized relationships between the men stationed at Fort Snelling in 1827, and the American Indians with whom they were sometimes in contact: "There may have been positive interactions between native people and soldiers on a regular basis, but I do not know of any such examples. Depending on the actual level of antagonism between these two groups of people at any given time, feelings toward each other may have ranged between contempt, fear, indifference, and curiosity." In addition to pointing to primary and secondary sources that shed light on the unequal power relations between soldiers, officers, and American Indians—with special attention to gender—this site supervisor offers: "There is no evidence that enlisted men had any access to American Indian women as a regular consensual sexual outlet. The only regular access enlisted men may have had was from each other, either as consensual homosexual relationships, or as power based

homoscxual relationships. The social environment at Fort Snelling may have been more comparable to a prison or work farm society on many levels." Site Supervisor email to staff, May 01, 2007; email forwarded to the author September 27, 2008.

68. Site Supervisor A, interview by author.

69. Site Supervisor B, interview by author.

70. Jeff Boorom, "Slave Treatment Question," May 23, 2007, email to Fort staff. For a thoughtful assessment of how staff at Boston's Old North Church dealt with gaps in the historic record by openly acknowledging the those gaps see Christine Baron, "One if by Land! Two if by River! Or, What if Everything You Thought You Knew were Wrong?" *History Teacher* 43, no. 4 (2010): 607–15.

71. Author's field notes, Historic Fort Snelling, October 17, 2008.

72. Patricia West, "Uncovering and Interpreting history at Historic House Museums," in *Restoring Women's History Through Historic Preservation,* ed. Gail Lee Dubrow and Jennifer B. Goodman (Baltimore: Johns Hopkins University Press, 2003), 83–95; 93.

73. Jeff Boorom, "Slave Treatment Question."

74. Historic Fort Snelling and Sibley House Historic Site Opening Weekend, May 29, 2010, May 30, 2010, http://events.mnhs.org (no longer available).

75. Kevin Maijala, "Historic Fort Snelling's Interpretive Transformation," conference presentation at National Council for Public History Annual Meeting, Portland, Oregon, March 12, 2010.

76. Minnesota Historical Society, "Visiting Historic Fort Snelling," www.mnhs.org/places /sites/hfs/visiting.html.

77. See Minnesota Historical Society, "New Fort Snelling Visitor Center: Response to Questions Raised during the Section 106 Consultation Process," November 9, 2007, 2, www. nps.gov/miss/parkmgmt/upload/November%209%20History%20Report.pdf.

78. For further readings on the U.S.-Dakota War of 1862, see Chapter 1, note 4. On the issue of historical trauma for the Dakota as related to Historic Fort Snelling, see especially the special issue of *American Indian Quarterly* 28, no. 2 (Spring 2004), which focuses largely on Dakota memory, historical trauma, and the events that preceded and followed the U.S.-Dakota War of 1862. On the issue of historical trauma, writ large, see Cathy Caruth, ed. *Trauma: Explorations in Memory* (Baltimore: Johns Hopkins University Press, 1995); Ana Douglas and Thomas Vogler, eds., *Witness and Memory: The Discourse of Trauma* (New York: Routledge, 2003); and Paul Lambek and Michael Antze, *Tense Past: Cultural Essays in Trauma and Memory* (New York: Routledge, 1996).

79. Take Down the Fort, www.takedownthefort.com/. Dakota tribal leaders supported these demands in a unanimous Upper Sioux Community Resolution No. 27-FY2006.

80. Robert Erickson, "Dakota Activists Drop Banners to Challenge Proposed Funding for Fort Snelling," *Indymedia,* February 18, 2010, http://twincities.indymedia.org/2010/ feb/video-dakota-activists-drop-banners-challenge-proposed-funding-fort-snelling.

81. Kara McGuire, "Minnesota's Sesquicentennial: At the Capitol: Celebration, somber protest; Amid festivities at the state's 150th birthday, American Indian marchers also marked the day," *Minneapolis Star Tribune,* May 12, 2008; Tom Meersman, "Protesters decry 'shameful history'; A group halted the sesquicentennial wagon train at Fort Snelling, protesting the state's treatment of Indians," *Minneapolis Star Tribune,* May 11, 2008. A number of other states have also used the "wagon train" reenactment as a way to celebrate the anniversary of statehood. *Houston Chronicle,* December 12, 1985;

and "California Sesquicentennial Wagon Train Ready to Roll," *The Free Library*, May 3, 1999, www.thefreelibrary.com/California Sesquicentennial Wagon Train Ready to Roll.-a054531417.

82. Waziyatawin, "Minnesota's Sesquicentennial Protest Events. Update on Wagon Train Protesters at Fort Snelling," Press Release, March 1, 2009, http://waziyatawin.net/commentary/?p=40.

83. For a comparative case study see John Barnes, "The Struggle to Control the Past: Commemoration, Memory, and the Bear River Massacre of 1863," *Public Historian* 30, no. 1 (February 2008): 81–104; Kass Fleisher, *The Bear River Massacre and the Making of History* (New York: State University of New York Press, 2004). For studies of contested memories at military sites see Michael A. Elliott, *Custerology: The Enduring Legacy of the Indian Wars and George Armstrong Custer* (Chicago: University of Chicago Press, 2007); Edward Linenthal, " 'A Sore From America's Past That Has Not Yet Healed': The Little Bighorn," *Sacred Ground: Americans and Their Battlefields,* (Urbana: University of Illinois Press, 1991); Robert Hayashi, "Transfigured Patterns: Contesting Memories at the Manzanar National Historic Site," and Frank Hays, "The National Park Service: Groveling Sycophant or Social Conscience: Telling the Story of Mountains, Valleys, and Barbed Wire at Manzanar National Historic Site," *Public Historian* 25, no. 4 (Fall 2003), 51–80; Robert Utley, "Whose Shrine Is It? The Ideological Struggle for Custer Battlefield," *Montana: The Magazine of Western History* 42, no. 1 (Winter 1992): 70–74; Douglas C. McChristian, "In Search of Custer Battlefield," *Montana: the Magazine of Western History* 12, no. 1 (Winter 1992): 75–76.

84. Barnes, "The Struggle to Control the Past," 83.

85. Minnesota Historical Society, "Visiting Historic Fort Snelling," www.mnhs.org/places/sites/hfs/visiting.html.

86. Laura Peers, *Playing Ourselves: Interpreting Native Histories at Historic Reconstructions* (Lanham, MD: AltaMira Press, 2007), 53.

87. Ibid., 176.

88. Catherine M. Cameron and John B. Gatewood, "Excursions into the Un-Remembered Past: What People Want from Visits to Historical Sites," *Public Historian* 22, no. 3 (Summer 2000): 107–27, 109. On the relationship between museums and therapy, see Lois H. Silverman, "The Therapeutic Potential of Museums as Pathways to Inclusion," in *Museums, Society, Inequality,* ed. Richard Sandell (London: Routledge, 2002), 69–83. Roy Rosenzweig and David Thelen's 1,400 person survey—the results of which are the subject of their book, *The Presence of the Past*—confirms that the public seeks encounters with history that are personally meaningful. Roy Rosenzweig and David Thelen, *The Presence of the Past: Popular Uses of History in American Life* (New York: Columbia University Press, 1998).

89. Bruce White, "Tearing Down the Fort—Why It Makes Sense," MinnesotaHistory.net: a forum for discussing current events relating to the history of Minnesota, http://minnesotahistory.net/?p=1339.

90. Scott Magelssen, "Recreation and Re-Creation: On-Site Historical Reenactment as Historiographic Operation at Plimoth Plantation," *Journal of Dramatic Theory and Criticism,* Fall 2002, 107–26; 123–24. At Plimoth, Magelssen saw the gift shop offering "a soothing refrain which protects the nostalgic touristic consciousness from doubt[ing]" inherited myths about pilgrims, Indians, and Thanksgiving, despite the heroic efforts of third-person Wampanoag, and first-person pilgrim interpreters.

91. Although the Fort had only four original buildings when it was reconstructed begin-ning in the 1960s, when it was restored to its 1820s appearance, it literally erased the passage of time on the Fort—from removing the WPA murals in the Round Tower and the Spanish stucco on the Commanding Officer's Quarters—to rebuilding the remain-ing buildings, not to mention the stone walls. For a compelling narrative about the limits of freezing historic sites in time, see Scott E. Casper, *Sarah Johnson's Mount Vernon: The Forgotten History of an American Shrine* (New York: Hill and Wang, 2008).
92. Benedict Anderson, *Imagined Communities: Reflections on the Origin and Spread of Nationalism,* rev. ed. (New York: Verso, 1991). For an excellent study on monuments, public memories, and national memory, see Alan Gordon, *Making Public Pasts: The Contested Terrain of Montréal's Public Memories, 1891–1930* (Montreal: McGill, Queens University Press, 2001). See also Kevin Walsh, *The Representation of the Past: Museums and Heritage in the Post-Modern World* (New York: Routledge, 1992).
93. Cathy Stanton, *The Lowell Experiment: Public History in a Postindustrial City* (Amherst: University of Massachusetts Press, 2006), 146.

Epilogue

1. "Customer service superstars" is a reference to the training episode that introduces this book. See especially Richard Handler and Eric Gable, *The New History in an Old Museum: Creating the Past at Colonial Williamsburg* (Durham, NC: Duke University Press, 1997); Laura Peers, *Playing Ourselves: Interpreting Native Histories at Historic Reconstructions* (Lanham, MD: AltaMira Press, 2007); Stephen Eddy Snow, *Performing the Pilgrims: A Study of Ethnohistorical Role-Playing at Plimoth Plantation* (Jackson: University Press of Mississippi, 1993).
2. Handler and Gable, *New History,* 218–19.
3. For complementary conclusions about the National Park Service, see Anne Mitchell Whisnant, Marla R. Miller, Gary B. Nash, and David Thelen, *Imperiled Promise: The State of History in the National Park Service,* Organization of American Historians for the National Park Service, 2011. https://s3.amazonaws.com/ImperiledPromiseHistory intheNPS/Imperiled+Promise.pdf
4. James W. Loewen, *Lies Across America* (New York: Touchstone, 2000); Thomas J. Schlereth, "It Wasn't That Simple," *Museum News* 56 (January/February 1978); Mike Wallace, *Mickey Mouse History and Other Essays on America Memory* (Philadelphia: Temple University Press, 1996).

INDEX

Notes: The abbreviation HFS is used for Historic Fort Snelling; MHS, for the Minnesota Historical Society. Page numbers in *italics* refer to illustrations.